WHAT THE DOCTOR SAW

WHAT THE DOCTOR SAW

DR MAURICE GUERET

Editorial Note: This is a collection of writings and columns by
Dr Maurice Guéret from the years between 2003 and 2013. Some are
unpublished, and others have appeared in print, especially in his Rude Health
column of the Sunday Independent's Life Magazine. Some of these have
been re-edited with footnotes and postscripts added where appropriate.
They are opinion pieces and should not be treated as medical fact.
Doctors differ, and so do their patients.

WHAT THE DOCTOR SAW

First Published in 2013 by IMD.

IMD
PO Box 5049
Terenure
Dublin 6w
Ireland

www.drmauricegueret.com

ISBN 978-0-99552701-8-5

A CIP catalogue record for this book is available from the British Library

1 2 3 4 5 6 7 8 9 10

**Printed in County Kerry by
Walsh Colour Printing**

All Design by John Brady

iMD

For Mimi and her Maman.
With love.

CONTENTS

PATIENT BLOOPERS
February 2005

After long days tinkering with the malfunctioning organs of life, there is nothing that doctors enjoy more than a spot of merry-making at their patients' expense. There is nothing malicious about this age old ritual. It's a darker humour, carried out away from listening ears and conducted in the best possible taste. Laughter is after all the best medicine.

Medical malapropisms, better known as patient bloopers, are a perennial favourite. We have Irish dramatist Richard B. Sheridan to thank for the very existence of malapropisms. Mrs Malaprop, an enchanting character of his 1775 comedy *The Rivals*, was noteworthy for her mangled misuse of words. The oldest one in the clinical book is the tale of the Dublin nun who was overheard telling her superior that she had *fireballs in her eucharist* as they left gynaecological outpatients. The unfortunate sister had just been told her menstrual difficulties were caused by fibroids in her uterus. A GP colleague once told me how a patient declared he was born with a *biblical hernia* (umbilical hernia). And a young lady once sexed up her medical history on a job application stating that she once suffered the effects of *multiple micro-orgasms*. An infection with multiple micro-organisms, perhaps. And a young man informed his doctor that he once had a painful twisting condition of his testicles called *testicular extortion*. He meant testicular torsion. A consultant anaesthetist once told me of a patient who said she had trouble waking up every time an *atheist* put her to sleep. And a legally minded lady who once had a female sterilisation (or tubal ligation) said she had undergone a *tubal litigation*. Mechanics and couriers are prone to describing *hiace hernias* (hiatus hernias).

The pronunciation of medicines can be as difficult for doctors as patients, but medics still like to giggle at some bloopers that crop up when requesting repeat prescriptions. One man asked his doctor for more *durex* for his constipation, when he really wanted a laxative called dulax. Thankfully this error was spotted. Augmentin is a commonly used brand of antibiotic in General Practice and doctors often get a giggle when contrary patients request *argumentin*. Recently I heard about a patient who rubbed *taxman gel* on his hip twice a day (traxam gel). And a farmer with gastric problems once wrote *muck-o-gel* on his request for a repeat prescription (mucogel). Another patient who underwent a double bypass heart procedure proudly told his doctor that the *dual carriageway* operation was a great success. A consultant who spent time in America once told me that *sick as hell anaemia* (sickle cell anaemia) and a rather apt *oldtimers's disease* (alzheimers disease) were common misnomers on the other shore of the Atlantic. A GP once treated a patient for a *fractured spatula* (scapula) and finally I'm told there were red faces all round when an elderly man told a young lady doctor that he was having trouble with his *prostitute gland*.

A FOOTNOTE FOR ALEX HIGGINS
July 2010

Last month's lonely and protracted death of Alex Higgins reminds us of the fragility and unpredictability of life, especially those lived on the margins. His obituaries mention a career that was 'blighted by alcohol and drugs'. All the old clichés about the 'people's champion' were trawled from the depths - dancing too close to a flame, living life at full throttle and burning the candle at both ends. The wonder is that Higgins lived to the age of 61 at all.

His 13 year survival with carcinoma of the palate/throat, considering that his lymph glands were affected at initial diagnosis, bears testament to both an innate toughness and very good oncology services in Belfast. But reading between the lines and looking at the quality of life Higgins endured in his final decade, really you would not wish this on anyone. Life on state benefit in sheltered housing, flitting between bars, social welfare, chemists and bookie shops. Photographers always ready to pounce - flogging weekly updates on a skeletal frame before they get to bury it. Unremitting post-radiotherapy pain. An absence of teeth. Attendance at charity events when you could barely hold a cue. Fund-raising events for the insertion of dental implants in sunny Marbella. Sisters calling by with roast dinners that are blended so he can drink them. Anti-depressants, pain-killers and mogadon to put your lights out at night. A website in your name flogging ads for casinos and pizza. Ever-dwindling offers for product promotion, poker events and exhibition matches. Suicidal thoughts. Pennies, that once were pounds, for a slice of your limited time.

Perhaps the finest achievement of Alex Higgins in his declining years was his endearingly blinkered but extraordinarily honest autobiography. *From the Eye of the Hurricane*, published three years ago, was a keen appraisal of forty years in the limelight. It was peppered with some priceless quotations, not least his claim that snooker introduced him 'some of the world's most obnoxious, rudest and saddest people'. Alex Higgins was a man of extraordinary contradictions. The woman-beater who wept like a babe in his family's arms as he was crowned world champion. The heavy drinking chain-smoking gambler who briefly fronted a campaign to sue tobacco companies:

"I was due to get around £200,000 from the claim. Mind you had it come off, I would probably have spent it all on cigarettes, drink and gambling. So it was probably a blessing that in 2002 the courts ruled against us and the claim failed."

The head-butting of a tournament director. The punching of a press officer. The referee in a headlock. The attempted spearing of a loud fan with his cue. An idle but menacing threat to have fellow Northern Ireland professional "po-faced" Dennis Taylor shot. All contrast with a reputation for quiet generosity and capacity for gift-giving. His recollection of first meeting with Jimmy White at Pontin's holiday camp in the 1970s is hilarious, assuming you are not a bird lover. White found Higgins throwing bread from his chalet for visiting seagulls. When the gulls landed he was trying to pick them off one by one with some accurate knife-throwing.

Higgins, by all accounts always a poor gambler, and he played the victim card far too often for his own good. From an early age he prospered at the art of earning 'a few shillings' but tempered this talent with an all too ready line in weak excuses. Snooker commentators have long noted wryly that Higgins was a master of self-justification. The table could be blamed, the cue, the opponent, the referee, the heat, the cold, but Alex was a stranger to himself, choosing not to see his own behaviour in a mirror.

Abingdon Street Belfast. 1950s. Only son of adoring parents.

Three spoiling sisters who wouldn't let him out of the house unless he was immaculately turned out. Council estate where "kids got by on their own wits and everyone was into some scam or other." Skinny kid who stayed out of trouble at school and kept well away from the "tough lads". Known at home as a "money machine" - earned cash at local snooker hall keeping score for punters who couldn't add or subtract. Hustling and scheming. Always honest, never stealing. The Protestant way. Enjoyed girls without guilt. Fondness for nice clothes. Sharp dressed man like his Dad. As for those mannerisms - sniffing, constant fidgeting, body twitching, chain smoking and the manic shuffling gait around the table- who knows? Self-Consciousness? Substance withdrawal? Anxiety? Attention deficit hyperactivity? Higgins own explanation was simpler, it was to "win games in record time to get to the pub and the girls quickly."

And that allergy to dicky-bows? Snooker bosses wanted to tidy up the game for its new female audience. Higgins said they wanted to turn it into a posh sport like polo and chose to pester him with their pettiness. He detested the bowtie, particularly under hot television lighting, and enlisted a medical specialist who confirmed in writing to snooker authorities that Alex had a 'sweat rash' that could be brought on by the wearing of any kind of tie. The WPBSA weren't having this and sent him off to their own medical man. Their own doctor then embarrassed the blazers by confirming the original diagnosis.

There were his marriage problems. One might forgive some brat-like behaviour in the all-male environs of the snooker fraternity, but it was in his treatment of women, that Higgins most let the side down. The hurling of ashtrays and throwing of televisions become not just predictable, but symptomatic and suggestive after a while. There is no official medical condition called spoiled child syndrome but perhaps there should be. Little surprise that treatment failed. Spate of counselling, spell in a nursing home and even a short-lived admission to a mental hospital "full of crazy people" where "they had us sitting around in groups, playing silly games and talking about our problems." Someday, we will have a thoughtful, retrospective and complete biography of Alex Higgins - carefully considered and not rushed to market. Until then we can remember this man's skill and the passing of a most extraordinary life. As someone wise once said to me "Sure aren't we all full of contradictions?"

HEALTH AT
HUNDRED ACRE WOOD
October 2009

Winnie the Pooh resurfaced this month after an eighty year absence from the forest. The family trust which administers AA Milne's estate has authorised a new volume, *Return to the Hundred Acre Wood*, which should enthral thousands of children this Christmas and bring a new generation of young readers back to the originals. The most dangerous doctor of all is the one with time on his hands, so this week I am going to rove my clinical eye over the original cast of *Winnie the Pooh*. Yes, it's check-up time for Christopher Robin's small band of friends.

Back in 1926 when Milne's first volume was published, Pooh was living alone, composing doggerel, and getting himself involved in a catalogue of accidents. In the first chapter he gets stung by bees, shot by Christopher Robin and falls from a high tree into some gorse. It took him six days to remove all the prickles which begs the question - did Pooh suffer from excessive clumsiness, what we now call dyspraxia. Further evidence for this diagnosis can be garnered by the fact that Pooh has trouble with simple tasks like putting his boots on. Further misfortunes include getting wedged for a whole week in the entrance to Rabbit's house and being unable to remove an empty honey pot from his overlarge head. These could be accounted for by the fact that Pooh is overweight, perhaps even morbidly obese. His body mass index or BMI is not stated in the text but it is safe to assume from the excellent illustrations that he is well up in the top 5% weight category for ursine creatures. He does walk a lot which raises the possibility that rather than sloth, his corpulence may be inherited or due to an underactive thyroid gland. Pooh's diet passes the five a day test, except that all five portions seem to be of honey. Pooh's honey fad is obsessive, dominating his social interactions to the extent that he really only calls on friends when their larders are full. Mentally he is sluggish, again perhaps hypothyroid, but evidence for a low IQ is suggested by his heavy use of malapropisms. On one occasion he misinterprets the words 'customary procedure' as crustimoney proseedcake. Pooh's concentration wanes when he is hungry and he 'comes over all funny' and has to hurry home for a snack to sustain him. This raises the possibility of a sugar regulation problem - hypoglycaemia perhaps. Pooh also suffers from insomnia. Once when counting sheep didn't work, he counted 587 heffalumps. He also falls asleep midway through supper which raises a possible diagnosis of sleep apnoea, although the fact that he is a good dreamer makes this less likely.

As for Eyeore, the old grey donkey from a thistly corner of the forest, sadness is the leitmotif that pervades his existence. His mindset is very negative, suggestive of an endogenous depression. He has some insight into his condition, admitting that he sometimes doesn't know what he's talking about. His speech is gloomy and he has poverty of movement. He mopes, spends much of his day gazing at the ground and his symptoms are more pronounced in the morning. In an early chapter he mislays his tail, but it seems his depression pre-dates this loss, which simply magnifies it. On another occasion he studies his own reflection in water and utters the telling word 'pathetic.' The only activities he enjoys, although enjoys is probably too forceful a verb for Eeyore, are invoking sympathy and predicting the worst. His friends comment on his demeanour. Pooh tells Piglet that their friend is 'in a very sad condition', 'very gloomy' and possesses a 'melancholy way'. Eeyore's personal hygiene suffers too as he is not keen on washing. His diet consists solely of thistles which raises an outside possibility of poisoning. Perhaps a toxic variety like Yellow Star Thistle prevails in Hundred Acre Wood. In one later chapter. Eeyore places his own tail in cold water, so that he can moan about it being numb. Could he have munchausen's syndrome, the rare factitious disorder well known to personal injury lawyers?

Tigger escapes scrutiny as he doesn't figure in the very first volume of Winnie the Pooh. Rabbit is argumentative, tells white lies and comes from a large family of layabouts who feed on the scraps of others. He is the main instigator of the plot to kidnap baby Roo from his mother, although all the friends are equally culpable in this distressing episode of child kidnap. I suspect Rabbit has antisocial personality disorder. Piglet is the character who appeals to any heart splashed with liberal blood. In one episode he is ashamed of something or other and goes to bed with a headache. He is weak-bodied, misses company at home and his loneliness sparks anxiety. But he's an optimist and his first thought in the morning is what exciting thing will happen today. A good observer and shrewd judge of character, his lack of height is a serious issue for him. Despite these feelings of inadequacy (napoleon syndrome) he is up for any adventure. Owl is a strange individual. He is always trying to say something wise, and when words fail he flies off with a loud squawk. He is the John Banville of Hundred Acre Wood, relating long stories using even longer words. When it rains he says 'the atmospheric conditions have been very unfavourable'. Piglet says Owl is not exactly a brain, but he knows things. There's a touch of the aspergers about Owl. Finally we have Kanga, lone parent of baby Roo, defined by her motherhood and the contents of her pouch. A fierce animal, especially in winter, she is protective of her charge and feeds him quack medicine - probiotics perhaps, to make him 'grow big and strong'. She is streetwise and performs good deeds without thought.

Disclaimer: These medical impressions are personal and based solely on a single re-reading of the first *Winnie the Pooh* volume. In 1928, A.A. Milne wrote *The House at Pooh Corner*, his second and final Winnie adventure. It deals with property development and the borrowing of money from a close group of friends who were all executives, shareholders and board members of the same bank. As a simple doctor, I know nothing of these matters. But in 1929 the inhabitants of Hundred Acre Wood heard a loud bang coming from a nearby clearing called Wall Street. Plus ça change.

THE RUDE CONSULTANT
August 2004

Last Christmas, I had a boozy night out at an over-rated restaurant on Dublin's Kildare Street. It was a re-union of old pals and as the resident medic in attendance, conversation turned, as it always does, to matters of health and death. One diner had cause to visit a hospital consultant recently and wasn't too happy about forking out €150 for a bedside manner that 'befitted a pig'. The name of the specialist gave me a clue to the nature of the diagnosis - to be polite about it, my friend had a small problem with his bottom. I told him to tell his GP about the consultant's abrupt manner so that he might consider sending his referrals elsewhere. But my friend had already done that. His GP replied "How would your own bedside manner be if you spent every working day looking up a*******s like yours?" There's no answer to that. Perhaps my friend needs a new GP too.

Every line of work has its share of cads, cranks, and caustic cretins. But the hospital consultant seems to reign supreme in Olympic rudeness. Now I have to say, it is a small minority that gives the majority a bad name. But what the uncouth lack in numbers, they do make up for in words. I recently invited medical colleagues to send me reminiscences of the rudest doctors they had ever worked with. Allow me share some of their recollections.

A consultant told a woman that he was very sorry but she was far too fat to operate on. She burst into tears. 'I don't understand why I'm so fat Doctor', she said, 'I'm a vegetarian'. To which he replied, 'So what have you been eating Madam. Trees !??'

In similar vein, another obese woman was lectured about appetite by her consultant.

"But Doctor I eat like a bird." she protested. "Yes Madam, a vulture" was the scurrilous reply.

And a very pious gynaecologist once removed an IUD contraceptive device from a woman during his clinic, and holding the offending object aloft went into the waiting area shouting theatrically "this is a mortal sin !"

One Dublin surgeon's pet hate was not children, but women who in his book had far too many of them. One day at outpatients he met with a lady who admitted to having seven children. He invited her to take the pill but she said it was out of the question. 'Why not?' he retorted 'Haven't you got a bloody mouth on you?' At this stage her irate husband stepped in to defend his wife's honour and roared that his wife was prone to clots in her legs and couldn't take it. Unfazed, the consultant pointed at the woman's husband and shouted to his intern 'Arrange to sterilise that libidinous brute !'

Another eminent specialist was asked by a patient whether she should seek a second opinion on his diagnosis. "Certainly Madam" came the reply, I'll tell you AGAIN, you have carpal tunnel syndrome."

And a pompous chest specialist showed his sensitive side to a smoker when he made a diagnosis of lung cancer. "Well Sir, you've read about it, you've heard about it, and now you've got it".

It's not just patients who suffer. Junior doctors also run the gauntlet of abuse from the proverbial rude consultant. One tardy house doctor who could never make the ward round on time was told "Murphy, You're like an undescended testicle - you're always late and when you finally appear, you're no bloody good!"

So what can you do when you have the misfortune to be treated with a complete lack of respect? Not an easy question to answer. You could write to the Medical Council, but delays in dealing with complaints are legendary, and unless they consider it a matter of serious professional misconduct you may not be satisfied with the response. GPs who hear horror stories about consultant colleagues will often strike them off their referral lists so you may get a more sympathetic hearing there. And remember, there's nothing a bully hates more than a taste of their own medicine. I met a lady patient once who had been treated by a notoriously rude medic. She got great satisfaction from sending flowers to his wife. The accompanying card read simply "Commiserations - from a former patient of your husband."

G'DAY DOC
April 2009

When I passed out as an apprentice doctor in 1988, medical newspapers were full of adverts inviting us to practice our newfound skills on guinea pigs down under. Australian recruitment agencies inevitably mentioned hot sun, hot sand and hot salaries. Strict editorial rules drew the line at any mention of hot sheilas. Proud to say, I resisted all temptation, but many colleagues did venture to the Antipodes and like those picnic-goers at Hanging Rock, some have never been heard of since. Now that the Irish economy is going to ground, and medical salaries are set to plummet, the advertisements are starting to re-appear. Some time ago a friend sent me a complete Dictionary of Aussie Slang, a must for anyone searching for ANZAC citizenship. I was writing a column in the medical press back then so I invited doctors who might have served time down south, to send in their own observations on Australian medicine. A right good post bag resulted.

I'm feeling crook is something medics heard on a daily basis. It has nothing to do with ancestors having chains removed in Botany Bay, it simply implies that you are ill. If you happen to be admitted to intensive care then *I'm feeling proper crook* is the appropriate term. Should the treatment not go so well and the services of the hospital mortician are required, *rellies* (relatives) are told that their loved one has *carked it* or *kicked the bucket*. Your bladder is your *goon bag*, an organ that fills up rather quickly when you imbibe *amber fluid* (beer). Doctors who wish their patients to produce a urine sample from the goon bag must provide them with a beaker and ask them to visit the *dunny, toot* or *thunder-box*. Never ask for a *piece of piss* - that simply means something is easy. Other anatomical variants to watch for are *clod hoppers* (feet) and *ivories* (teeth). Paediatricians in Ireland look after children, but the clinics of their Aussie equivalents are over-run with *ankle-biters, tykes, sprogs, nippers* and *billylids*. For rectal examinations or buttock injections, patients are instructed to *chuck a brown eye* which in our vernacular would simply be 'lower your pants' (*underdacks*). Little flies that spread malaria are called *mossies* and those rubber receptacles which offend popes but offer wonderful protection against reproductive and genito-urinary mishaps are called *frangers*. Casualty officers should know that *fell off my pushy* usually refers to a recent bicycle accident. A *prang* is a minor road accident, whilst a *bingle* is a more serious one. Patients involved in a bingle often require the attention of an orthopaedic surgeon, sometimes called a *panel beater*. Both types of accidents may be caused by reckless drivers known as *lead-foots*. Rowdy queue jumpers in the emergency department are likely to be told by the charge-nurse to b*ite ya bum*, an endearing advisory term requesting a bit of peace and quiet.

Giving somebody the optics has nothing to do with examination of the retina. It means you are probably devoting too much time to ogling the fairer sex or indeed the above-mentioned charge-nurse. Ear, nose and throat specialists who visit Australia will be told early in their careers that a *bushman's hanky* involves holding one nostril closed and blowing rather energetically through the other one. Being a teetotaller in Australia, a hanging offence in rural parts, has its own peculiar term of abuse - those who wear pioneer pins are known as *wowsers*. And a *root* is how Australian men boast of their endeavours in bed. A visiting politician found this out to his cost when he informed his bemused hosts in a speech that 'all my early *roots* were here'. A *root rat* is a gentleman, a politician perhaps but not exclusively so, whose vocabulary does not include the word monogamy. Ladies who are keen on over-visiting *gynos* (obstetricians/gynaecologists) are said to be *clucky*.

Chucking a sickie has nothing to do with forceful or projectile vomiting. It means a day off work, usually without pay as Australians are not renowned for state-sponsored generosity. Getting physically sick is a *chunder*, especially when there is drink involved. When the whole contents of the barbie come back up, the descriptive term is changed to a *technicolour yawn*. *Vegemite* is a legendary Australian hangover cure, an extract of yeast you spread on very hot toast. Vegemite is also hawked around as a general tonic for the children of Oz, just as we in these parts are assailed with yarns about over-priced bacteria-ridden yoghurts. Doctors, nurses or indeed any worker who toils hard are delightfully called *yakkers*, whilst *bastard* is still a term of great endearment and not worth *packing a wallop* (throwing a punch) over . Those who shirk their share of work are sometimes accused of *fat-arsing around*, a term that has nothing to do with general shape or body mass index. A psychiatric diagnosis yet to reach clinical textbooks in the northern hemisphere is *a few kangaroos short of a top paddock*. Doctors who ask rather too many questions might get a reputation as *stickybeaks*. Irish dieticians seeking Ozzie visas also need to do their homework. Sausages, renowned for non-disclosure of entire contents are known as *mystery bags*. I rather like their description of milk as *moo juice*, not to mention the delicacy of Australian rabbit - known locally as *underground mutton*. The natives don't waste too many letters. That stringy Italian dish of pasta and mince is known by culturally adept Aussies as *Spag Bol*.

And don't forget a bit of geography before you pick up your Irish stumps. *Sandgropers* come from Western Australia, *Top Enders* are residents of Northern Territory whilst *Banana Benders* are those who hail from Queensland. You'll always be a *Paddy*. But now that you know how to converse with the natives, they'll consider you a decent *larrikin*. G'day mate.

WHAT THE DOCTOR SAW
November 2013

On the cover of this book is an old photograph from my mother's side of the family. It was taken in the grounds of Ireland's most notorious criminal asylum, the Central Mental Hospital at Dundrum. Neddy was the asylum donkey, newly retired from its fourteen acre farm and allowed to roam the Hospital grounds. The man with the reins is Billy, my late grandfather, who was resident at the Central Mental Hospital between the years 1948 and 1965. Billy was the hospital's Governor and Chief Psychiatrist, otherwise known as Dr William J. Coyne. Behind those imposing high walls known to generations of Dubliners, he worked as a doctor and administrator, practised his golf and with his wife, my Granny Catherine, brought up a family of five girls.

To his wife and daughters he was Daddy. His grandchildren all knew him as Pop. But to everyone else, he was simply The Doctor. Pop was born in 1900 and grew up on the seafront at Clontarf on the north side of Dublin. His father's family, the Coynes, were once well-to-do merchants from Urlingford in County Kilkenny. His mother's family were Republican Murphys from Dublin's North Strand. Billy was a bright student at O'Connell Schools, a regular prize-winner like his friend, the Lemass boy in the class ahead of him. Armed with a City of Dublin Scholarship after his Leaving Certificate, he enrolled at the medical school of University College Dublin, then on Cecilia Street at Temple Bar. Whilst studying at UCD, Pop's youngest brother contracted diphtheria and died. Family lore has it that my grandfather took blame for this tragedy, or was made to feel somehow responsible for his baby brother's death. Pop had been in attendance at a notorious fever hospital at the time and it seems he was blamed for 'bringing the disease home'. This was the explanation suggested to us for Pop's pre-occupation with hand washing, which bordered on the obsessional. He washed his hands so frequently that the skin became wafer thin and ulcerated in later life. In the late 1960s, Pop had one of Ireland's first electric hot air hand-driers installed in his bathroom. It made quite an impression on his grandchildren, especially those for whom hand-washing was a foreign country. His main teaching hospital was the Richmond and he once told my father about a strange episode there during the Irish Civil War when he and other clinical staff were kidnapped at gunpoint and marched down O'Connell Street towards Westmoreland Street by an armed group. They were taken to a house where a number of casualties of the war had been hiding and told to minister to their wounds. All Pop would say about this event was that the people involved were 'Bolshies' and I have not heard of this episode in any chronicles of the Irish Civil War. He qualified from the Richmond Hospital in 1923 and immediately began studying for a post-graduate qualifications.

Armed with a glowing reference from Dr Denis Coffey, UCD's first President, he migrated to London for further training. His experience in the city's Bethlehem Hospital, better known perhaps as Bedlam, set him up for a career in psychiatry and he later became Deputy Resident Medical Superintendent at the private Chiswick House asylum west of London. He met and married my London born grandmother, started a family and even found time for some personal golf lessons from legendary professional Henry

Cotton. In 1934 he returned to Dublin to a house on the grounds of Mountjoy Prison to take up the position of Resident Medical Officer. We have other archive photos of Pop and his extended family enjoying sunny weekends on the prison's tennis court. But they don't tell the complete story. One of the Medical Officer's duties at Mountjoy was to witness executions and to certify the prisoners' deaths by hanging. To our knowledge, he had only to perform this task once, in June 1937. (I have written about the case in a separate chapter of this book called The Anatomy of Hanging). The memory of this event stayed with him a lifetime. He and his young family left Mountjoy very soon after that execution for the rolling hills of Monaghan. He was appointed R.M.S. in the District Mental Hospital there, where he stayed for the duration of the war and beyond. By all accounts his decade there was extraordinary. According to Joseph Corcoran, chairman of the hospital worker's union, conditions for staff and patients improved 100% under his stewardship. Corcoran said that Monaghan went from being a hospital with the worst conditions for staff in the country to one of the best. Pop's favourite four prescriptions were occupational therapy, industrial therapy, agricultural therapy and recreational therapy - for patients and staff. Sports days, work parties, outings, picnics, sing-songs and traditional dances were regular events he placed on the hospital calendar. He recognised how little the drugs of the day did to help patients and focused instead on the idea that an institutionalised body and an idle mind are less inclined to get better. We have some extraordinary black and white cine film that he took of the hospital sports day in 1939, shot days before the Second World War began. The Nurse's Obstacle Race and the Patient's Slow Bicycle Race being particular favourites.

All this time, Pop was still studying, taking a Fellowship in the Royal College of Physicians in 1939 and a Diploma in Public Health in 1945. In 1949, he moved back to Dublin taking up the position of Governor at Dundrum. A loyal and generous staff at Monaghan gave him a beautiful set of new golf clubs as a departing gift.

The Central Mental Hospital opened in 1850, as Ireland's first criminal lunatic asylum. In fact it was the first such institution on these islands, predating Broadmoor by a full ten years. What differentiated this mental hospital from others, was the fact that most of its patients had committed serious crimes, usually manslaughter.

On the day he arrived at the Governor's House at Dundrum, Pop noticed that his full length hall mirror had been removed from the furniture van but there was still no sign of his golf clubs. As a keen student of golf mechanics be began to practice his swing, with an invisible club, whilst watching his reflection in the mirror. Two patients were passing and one asked the other if a new inmate had just arrived. His pal had a seriously worried look as he replied. 'No, I think that's our new psychiatrist !'

Pop took his golf almost as seriously as he took criminal law and forensic psychiatry. He had 52 different golf swings, one for each week of the year. All were modelled on touring professionals of the day. He might play a Saturday medal as Gary Player and then a Wednesday fourball as Ben Hogan. According to the club's professional, the late Christy Greene, Pop had the most elegant swings ever seen at Milltown Golf Club. But records show that The Doctor never once got his handicap down below a hacker's 18.

In his first year at Dundrum, he was asked by the Dáil's public accounts committee what he was going to do to staunch expenditure at his hospital. True to form, Pop replied that he would be doing the exact opposite and went on to list all the measures he would need extra money for. Within a few years of arriving, he had managed to double the hospital's financial allocation, and none of it went on bigger salaries.

He banished the practice of patients sharing communal ill-fitting garments and insisted that each person would have their own personal clothing, tailored in their own size. Twice a year he would hire buses to bring patients out from Dundrum on day trips and picnics. The beach at St Ita's in Portrane was a favourite destination, a busman's holiday of sorts, but greatly enjoyed by staff and long-stay patients. One of his charges, a man who had killed twice, was very interested in sailing. Pop allowed him to build boats in the hospital grounds for the duration of his stay.

Every year Pop was hauled before politicians on the public accounts committee to explain matters like failures of the carrot crop on the hospital farm, low prices from sales of hospital sheep, victualling rations for staff and the late delivery of spring seeds. Never once was he asked a single question about his patients. To the Oireachtas of the day, patients with mental illnesses were simply a burden and a cost. I'm not sure too much has changed today.

In 1958 he was forced against his will and judgement, to accept Nurse Cadden as a patient. She was a well known figure in Ireland's back street abortion business who had a death sentence commuted to life imprisonment and it was Pop's contention all along that she had no mental illness and should never have been sent there in the first place. It has been suggested that she was sent to Dundrum from Mountjoy jail to silence her. What exactly she knew, that some wished to silence is not recorded. Nurse Cadden died in Dundrum just one year after her arrival.

Pop retired in 1965 and lived another 20 years in happy and busy retirement. The condition of his hands meant that he had to give up golf, but the game of bridge at which he excelled, provided ongoing skills to master. He is buried high up in St Fintan's Cemetery in Sutton, still keeping watch over the shenanigans of his native city. His grave is just few feet away from the remains of a Taoiseach who once boasted to have 'done the State some service, and they know it.' 'No more of that' I can hear Pop whisper.

HAPPY BIRTHDAY SIGMUND FREUD
May 2006

We have just celebrated the 150th anniversary of the birth of psychoanalyst extraordinaire, Dr Sigmund Freud. I once had the great pleasure of visiting Freud's residence at 19 Berggasse, Vienna. He wasn't at home. Indeed he had left rather abruptly for Paris in 1938, and then London, where he died a year later. Freud was of Jewish faith and Vienna was no hotbed of European tolerance or religious diversity at the time. Vienna is quite a beautiful old city but I could not say the same for its inhabitants. The correct psychiatric terminology for its uptight and rule-loving citizens is hard to find but if I said 'up their own bums' you might catch my drift. I have never quite forgiven the Austrian coach driver who stopped his bus in the middle of rush hour traffic and came clambering down an aisle packed with tourists saying "'Zombody iz eating ze Packetz of ze Crisps on ze bus." He refused to move until a certain Irishman owned up to opening a bag of Tayto.

In the 1970s, a museum was developed on the Berggasse in the house where Freud reared his talented family and saw his patients. Though austere by today's standards, I found it quite haunting and beautiful. Medical students in my day were given quite a cursory education on Freud so I was delighted to use the visit as an opportunity to read up on psychiatry's greatest celebrity. In his day, Freud was an important thinker - a great man for theories. He had that great advantage over today's medical talkers and opinion-leaders in that he actually met and treated patients. If he was around today, he would perhaps be tempted into the circus of the courts system where psychiatrists and psychologists can be hired out like monkey suits at a debs dance and earn huge amounts of money disputing each other's theories in public without ever having to effect a cure.

Freud began his medical career by studying the genitalia of eels. Later he undertook studies of a new drug called cocaine declaring that both he and his patients (those who were not already morphine addicts) had broad experience of it over long periods of time and perceived it to be non-addictive. He then drifted into hospital neurology. The greatest career influence on Freud was Jean Martin Charcot whom he first encountered on a trip to Paris. Charcot was a giant of 19th century medicine. It is alleged that he married an exceedingly plain lady for power and wealth, and let his medical training and skill do the rest for his advancement. A renowned hypnotist, who specialised in neurology and diseases of the mind, it was Charcot who lent Freud the idea that sex was the root cause of all hysteria. *"C'est toujours la chose genitale - toujours... toujours... toujours."*

In the 1890s Freud began theorising about early sexual traumas, usually at the hand of the father, and how they were the root cause of neurosis in his predominantly female hysterical patients. He invented seduction theories and the concept of repressed memory and went public with his thoughts on the Viennese lecture circuit. Within months however he had abandoned this

29

conjecture to replace it with his Oedipus theory - the idea that infants are sexualised from birth, with sexual fantasies towards their mothers and violent urges towards their fathers. He held rigidly to this doctrine until the end of his life in 1939 and to this day, Freud revisionists like nothing more than to convene anniversary conferences and fantasise about whether he dropped the wrong theory. Twenty years ago as a medical student in St Patrick's Hospital in Dublin, we had a coffee shop discussion on Sigmund Freud with fellow inmates. Scepticism was my middle name back then for I recall saying that Freud was just one vowel away from being a complete charlatan. But his patients loved him, they spoke highly of his skill, and he certainly left us with a legacy and plenty to talk about. That's surely worth commemorating so Happy Birthday Sigmund.

THE LAST CASTRATO
October 2004

You have probably read plenty of biblical references on placards at football matches. But my guess is that Matthew 19:12 is not one of them. Here is what it says:

There are some eunuchs which were so born from their mother's womb: and there are some eunuchs, which were made eunuchs by men: and there be eunuchs, which have made themselves eunuchs for the kingdom of heaven's sake.

I must admit, Matthew had a nice turn of phrase. In a few well chosen words, he has managed to describe the aetiology of one of man's oldest anxieties - the fear of castration.

Of course Matthew was not to know that his theory would become outdated. In the sixteenth and subsequent centuries, it was the pushy stage-mom who became the greatest threat to male pouches.

It became commonplace in the so-called age of Enlightenment, for castrated male children to be used for choral music. In most cases this was at the instigation of opera loving mother. If she couldn't afford the extravagance of a doctor to do the chopping, she often did the dirty deed herself. Poor families were quite happy to go along with the practice. Like today's X-Factor, singing provided a ticket out of poverty or oblivion into the respectable and potentially lucrative world of church sanctioned popular music. But unlike today's talent shows, Castrato Factor required something known in the surgical trade as a bilateral orchidectomy.

This old surgical procedure is well described in the medical literature. In the absence of a hefty dose of opium, the young patient was placed in a warm bath and had his jugular neck veins compressed until rendered semi-conscious. The knife was warmed. Cutting and sewing took just minutes, particularly if Mum was also a kitchen-goddess who could do wonderful things with a plucked chicken.

Officially, both church and state expressed disapproval of this barbarism, but commentators suggest that they were all too willing to believe 'cock and bull' stories about dog attacks and kicking horses. Even today, male victims of accidental groin traumas get ribbed about future soprano careers. But this teasing is far off the mark. Castration has no effect on the vocal cords of an adult male. Only if carried out before puberty does it prevent the cords from thickening and maintain the child's falsetto voice.

There was a captive market for ten year old boy singers whose voices were guaranteed not to break. Principally because the Catholic Church took St Paul at his word over his infamous dictum *'Let women be silent in Churches'*.

For nearly three hundred years the castrato found ready employment and generous pay-packets in the twin worlds of Opera and Church Music. According to the *Rough Guide to Opera* castratos developed uncommonly thick hair yet many remained bald everywhere else. They were taller than average and prone to adult obesity. Both Catholic and Protestant churches refused castrati the rite of marriage so they became popular consorts for both sexes. Women were particularly enamoured with this early form of male contraception.

The last castrato was a Professor Alessandro Moreschi who was born near Rome in 1858. He became conductor of the choir at the Sistine Chapel. Moreschi died in 1922 and bears the distinction of being the only castrato ever to have been recorded. You can listen to samples of his recordings on the internet. But be warned, it's eerie. Not the sort of stuff to listen to in a warm bath.

TWO WISE MEN
September 2007

For some years I have had the privilege of being a friend, board member and trustee of Alice Leahy's TRUST organisation which does so much to alleviate the pain of people who live on the streets. The little entrance hall at TRUST is a lovely room to meet in. One Wednesday lunchtime, late last year, we were about to have our monthly board meeting in the hall, when one of our dearest friends, Eddie, was letting himself out. He looked a million dollars in his crombie coat, having had his daily shower, shave and change of clothes. I took the opportunity to introduce Eddie to James, our chairman at TRUST, and the two men smiled, shook hands, and wished each other well. Nine months on, as I write this piece, Eddie and James are no longer with us. James passed away at home just a few weeks after that board meeting and in August of this year we lost Eddie to cancer in Our Lady's Hospice in Harold's Cross. They were two extraordinary men - as Eamonn MacThomáis used to say, both professors in the 'university of conversation'.

James was first and foremost a family doctor. One obituary described him as the architect of modern general practice in Ireland. He abhorred the old dispensary system where poor patients were treated in Dickensian clinics run by the state, whilst private patients were invited into the doctor's parlour for after hours consultations. James was elected chairman of the old Eastern Health Board (a rare achievement for somebody who was not a party hack) and he was instrumental in reforming this blight on Irish General Practice.

I first came to know James as one of my professors in Trinity College Medical School and it was clear to anybody who attended his lectures that he was very much more than a disease merchant. He spoke about people - not about their symptoms. He spoke of their needs - rather than their tablets. He spoke about the fears of patients rather than the fears of medical practitioners. One of his greatest regrets about the state of modern healthcare was that doctors were so slow to recognise their own limitations.

Together with his Trinity colleague Professor Petr Skrabanek, James set out to challenge all sorts of medical orthodoxy. When pompous doctors made pronouncements, James and Petr were first to stand in line and ask for proof. All too often it was not forthcoming. They read widely and published many books between them. They challenged some of the life-long labels doctors stuck on patients, particularly in the field of psychiatry. They poured icy cold water on those who claimed to specialise in 'preventing illness'. They asked why doctors were so sensitive to professional criticism and independent appraisal when this was what they themselves should have been trained to do. James had a particular warmth and empathy for those who were 'different' and channelled his steadfast principals of freedom of expression and tolerance through his work at TRUST. He accepted you as you were, and saw the role of a doctor as one who should offer comfort and friendship above all else.

Eddie was a true character who touched the lives of so many in his native city. He probably knew more people in Dublin than the rest of us in TRUST put together, yet despite having so many friends and acquaintances, he felt removed and apart from his people. His first job as a teenager was in an abattoir - something that must have been very hard for somebody who loved, cared for and confided in animals. He married young and had two fine children of whom he was very proud. Later he worked in maintenance for Dublin Corporation - at one stage held down two jobs to sustain his young family. Through no fault of his own, Eddie succumbed to mental illness and spent much of his thirties and forties in psychiatric hospitals - often against his will. His doctors might have described him as difficult to treat - Eddie saw it differently. He wanted to talk - but he found it hard to get anyone to listen. Instead he was offered tablets, when he refused he was forcefully held down for injections. He used to say 'they know all about tablets, but nothing about the mind - they don't know how I feel.'

When medication didn't work, Eddie was sent for electro-convulsive therapy. He never forgot this treatment - it was perhaps the greatest trauma of his life. A rubber bit was placed in his mouth, he was injected with tranquillisers and an electric shock was delivered to his brain. 'It's like a horse kicking you in the head, you feel like an animal too !' he told Nurse Alice in his final days.

Eddie had few 'little luxuries' as he called them. He liked his John Player Blue and a few cans of beer if there was sport on TV. Anyone could call to Eddie's pad - for money, to share a can, borrow a cigarette, discuss their troubles - and he would always let them in. He liked to set quizzes - 'Name six streets in Dublin named after counties in Ireland' was one he enjoyed best with new friends.

I thought of Eddie as a kind of psychiatrist, trained on the streets and the hospitals he was marched into. He spoke knowledgeably about people's problems and could do wonderful imitations of the many doctors who treated him over the years. I'm sure he did me too. He tolerated my dull company and occasional home visits probably because I would share a few of his cigarettes with him.

Eddie knew he had a mental illness, and he knew where it came from. 'It's inherited and there's nothing I can do about it only accept it' he would say. His problem was not his illness, it was how others treated him because of it.

In a one room flat on the upper floor of a complex off Francis Street lived Eddie, his three Jack Russells, his crombie coat, little television, a bed, a chair and his hob cooker which doubled up as a heater in Winter. He carried a photograph of himself looking very dapper as a young footballer.

'I have lived a weird life, like a hermit, lost for company - the stigma of mental illness lasts. Look at the new hospitals, you have to go in a separate entrance if you are mentally ill.'

Eddie had a twinkle in his eye and always found the right words in the company of ladies. He was considered a 'great catch' in his youth. He had the gift of the gab, liked his clothes and knew just the right words to make others feel comfortable with him.

Like James, he would challenge those who assumed authority as their mantle. He noticed little things. Being a former boxer, he liked to keep people on their toes. During his final illness, he would query why nobody seemed to have time to sit down and chat. 'The way they say how are your bowels today instead of how are you'.

When Eddie's time was up, the hospice rang TRUST to say they were having difficulty getting him attached to a painkiller pump. His fear of injections was very real - it reminded him of the sometimes brutal ways his mental illness was treated. Nurse

Geraldine rushed off to Harold's Cross to comfort him. She held out her hand and he squeezed it. Gerri asked him to close his eyes. His last words were so typical of Eddie. He said 'Thank You'.

Two wise men have left us this year at TRUST. We cherish their gift of wisdom and thank their families and friends for sharing them with us. Oh, and Eddie's six counties that have Dublin streets named after them - they are Clare, Wicklow, Meath, Wexford, Cork and Kildare. The last one, Eddie would giggle, has the real madhouse on it .

Postscript: This piece was originally published in a compilation edited by Alice Leahy called Wasting Time with People - Gill & MacMillan. See www.trust-ireland.ie

FITZWILLIAM SQUARE
June 2011

A consultant in Dublin's Mater Hospital had some planning bother recently when neighbours on a street adjacent to the hospital objected to the opening of private medical rooms in his house. They expressed concern that their neighbourhood might become a commercial extension of the nearby hospitals, however I understand they lost the case. Similar planning battles have been fought over the years in the Crumlin area of Dublin where plans to build private consulting rooms in the vicinity of Our Lady's Children's Hospital hit choppy waters. How different things were in bygone times when the presence of doctors living or working on the street was a source of great comfort and pride. On my desk this week is a wonderful new history of Dublin's Fitzwilliam Square, called *Lives Less Ordinary* by Andrew Hughes (Liffey Press). The Square in the 19th Century was more likely to have housed academic doctors or doctors of divinity but in the early decades of the 20th Century, it became the 'Harley Street' of Irish medicine, attracting 'the cream' of the profession. By the 1960s, it had ninety five practising doctors and only four of the sixty nine houses were in private residential accommodation.

Not every 'healthcare professional' was made welcome on Fitzwilliam Square. In 1841 a Dr Thomas Massey took out a sub-lease on Number 4, supposedly because his wife had 'a particular fancy' for living in the residential enclave. Massey was both an apothecary and an accoucheur (obstetrician), specialties that were fairly low down the pecking order of 19th century medical hierarchy. Within months, he had alarmed his neighbours by converting his front room into an chemist shop, complete with business counter and a glass door. Letters started to flow between Massey and concerned residents who feared 'the value of our residences will materially deteriorate by receiving so unwelcome a neighbour as an apothecary'. A court order promptly settled the matter against Massey . The original Fitzwilliam Square leases forbade the use of front of house for umpteen businesses including ale making, soap boiling, skinning, butchering, baking, lime burning, brewing, hat-making, druggist or apothecary. Pharmacists weren't always the eminently respectable profession they lay claim to now.

When I began re-publishing the *Irish Medical Directory* way back in 1994, there were perhaps a dozen specialists still plying their trade on Fitzwilliam Square. What's astonishing is that today, aside I think from one GP surgery, there is virtually no specialist representation left there. The wizardry of fancy clinics and private hospitals with their scanners, laboratories and opportunities to share insured patients with other doctors and therapists, has drawn them all away. The Fitzwilliam Square bodies have been buried. Only the ghosts remain.

DEATH OF IL PARATA
March 2004

I purchased my first 'proper' camera in the summer of 1998. One with zooms, aperture, shutter speeds and other things that still go over my little tête. The Tour de France and its urinalysis testing was marking out new territory in Dublin's fair city, and where better to experiment with fancy camera buttons than Fitzwilliam Square, where the city council had conveniently filled in all the potholes.

Kelly and Roche, those magnificent men with funny accents, had whetted our appetites and now Ireland had a glimpse of what the French called the greatest sporting event on earth. My snaps were appalling. All I caught were innocent bystanders, occasionally obscured by the colourful blur of a passing hero. From many dozens of photos, the only one I was proud of was that of a shaven-headed Italian with a little goatee beard and a spotted bandana. It was Marco Pantani, known affectionately to his Italian country men as Il Parata. Last month, on St Valentine's Day, a bloody-faced and overweight pirate was found dead on the floor in a cheap hotel room in Rimini. Pantani was half naked and his face was bloodied. He was 34 years old. Ten bottles of tranquillisers and anti-depressants littered the room. The post mortem is ongoing, evidence has been delivered of a heart attack, there is talk of swelling of the heart and brain and lung damage too. Five years ago, Pantani's career went into an irreversible decline on home territory. He was hours away from winning the 1999 Giro d'Italia when officials ejected him from the race. A doping test revealed an unnaturally high number of red cells in his blood. Pantani would be tainted from that day with a suspicion that he took the blood hormone Erythropoietin, or EPO. A comeback failed miserably, he became a social recluse and entered a clinic for treatment of depression.

Just two days before Pantani's death, a Belgian rider Johan Sermon died in his sleep. He was 21 and his autopsy revealed heart failure. Last year, six riders died of heart failure, most of them young men in their twenties. In June, French cyclist Fabrice Salanson died in his bed aged 23. 32 year old Denis Zanette collapsed after a visit to the dentist. Marco Rusconi dropped dead in a supermarket car park, he was also 23. A promising amateur Marco Ceriani suffered a heart attack during a race - he was just 16. These deaths in the world of élite cycling suggest that all is not well.

Use of drugs is not the only reason that young men who have reached extraordinary levels of sporting fitness suddenly expire. A rare often hidden heart defect called hypertrophic obstructive cardiomyopathy (medics abbreviate it to HOCM), claims a small number of lives every year in Ireland. Catastrophic and sudden brain haemorrhage, usually caused by bubble-like blood vessels or aneurysms, can also cause deaths out of the blue in young men and women.

But clusters of unexpected deaths in professional cycling suggests that pharmaceutical enhancement of prowess is alive and well. There were 17 sudden and unexpected deaths of European cyclists in the 1980s, the decade in which mass production of EPO began. Cycling authorities want us to believe that the scandals are over and offenders have been dealt with.

But fit young men continue to keel over like flies. Pantani's pathetic death may act as a spur to get to the bottom of a crisis in this murky sport. The powers that be in cycling have much to lose by passing their yellow jerseys over to an independent tribunal of inquiry - nobody likes to break spokes in the wheel of a well oiled and lucrative business. But if somebody doesn't start explaining the inexplicable, and soon, this sport will suffer the same fate as its riders.

THE IRISH DADDY
September 2005

Dr Harold Shipman was a teenager when his mother Vera died of cancer. And it was he who took particular care of her as the curtain was coming down on her short life. It was Harold who kept the house clean. It was Harold who sat long hours by her bedside. And it was Harold Shipman who took her death particularly badly. Legend has it that on the night of her death, he went out in the heavy rain and ran and ran until the new day broke. He returned home shattered and exhausted. Shipman wore a black armband over his school blazer at her funeral and never again spoke about her death. The rest, as they say, is history.

Another boy who lost his Mammy to cancer during childhood is celebrated Irish writer John McGahern. He has just published his first work of non-fiction, *Memoir*, an autobiography of childhood and early adult life. *Memoir* is a magical blend of the ordinary and the extraordinary. A powerful piece of writing, yet as is McGahern's way, gently understated and tending to tug on brainwaves rather than heartstrings. On the one hand it is a simple story of a young boy, the eldest of many siblings, who has the carpet of an idyllic childhood pulled from beneath him with the loss of his mother to breast cancer. McGahern's poignant response was to lock himself into a clothes cupboard under the stairwell where he could have a silent weep.

Into the breach stepped a forbidding father. *Memoir* depicts a father of such menace, manipulation and malevolence he cannot be ignored. The fact that Garda Sergeant Frank McGahern lived a few miles away from his wife and young family is simply explained by the fact that he ran a Barracks in Cootehall, Co Roscommon. The fact that he did not visit his dying wife in her final weeks, yet kept up secret correspondence with her hospital consultant in Dublin, is less easy to explain. Dominating the pages of this work is the brooding and forbidding presence of the repressed and oppressive Irish Daddy. The Daddy who can beat his young daughter senseless with a shovel yet still drag her and the rest of his sorry flock to the front row of his church each Sunday. The Daddy with the physique, good looks, public posturing and outward charm to make it in politics. And the inward boot camp Daddy whose world revolves around order and control for its own sake. Charged, like so many rural Gardaí, with minding areas that are virtually crime-free, he finds his children guilty of childhood and sets about them viciously as if they were the Krays. The Daddy who pigeon holed everything and everybody. You were either too good for him and respected or not good enough and despised. The Daddy whose moods swung as often as his strap. The Pioneer Total Abstinence Daddy. The Sexually Repressed Daddy. The Charming Daddy. The Courting Daddy. The Daddy whose own Mammy was perhaps as strange as he was.

McGahern's *Memoir* is a warm tribute to his mother. It is much less benevolent towards her husband. McGahern has said in interviews that writing the book has not helped him understand his father any better. That may be, but that is not to say it won't help others. *Memoir* richly deserves a good readership.

BROOKLYN
May 2009

Homelessness isn't a hotbed of literary activity these days. Though many folk still put their heads down at night in Dickensian conditions, there are few bestsellers set on the streets where they live. Homeless folk make best copy when they are found dead in skips or rubbish tips. Two weeks ago, just as the shiny new Samuel Beckett Bridge was being towed up the Liffey, twenty homeless people were evacuated from a burning squat in our capital city. Their plight barely registered in the following morning's news. The lives of these non-commuters in our city are not exciting - their days are long, difficult and intolerably dull. Fleeting moments of kindness and the temporary warmth of alcohol are all that many have to live for. We are a fine little nation for protecting the unborn and commemorating our dead. It's the living, the breathing and the suffering who are so far down the batting order, many never make the team.

Colm Tóibín's new book, *Brooklyn*, demonstrates a rare insight into the subject of homeless men and our attitudes towards them. I have been hoarding first editions of Colm's books for years and will extol his literary virtues and future worth to anyone who cares to listen. He is a true Irish gem, a writer whose mastery of the ordinary has reached extraordinary heights. And you don't need a dictionary beside you to appreciate his skill.

Tóibín's new heroine, Eilis Lacey, has left her native Enniscorthy in the 1950s for shop work in Bartocci's Department Store on New York's Fulton Street. She spends her first December away from home helping to serve Christmas Dinner to 'leftover Irishmen' in a parish hall.

'At first the men seemed shabby to Eilis and she noticed body odours from a good number of them. As they sat down and drank their stout waiting for the soup or the food, she could not believe there were so many of them, some so poor-looking and so old, but even the younger ones had bad teeth and appeared worn down. Many were still smoking, even as the soup came.'

They reminded her initially of the men in her home town who congregated at the bridge, or drank too much or had the misfortune of hailing from the County Home. But things changed.

'By the time she served them and they turned to thank her, they seemed more like her father and his brothers in the way they spoke or smiled, the toughness in their faces softened by shyness, what had appeared stubborn or hard now strangely tender.'

Homelessness has been a fact of Irish life for generations, in our own cities and in cities abroad. Governments come and go, and have their half-baked strategies for dealing with it. I am old enough to remember the Homeless Forum which was followed by the Homeless Initiative only to be followed by the Homeless Agency. And sure if I live long enough I will surely see a Homeless Enterprise, a Homeless Authority and heavens-forbid, perhaps even a Homeless Tribunal. There are lots of people who eat handsomely from the homeless pot, and many of them have very fine homes indeed. The whole culture of our industry in homelessness has changed utterly in recent years. It has followed the health bureaucracy model where buzz words, management speak and well-attended conferences have taken over from human contact. It's all about wordy reports, careless promises and meaningless slogans.

Our current Homeless Agency is going to eliminate homelessness in the capital by 2010. By my reckoning, this means they are either seriously deluded or have six months to do something that no city on earth has ever achieved. Their first report for 2001-2003 was called *Shaping The Future*. Their second report for 2004-206 was *Making It Home*. Their third report for 2007-2010 is almost child-like in its optimism it is called *Key To The Door*. Whatever might come next? *Somebody Pissed on my Sleeping Bag Again 2011-2014* is odds on favourite.

Recently I have been trying to digest some of the copious literature that seeps from the bowels of the Homeless Agency. Doing this without succumbing to nausea is no easy task and it's hard to avoid the feeling that the people who write these reports and journals live on a very different planet to the one the rest of us would choose to explore. There are case-management initiatives, inter-agency protocols, holistic needs assessments, progression route networks, facilitator role clarifications, partnership action plans, common operational definitions, pre-determined case studies, housing support pathways, key performance indicators, group knowledge schemes and more of this babble if you cared to read on.

In my native Dublin I know many good people who spend every working day caring for the downtrodden. They don't use these terms. Nor have I ever heard homeless men or women use them. They talk principally of the weather, the warmth and the cold, the wind and the rain, their blankets and their shelter, their tea and their buns, their dark moods and their recent injuries, their foot sores and their leg ulcers, their sleeping bags and their favourite doorways, their socks and their woolly hats, the casualty department and the ambulance trips, the price of drink, the next fag, the occasional kindness of strangers, their friends and foes on the street, their little money, their little futures and their certain death.

Homeless people have little need of research officers, housing consultants, strategic planners, policy advisors and specialists in communications. They don't read quarterly magazines or annual reports and they know little about how to compile and present statistics in a positive light. They are rarely if ever asked to speak at conferences. I can't claim to speak for people who have no homes to go back to. Like Tóibín, I can just imagine that it's life's little things that can make a bit of a difference. The kind word, the gesture, the smile, the pat on the back, the wave, the invitation to eat together, the simple acknowledgement that we are all the very same, we all came down the same canal and someday we'll all go home in a wooden box. Even those whose remains are found in a skip.

HILLERY & BROWNE
July 2009

In April last, my email inbox filled up with requests that I vote in the Irish Book Awards. A campaign was underway, viral I think was the word used, to secure support for certain authors. I thought it rather strange that the prerequisite that you should read the books before you vote was not in operation. I never did hear the result of these awards, and in truth I didn't really care. One motto in life is to treat all awards with great suspicion, and you won't go too far astray.

This summer, long after the best book ceremonials, I took on the pleasing task of perusing two of the medical biographies on the list. One was John Walsh's *Patrick Hillery - The Official Biography*, a studious portrait of the late President. And the other was *Music and Madness*, a sort of memoir by Professor Ivor Browne the psychiatrist. All biographies of Irish medics struggle for air when pitched against the rage of Noel Browne's *Against the Tide*, but both of these titles are worthy reads in their own right.

Paddy Hillery was a remarkable man. All his life he was portrayed as the reluctant public representative, dragged kicking and screaming from his beloved Miltown Malbay and forced to abandon his patients for the vagaries of Irish politics. Yet he continued to win election after election and his career rose to heights seasoned politicians only dream of. Following a short induction on the backbenches, his ministerial career blossomed, taking him from Education to Labour to Foreign Affairs. He departed to become our first European Commissioner and then served two terms at Áras an Uachtarán, the only medical doctor to achieve the highest office in the land. What comes across between the lines of John Walsh's study is that Hillery's understanding of politics was innate, almost Machiavellian. Small but positive reforming steps were the hallmark of his departmental career. In Education he extended school-leaving age to 15 years. He overhauled scholarships for less well off students and developed libraries in primary schools. He fought to keep relatives of politicians off state-appointed boards and instigated the idea of an Irish comprehensive school, currying little favour from bishops. Dr Hillery would not like to be remembered as the Minister who introduced portacabin classrooms to Irish schools, but his original intention was that they were to be used in the short term to deflect an immediate crisis in Dublin schools. Almost 50 years later they still sully school yards across the land. Hillery's handling of the early crisis in Northern Ireland was exemplary. In the Autumn of 1969 he wrote a private note about a cabinet meeting where he described militant colleagues as 'smothered in lashings of creamy patriotic ballad singing'. His own ethos was as nationalistic as the next man in his party, but he had the good sense to know when dangerous fires should be put out. He was a the sort of doctor you would be glad to call in an emergency, and his skills were recognised with promotions by de Valera, Lemass and Lynch.

Reading through this book for a sense of what Hillery might have been like as a doctor, you reach the final chapter when his own health raised concerns. According to the biographer, Hillery himself was wary of doctors and was quite a reluctant patient. He didn't want a fuss made of his symptoms and told his son that 'If you talk to doctors, they'll find something wrong with you.' He was neither the first nor the last to hold this view. Dr Hillery died in April 2008, at the age of 84.

Professor Ivor Browne is still very much alive, well and residing in Dublin suburb of Ranelagh. I took his book, *Music and Madness*, to London recently and became so engrossed that I got great value from the plump pillows of my hotel. Described in the forward as 'a towering figure in Irish psychiatry', I had in fact been quite ignorant of his career until I picked up his memoir. Though I had worked in St Loman's Hospital where Browne once ruled the roost, he was rarely mentioned there by staff who were his contemporaries. I had come to the conclusion that his life, practice and philosophy had perhaps met with furrowed brows amongst some colleagues. Browne was in the news just a few years ago when he was shamefully treated by the Medical Council for his honourable actions in the Fr Cleary paternity case. His perspective on these events, and on the pitiful way fellow psychiatrist RD Laing was treated on the *Late Late Show* in 1982 are well aired in his new book.

Psychiatrists are masters of the small detail. And Ivor Browne doesn't disappoint. His tome begins with the moment of his conception. We are told that his birth was considered a mistake by his own father, who had imposed celibacy on himself when the family was complete. This denial was accomplished by advising Mrs Browne to lock her bedroom door. But one night after a few drinks he climbed through her window at Number One Sandycove Avenue East. And a very tall psychiatrist was born. Professor Browne's childhood is appealing but one suspects that he has spent perhaps too much of his adult life trying to make sense of it.

He describes his father, a banker who hated banking, as a man's man, with inhibited attitudes and a decidedly contrarian outlook. Browne's mother was warm and loving, though her sensuality was suppressed by her husband and she lacked self-confidence. One gets the impression that these are details of vital importance to Browne. But to the reader they might refer to any other family in the state. Browne's book is fascinating and its honesty almost too painful to bear at times. He describes how his father and his childhood friends thought him 'not the full shilling', prone to losing contact with reality and perpetually living in a dreamy state. On one occasion Ivor's own friends suggested to Mr Browne that he refer his son for help of the psychiatric variety. His father was too pre-occupied by his own problems to act on their advice and for that Ivor Browne was unusually grateful. Another case of a doctor being glad to escape the clutches of his own profession.

THE CHRONICLES OF HERNIA
July 2010

The Guéret family history is not quite as exotic as the name sounds. We had long assumed that the label sewn on our school blazers was a proud derivation of the French verb Guérir (to cure) and signified descent from a long line of Gallic healers, who exchanged clinical services for fine wines, blue cheese and loose francs. But when a French scholar in the family told us the truth, it was a bit of a let-down. The surname Guéret directly translates as *Fallow Field* - and may be broadened out to signify a place (or person) who is uncultivated, coarse and lacks some sophistication. Such an early snub may discourage an interest in genealogy but with all this current *Who Do You Think You Are* mania, we are all being egged on to discover secret heirlooms, unspeakable skeletons or stultifying dullness in the family closet. What we now know is that the family left Paris for Dublin (with mother-in-law Madame Marie-Victoire Guigon in tow) on the very day in 1870 that Napoleon III, President of the Second Republic, surrendered to the advancing Prussians. Our family of Bonapartists imported with them a church supply business which thrived for some years as the 'Maison Français' on Wellington Quay. Timing was everything, and the sacking of Paris provided la famille Guéret with a lucrative escape route to capitalise on Ireland's newfound devotion to all things religious and superstitious. They certainly knew how to move a few statues before being laid out horizontally in Glasnevin. Highlights of the family advertisement in the 1873 *Irish Catholic Directory* included 'mortuary cards in sheets of one hundred, the best incense of Jerusalem (same quality used in Rome), ornamental chapels, holy water fonts and statues of Our Lady of Lourdes'.

Which brings me rather circuitously to the subject of this Sunday's sermon. Whilst excavating old newspapers and directories for lost nuggets of family lore, I became interested in other businesses that were plying their wares along the Liffey at the same time as my great grandfather. Across the stench at 22 Bachelors Walk, was the premises of McAdams and Corcoran, supplier of 'artificial limbs, surgical appliances of every description including trusses'. They advertised only in Saturday newspapers and it was on the sale of trusses that they focused their sales pitch. For the uninitiated, a truss is a medicinal cross between a jockstrap and a g-string. It was a narrow garment which offered support where support was especially needed. Trusses were the mainstay of hernia treatment for many years. At least until the public began to be able to trust or afford the fees of surgeons. If you had a bulge from your abdomen, be it the size of a cherry or a watermelon, there was a custom made truss waiting for you in town.

In October 1876, McAdams and Corcoran announced to the public that their particular trusses were 'of the most approved principals, easy to wear and afforded effectual support' . Sensing that hernia patients could be a little embarrassed about the inguinal location of most swellings, the shop promised 'the greatest care in fitting'. Two-tier healthcare was alive and well a century and a half ago for they invited 'poor people' to attend for fitting between 9am and 11am where they could avail of reduced prices. This was a most generous ploy for a surgical supplier, but also perhaps lent a subliminal message to better off customers that they might attend later in the day to avoid mingling with bargain-seeking riff raff.

McAdams and Corcoran weren't the only lumps, bumps and amputee show in town. Up on the more salubrious Grafton

Street at Number 41 was the premises of Fannin & Company, who also advertised their trusses on Saturdays. Keen to seek out an end of the market commensurate with their prime location, they advertised their hernia supports as 'of the most superior description'. They even took some liberty with medicinal claims by suggesting that their accurate adjustments could not only relieve but could 'frequently cure the various forms of rupture'. If Sir or Madam was too embarrassed to submit to a tape measure in the shop, they would even send out directions for self-measurement at home.

The truss business is not what it was. Demand for the exquisitely named 'Rat-Tailed Spring Truss' and its competitors flailed in the early decades of the 20th century. Irish Surgeons returned from abroad with new-found expertise in the anatomy of nether regions. Their sewing techniques had improved and warnings were ringing in their ears about endangered nerves and hazardous blood vessels the sharp end of scalpels should avoid.

In my junior doctor days at the old Adelaide hospital, there were always a few hernia cases to be prepped and shorn each week. Spare blood had to be cross-matched in case of knife slippage and patients were kept in the recovery ward for a full week before being offloaded home with a sick cert for six to eight weeks. Today all has changed utterly. With tiny wounds and laparoscopic repair by hidden cameras, you can go home on the same day, just as soon as you pass a post-operative pee. Gentle exercise is usually encouraged straight away and the self-employed will often return to work in 24 hours.

But the tried, tested and trusted truss is still available. On-line if you don't mind. For patients nervous of, or too frail for surgery, only the advertising patter has changed. 'Gentle Relief - in a Brief. No antiquated designs or buckles necessary. Removable foam cushions. Advanced, plush micro-soft materials . The very latest Anatomical Design.' I wonder if cheap rates apply on the internet between 9 and 11 in the morning?

GENETICS
June 2007

It's extraordinary to think that the brave new frontier we know as genetics, had its origins in the tranquil vegetable patch of an Augustinian monastery garden in Bohemia. It was there that one of the priests, Gregor Mendel, conducted his experiments on the common garden pea. As is not uncommon in science, it was only after his death that the real importance of his work was appreciated. Though few listened at the time, Mendel proved that the inheritance of traits, good and bad, tends to follow defined laws. One hundred and fifty years later, we are still talking about the genetic revolution. We are much the wiser. But are we any the better for it? Hype is everywhere so it's difficult to separate the pea from the pod. Take this month's much publicised research in *Nature* magazine. Scientists, led by a team from Oxford, looked at the genetic make-up of 17,000 volunteers to see if the DNA of those who had common diseases looked any different from the DNA of healthy folk. They found that it certainly did. In cröhn's disease, a chronic inflammatory condition of the bowel, they discovered eight regions where the DNA of patients differed from that of those without the disease. In rheumatoid arthritis they discovered three, in diabetes four and so on for heart disease, high blood pressure and bipolar disorder (formerly known as manic depression).

Headline writers had a field day. 'CURES FOR MILLIONS ON THE WAY' and 'SECRETS TO DISEASES UNLOCKED' were two that jumped out from the morning papers. One had to get right down to the small print to see what the truth was. The leader of the research team, Professor Peter Donnelly, said that his findings 'open a new chapter' which is spot on, because the book of genetics is far from finished. To date very few patients have seen benefits. Genetics in Medicine is akin to a giant jigsaw. A new piece is handed to us every so often, but we have no idea how many pieces there are, whether they will fit into one another and if we will like the final picture, if indeed there is one.

There's no reason to be a Luddite. Science will advance, as it always does. The danger is only of being carried away on hollow promises. This is an exciting time to be involved in science. It's not many years since the entire human genome was mapped out. There followed a flurry of research where genes responsible for rare diseases were uncovered. Now science is starting to focus on more common diseases, the big earners if you like - coronary heart disease, depression and arthritis.

Cures for everything is pi in the sky. What we are going to see first are more screening tests, and for the first time, many of you are going to confront the fact that whilst screening is good for the profits of screeners, it's not necessarily good for you. Would you have a test for dementia in your twenties when the condition may not affect you for another sixty years? Probably not. But if your family medical history is littered with early heart attacks you might well have a test for a predisposition to coronary heart disease. If positive, there is a slight potential benefit as you might try to modify risk factors like smoking or obesity, or take preventative medicines that prove their worth.

What genetic advances might also mean is that your treatments can be tailor-made. At the moment, many of our medicines, good as they are, have a bit of a blunderbuss effect. Trial and error is a large part of modern medicine, unappreciated by patients and unmentioned by their doctors. In conditions like depression and hypertension, it is not unusual for your physician to try a number of medicines before the correct bullet is found - one with minimal side effects and maximum effect.

I was on Matt Cooper's radio programme the other week debating genetic advances with Stephen McMahon, stalwart of the Irish Patient's Association. Stephen sung a wise and cautionary note when he wondered how advances in genetic screening might affect people's ability to gain mortgage protection and health insurance. Up to now, those of you who have applied for loans will be familiar with the health questionnaire approach of insurers, often followed by a medical examination with an independent doctor. Depending on the size of the loan to be secured and your risk factors, they may also ask for electrocardiographs, cholesterol, HIV and other tests. When more genetic screening is introduced, might they refuse to advance money if you refuse permission to be screened for diseases you would rather know nothing about. What about employers? Will they screen you for future disabilities and award jobs to candidates on the merit of healthier looking genes?

The frontier of Genetic Medicine is a wonderful place to be. Gold-rushing entrepreneurs have ridden wild horses in already, convinced that fame, fortune and future fitness awaits the pioneers. The rest of us are happy to stay on sentry duty, in watch, in wait and in contemplation. A brave new world may well be around a few corners. But we need to keep wits about us and explore it slowly.

JEWISH DOCTORS
January 2010

I have a particularly strong devotion to the memory of my own childhood doctor. The late Dr Manné Berber, a Dublin Jew, practised family medicine just off the Braemor Road in Churchtown. His religion was unknown to me on early visits, and wholly irrelevant on later ones. To us children, Manné was a dark, handsome bearded man with a mellow voice that would soothe afflictions long before he reached for a prescription pad. He had a small plastic doll in his surgery, a stethoscope-wearing doctor I think, in a white coat. The mannequin was used to interest and distract any toddler who was potentially troublesome. I recall him administering vaccines on sugar lumps and being well up on new-fangled inhalers that had just come into vogue for the management of my asthma. He ran an appointment system for all, and his premises was immaculately clean. He had an excellent lady secretary and to this day I can still remember the tidy and wide-ranging collection of magazines in his waiting room. Fees were never discussed. As far as I can recall he trustingly billed his patients afterwards. In guineas and shillings, as was the custom. My sister, a nurse, recently reminded me that Dr Berber was one of very few family doctors who upheld an honourable tradition of never charging nursing colleagues for his services.

One evening when a high temperature gave me a serious-looking convulsion at home, his locum, a Dr Shapiro, came out promptly and administered whiskey and anti-inflammatories, the favoured fever-quenchers of the day. Family lore has it that my esteemed brother (who had to share a room with his convulsing younger sibling) asked Dr Shapiro if Guéret junior was going to die. He has never since discussed the look of disappointment etched on his face when the answer was negative.

Dr Berber died suddenly 20 years ago, long before he was due to retire. I was tanning myself in Spain at the time and missed the chance to pay respects that were due. Manné was a saintly man, an excellent medic and a trainer of other family doctors. He was and still is sorely missed by very many. Regular lectures now commemorate him and an annual scientific award bearing his name is made by the Irish College of General Practitioners. I'm not aware of any personal discrimination he might have suffered in his life as a member of the relatively small Hebrew community in Ireland. But what I did become aware of in my teens and later life is that there still lingers a dirty puddle of anti-Jewish feeling in this country. Though it has diminished, the ugly affliction has never dried up completely.

In secondary school, an otherwise kindly priest once told us that we should never wear jeans to cricket matches as 'they were invented by a Jew'. Exactly what Levi Strauss had done to offend him, he didn't mention. But I think of this evil remark every time I try to squeeze into my now solitary pair. I didn't dare mention that our family doctor was a Jew, but I did discern later that many so-called Christian husbands in Dublin forbade their wives from attending Jewish doctors, with their own woes or those of their children. This discriminatory practice was more prevalent amongst the upper echelons of Dublin society and there is some evidence that it had official church, if not state backing.

Archbishop John Charles McQuaid came from an order that to put it mildly, hadn't a particularly proud record in fighting anti-semitism. In 1932 he preached a sermon in Cavan Cathedral in which he alleged that Jews were engaged in practically every movement against his own church. He branded them 'allies of Satan' and his disgusting remarks were proudly recorded without adverse comment in the local press. Throughout his reign, McQuaid fought many efforts to promote dialogue between Dublin's Catholic and Jewish populations, even in the wake of the Holocaust. In 1942 he received a private briefing about the *Pillar of Fire Society* which was set up to build bridges between religious communities. McQuaid was told that *'there was nothing hoity-toity about the Jews. They are uniformly humble, respectful and yet frank. They are afraid of persecution. They want justice and sympathy.'*

McQuaid exhibited scant interest in their national or international plight. His reply to his informant was telling. *'Their purpose, however it is masked by an appearance of suavity and accommodation, is and will remain material.'* Throughout his long and interfering tenure, dozens of excellent Jewish doctors who were born and trained in Dublin, left for work in the UK such was their difficulty finding salaried positions in the 'Free State'.

Similarly, many sports clubs in Dublin and beyond, operated unwritten exclusion rules for members of the Jewish Community, long after the dire horror of the Holocaust became known. Despite obstacles, the Jewish community probably contributed more to the Irish state than any immigrant group did before or since. In the medical arena, Dr Bethel Solomons played international rugby ten times for Ireland before going to become Master of Dublin's Rotunda Hospital. The mother of Dr Jonathan Miller, the internationally regarded medic, writer and opera director was the Cork-born Betty Spiro whose family were forced to move away from these shores for holding non-Republican views. She established a reputation for herself as a very fine writer amongst London's Bloomsbury set. Alas, there are a mere handful of Jewish doctors left practising in this country today. To quote Nick Harris from his recent book *Dublin's Little Jerusalem*, Dublin Jewry has reached a low ebb. If you still have one to care for you, count your blessings.

HEALTH ECONOMICS
November 2009

Health Economics doesn't rank on the curriculum of Irish medical schools. It didn't warrant a single lecture when I passed out two decades ago and it's probably safe to assume nothing has changed since. The first concept of health economics was born in the same year I was. It was 1963, and future Nobel laureate

Kenneth Arrow wrote a seminal piece titled 'Uncertainty and Welfare Economics of Medical Care' for the *American Economic Review*. America didn't take much notice at the time - too busy grieving for a President who perished in Dallas the month before. But Arrow, a young professor of economics at Stanford University, had written a paper that would stand the test of time. His legacy is every bit as useful today as the lessons from the short and unfulfilled life of a dead Kennedy. It's no accident that the United States is a leader in studying the economics of medicine. Health bills are its principal source of bankruptcies. Seventy million of its citizens have either existing medical debt or difficulty paying for everyday healthcare. It's often assumed that these are the poor, the unemployed who cannot afford any insurance. Not so. Sixty per cent of those in medical debt do have health insurance - it's just that their policies are rubbish.

Professor Arrow focused his landmark study on the operation of the 'medical-care industry' and looked at how it differs from all other markets. Demand for its services, unlike food, shelter or clothing, is irregular and unpredictable. It operates in an environment where there is an assault on personal integrity, a risk of death and a considerable risk of impairment. When you become ill, you run not only the risk of high medical bills, but also the risk to your livelihood too. In medicine, leaving drugs aside, there is little testing of practice. A strong element of trust has to exist, and to buttress this, there are ethical restrictions on your doctor and restricted entry to the trade. Uncertainty as to the quality of the product is more intense in medical care than for any other commodity in the marketplace. Recovery too, is a variable feast. Arrow described well the uncertainty that afflicts both patient and doctor in their relationship. One is assumed to possess infinitely more knowledge than the other, but that superior knowledge does not always translate into knowledge of the outcome. As for fees, Arrow described the pricing practices and economic attitudes of the medical profession as 'unusual'. He listed price discrimination according to patient income, the old fee per service model and vehement medical opposition to pre-payment as three examples of practices that depart sharply from the competitive norm.

In Ireland, health economics affect more people adversely

than swine flu will ever do. It behoves all of us to think about it, especially now that purse strings are being pulled tighter. There are difficult choices to be made and we have to decide whether we are going to go down the bankruptcy road that afflicts America or choose a more state-involved European model. Today, for your pleasure, you can read the world exclusive of my own paper. 'Milly, Molly, Mandy and their Granny - The Uncertain Economics of an Irish Back Sprain.'

Milly wakes up with a dreadful back ache. She hobbles down to the pharmacist who advises a day's rest and a packet of over-the-counter painkillers. Her bill is ten euro.

Molly has exactly the same pain. She visits her GP and receives an examination of her back, a urine test and a prescription for 28 painkillers to be taken for a week. Seventy five euro for the lot. Had her doctor been unavailable, she could visited an emergency care clinic where for an examination, a plain x-ray of her back, a urine test and the same prescription, she might have paid two hundred euro.

Mandy visits the emergency department of a private hospital. She is seen promptly by the doctor who suggests blood tests, urine tests, an abdominal ultrasound, a pregnancy test and rounds the whole lot off with an MRI scan of her spine. All is well - she is discharged within hours with the same prescription as her sisters, and a bill for €1,500.

Wise Granny woke up with the same pain. She rang her life-long consultant on his personal phone and he suggested that she come into hospital for a few days. The stay lasted for a week. Whilst in she had every test under the sun, courtesy visits from three more consultants, and left hospital hale and hearty without so much as a invoice. Her five figure bill was picked up by her insurance company.

Read into this parable what you will, but before we spend another cent of our annual fifteen billion euro on healthcare, we need an urgent debate about where, how and why we waste this kitty as we do. There is no 'healthcare system' in Ireland. A system implies some sort of order and basic ground rules. We have a lottery which handsomely rewards those who pull numbers from the drum, yet ignores the cries that care is substandard. In recent weeks we have witnessed heart-rending scenes of our health services letting families down. If this country wants GPs they should cease contracting them, and employ them like everyone else. They should be provided with premises where they have immediate access (like vets do) to diagnostic facilities. They should have back-up facilities to observe and monitor patients whose diagnosis they are unclear about. Health insurance also needs an injection of reality. The practice of not paying for outpatient care and paying through the nose for inpatient care is a sham and needs to change. Ireland needs a hefty dose of health economics. If only to point out that the duck is long dead, and continuing to feed a dead duck does not bring him back to life.

SURGEONS
January 2010

I have just put down the most entertaining book to come my way in years. Professor Barry O'Donnell, a Christian Brothers boy from Cork, toiled for decades at Our Lady's Children's Hospital in Crumlin becoming Ireland's foremost children's surgeon in the latter half of the 20th century. On retirement he took on the Presidency of the Royal College of Surgeons and he has now published the most extraordinary account of theatrical life in Ireland and the motley crew of surgeons who inhabited it. If you, or your ancestor had a major surgical operation performed in the last century, chances are, the colourful life of your carver has come under Barry's microscope.

Surgeons are a breed alone in the pantheon of doctors. When I trained there was a story about one who refused to operate on a well-upholstered lady until she dislodged half her body weight. The patient was mortified and ran from the consulting room shouting that she was going for 'a second opinion'. The surgeon obliged her request by calling after her 'Not only are you hideously fat Madam, you are ugly too.' In his tome, Barry has provided a 'warts and all' picture of a profession loved and loathed in equal measure by patients and colleagues. The black humour of modern surgery is well to the fore.

The late Dick Brennan of Dublin's old Adelaide Hospital studied under the leading rectal surgeon in England, William Bashall Gabriel. His master was inevitably referred to as the 'Arse Angel Gabriel.' Mr JC Flood of Jervis Street Hospital was known for his caustic personality. A colleague once said he had more degrees than a thermometer but zero capacity for registering warmth. His sworn enemy was the Reverend Mother of the Mercy Order who ran his hospital. When she died, Flood was admonished by another nun for not attending her funeral. 'Waste of time Sister. She is in hell.' he replied. Jack Cherry was a legendary Orthopaedic Surgeon at Dr Steevens Hospital, a man of immaculate appearance who was a very convincing witness in court cases. His sixty year career saw huge changes. 'When I was young, patients were happy to get out of hospital alive . . . now they want to be cured as well !' he once declared. There are copious tales of personal acrimony between surgical colleagues. One used to sit in theatre reading his newspaper, long after his theatre list was finished. His reason for so doing was to keep a better qualified surgical colleague from getting in. Robert Dancer Purefoy was a baritone singer and gynaecologist who became Master of the Rotunda Hospital at the beginning of the last century. He was one the last surgeons to wear a top hat whilst operating. Seymour Heatley of Sir Patrick Dun's was a phenomenally fast surgeon who once took a gall bladder out and stitched up in seven minutes flat. He refused to wear a white coat on his rounds and would chain-smoke whilst lecturing to students. It is said that he never spoke a single word to a surgical colleague who once 'subsumed' his beds. Not known for his flamboyance, Heatley's wife swanned around in a Jaguar whilst drove to theatre in a very ancient Ford Anglia.

Professor O'Donnell gives a lot of attention to the personal appearance of the 600 surgeons that populate his book. There are plenty of references to hair style, deportment, polished cars and the airs and graces which emanated from each of his subjects. Hobbies also feature noticeably. The late Gussie Mehigan was a 'favourite son of St Vincent's Hospital' without an enemy in the world. His only weakness was a fanaticism for keeping fit. Just in his mid 50s, he died of a heart attack whilst out running in his green tracksuit. Dark, bronzed and diligent, Bill Beesley's good work was well known in the Adelaide hospital. He became even better known when he won the National Lottery - not once but twice. Denis Kennedy was a Tipperary man with a 'no-nonsense style of operating'. For his children and grandchildren he insisted on nothing but the best - which meant he did all their operations himself. Another Tipperary man, Jamsie Maher, was 'strong as an ox', and was once on the fringes of making the Irish rugby team. A bachelor who loved nightlife, he would invite students, hospital staff and rugby players to parties at the basement of 32 Fitzwilliam Place. The doors were locked from the inside to ensure nobody left before dawn.

An appendix to Barry's book entitled 'Better Left Unsaid' features cutting and caustic comments made about surgeons by their colleagues or juniors. The comments are orphaned at the back of the book rather than being attributed to particular operators. And it's not difficult to see why. Here is an anonymous selection.

'A lifetime achievement award for the courting of controversy.'
'On the Richter scale of charismatic leadership, the needle barely moved.'
'A known skinflint and tightwad.'
'Liver made of brass.'
'Never put a foot right.'
And my own favourite -
'His retirement was early rather than premature.'

The above samples are just a taste of Barry O'Donnell's epic work on the surgeons who had our nation in stitches for the last hundred years. For the main course, desert, nightcap and cigar, you will need to put *Irish Surgeons and Surgery in the Twentieth Century* on your Christmas list. It's published by Gill and Macmillan and deserves to be out of print very quickly indeed.

A SPOONFUL OF SUGAR
April 2005

Surgeons are without doubt the hardest working creatures in our hospitals. I once worked for a surgical team in the old Adelaide hospital that started work so early, one had to get up each morning before one went to bed. By the time the grouches on RTE's *Morning Ireland* began moaning, the surgeons had a working day done. Ward rounds happened before the cows were milked, clinical meetings were over before nurses emerged from nighties and the operating team were scrubbed up in theatre wondering why anaesthetists sleep it in most mornings. My surgical career lasted a mere six months. I traded it for sanity and a later breakfast.

Surgeons can be a grumpy lot. Family life for many is pretty well non-existent. Across the world they have high divorce, suicide and alcoholism rates. Bedside manners are not always a strong suit. Surgeons are the skilled mechanics of the medical industry. But unlike those who tinker under the bonnet of the car, they boast that all daily operations take place with the engine still running. All work and no play can make Mr Jack a dull chap. Some professional cutters sparkle up their dreary lives by hiding bees under their surgical bonnets. Intuitions and hunches can verge on the obsessional. Just the other day, a surgeon wrote an opinion piece about the evils of sugar for the *British Medical Journal*. I didn't know whether to laugh or cry.

I shan't embarrass the gentleman by naming him but he began his rant by calling for the classification of sugar as a hard drug. He called on politicians to criminalise the sugar trade urging the creation of anti-sugar agencies. Not shy of opinions, he then declared that all the sugar fields of the world should be converted into rubber plantations for the production of condoms. Non-compliers, he went on, should be subjected to sanctions including the destruction of their crops with aerial spraying. Finally, without a trace of irony, he called for the eradication of sugar in the spirit of coercive healthism.

This sort of medical sermonizing and health evangelisation is not uncommon these days. We live in times when if you want to be heard, you need to exaggerate. The success of the passive smoking crusade has encouraged shy doctors the world over to go on the rant. Many welcome the new pub odours of flatulence and sweat, the clothes that can be worn again tomorrow and the modest decline in smoking rates the smoke ban has achieved. But remember, it was driven through accompanied by 'scientific facts' that were every bit as dodgy as those from a loathsome tobacco industry. The late Professor Peter Skrabanek of Trinity College in Dublin cautioned before his own passing about the rise of coercive healthism. He wrote that medicine has no right to be meddlesome in the lives of those who do not need it. Petr was of a small breed of doctors who bemoaned the fashion of 'disease-conquering' and 'death avoidance'. Medicine, he said, was about the alleviation of suffering, the minimisation of harm and smoothing the inexorable journey of man to his grave. Professor Skrabanek cautioned those who wished to extend health care to the healthy, arguing that it simply diverts limited resources from the needy sick to the worried well.

It sounds like the sugar doomsday brigade are banging their bin lids and preparing to march. If there is a grain of truth in their message, it may be lost, slipping between the hype and the hard sell. Go treat yourself to the odd lump or two until the noise dies down. Like a Dublin bus, the next fad will be just around the corner.

CHINESE MEDICINE
August 2006

Our Chinese community makes a tremendous contribution to both the Irish economy and stretch marks on the Guéret waistline. I have long been an aficionado of their cuisine and will gladly bore anyone with a lengthy dissertation on the best establishments for roast suckling pig or twice cremated once deceased duck. Chinese chefs I trust implicitly. Their quacks, less so. In fact their contribution to medicine - particularly the alternative variety - is highly questionable indeed. Just the other day I passed one such establishment which proudly displayed on its advertising hoarding the 'fact' that it was **APPROVED BY VHI AND BUPA**. Now it may come as news to readers, but I feel you should know that neither the VHI, nor BUPA, nor other premium collectors in the health sector, approve of anybody in the medical business. They are health insurance companies. They do not have roving teams of inspectors checking whether needles are used more than once. Nor do they employ pharmaceutical inspectors to check that steroids are not secreted into 'natural' creams or that avian viruses lie dormant in the powdered testicles of Giant Panda Bears. Nor do they have the expertise or interest in assessing ludicrous diagnostic methods or unproven cures that Chinese Medicine Clinics promote for diseases that may or may not exist.

Your chosen health insurers may happily cough up ten or fifteen or twenty euro towards the cost of your forays into alternative medicine. But in my book, that is very far removed from approval. In fact it suits health insurers very well to have every subscriber take themselves off for low cost 'diagnosis' and 'treatment' rather than clog up private hospitals where charges for real medicine are higher. Another Chinese emporium that I looked into recently was offering to diagnose hundreds of diseases from a single lock of your hair. This is arrant nonsense. A trained doctor in any rational branch of medicine can tell very little from a lock of your hair. Hair is a dead structure - it keeps its sheen from the secretions of sebaceous glands on your scalp. Like a thatched roof it can be dyed, brushed, combed, highlighted, untangled, curled, cut and styled - but, and with due apologies to the multi-billion hair products industry, it cannot be fed, nourished, hydrated, elasticated, energised, strengthened or indeed pampered. Hair has the same physiological properties as the feathers on the Monty Python parrot. Any clinic that offers to diagnose 'hundreds of diseases' in exchange for cash or tries to sell you a list of personal 'allergies' based on a hair sample deserves, at the minimum, to be politely ignored.

Much is made these days of the 'long history' of Chinese Medicine as if it's entitled on age grounds alone to some form of recognition or clinical authority. In fact, for most of Chinese history, traditional healing methods have been bound up with religious beliefs. Less trumpeted facts about traditional Chinese Medicine are that the stalwarts who promoted these treatments tended to believe that all illnesses are caused by the spirits of unhappy ancestors, mean-spirited ghosts and easily offended Gods. If none of these could be blamed, then the patient was at fault, for the wages of sins. Medical historians record that rural populations were treated by an array of 'quacks, vulgar doctors, itinerants, priests, shamans, acupuncturists, masseurs and old women'. They had little prestige and even less learning. Two hundred years ago, visiting medics from Europe were appalled at the ignorance of even basic anatomy that existed in the traditional Chinese medical community.

We are sometimes deluded by purveyors of traditional Chinese Medicine into the belief that these are still the treatments of choice for the modern Chinese citizen. In fact that is far from the truth. Acupuncture, Herbalism and other bygone fads have been unfashionable in China for almost a century. Republican China which lasted from 1911 to 1949 developed a modern medical system based very much on the eclectic use of science and discovery that we have in the West. This was continued under Mao and the Communists, although for nationalistic (and financial reasons) they tried to resurrect some of the older (and cheaper) methods and lending them a kind of false kudos. The growth of acupuncture in the West is often attributed to the visit of Richard Nixon in 1970, when the US President was duped into believing that a patient underwent surgery using acupuncture instead of anaesthesia. The truth was in fact rather different. The employment and promotion of traditional Chinese Medicine under Chairman Mao was a sham, conducted out of economic and symbolic necessity rather than anything else.

With the death of Mao, and the encroachment of Western medicine, things have never been so good for the world's most populous nation. According to the most recent report from the World Health Organisation, the overall disease profile in China is now very similar to that of a developed country. Life expectancy, appallingly low before mass immunisation was introduced by Mao, has almost reached the levels of the affluent West. As for traditional Chinese Medicine, the Chinese Government is now firmly wedded to medical training based on rational proof and scientific fact. A recent editorial on China's Healthcare system in the *British Medical Journal* suggests that the professional behaviour of all healthcare providers will in future be subject to stringent regulation. Treatments will be properly evaluated to reduce unnecessary expenditure of medicines and diagnostic tests. Good news for the people of China. Bad news for quacks. Though rising tuberculosis rates and bird flu outbreaks are of concern, some of our more western worries are taking over. I read recently that one fifth of the world's obese people now live in China. We were warned about this sort of thing at school. Let's hope they don't start jumping up and down.

THE IRISH TRANSSEXUAL
June 2005

There are mixed views on the performance of Ireland's Equality Authority. I would take up a putter to defend the inalienable right of consenting club-wielding male adults to congregate and knock tiny white spheres about in the privacy of sand dunes. And equally I would defend the turf of ladies who dress as maids and hike off to the mountains with jolly hockey sticks for the purpose of inflicting dark bruises and knocking lumps out of each other's shapely pins. I do worry that our Equality Authority devotes equal time to daft notions (such as single sex clubs) as they do to very worthy issues of public concern. When engaged with the latter, they do perform some excellent work.

The Authority recently launched a report on *Access to Health Services for Transsexual People*. Like many reports from officious Ireland, it will probably gather cobwebs and attract dust mites until such a day that a Minister denies to a committee of their peers that they ever had sight or sound of it. But it is a fascinating document on an area of hidden Ireland that the public and their doctors know very little about. Facilities for assessment and management of transsexual people in Ireland are virtually non-existent. There are a tiny number of specialists with an interest in the field, but GPs are not told who they are. This report clearly shows that the experience transsexuals have of the Irish health service can add to their mental trauma. I'm glad to read that most family doctors, though unsure of what to do, were sympathetic. But one transsexual was told that their concerns were 'all nonsense'. Another described being 'thrown out by the scruff of the neck.'

The transsexual male is neither a transvestite who gains sexual excitement from wearing female clothes, nor is he a Lily Savage or a Dame Edna who cross dresses for the titillation and entertainment of polite society. The transsexual male (female transsexuals do exist in smaller numbers - it's males we'll concentrate on here) is a person whose physiological sex is opposite to the gender they perceive themselves to be. The tabloids have their own spin on it - a woman trapped in a man's body.

It's over fifty years since the world was introduced to the male transsexual and the treatment options that are now commonly available outside of Ireland. In 1952, George Jorgensen, a former US soldier from the Bronx travelled to Denmark, the native country of his parents, for a surgical sex change. He had been treated experimentally with female hormones for a year prior to surgery and underwent two surgical procedures to remove his testicles (orchidectomy) and a penectomy (self-explanatory, I think). Nowadays the construction of a vagina is part and parcel of the treatment, but this was not offered to George who restyled himself as a much happier Christine. Though officially not the world's first genital reconstruction surgery (the Germans and Swiss had conducted prior experiments) Christine Jorgensen was the first patient to hit the headlines. New York's *Daily News* titillated readers with 'Ex-GI Becomes Blonde Bombshell.' Despite much ridicule Christine rose above the sniggers and catcalls to forge a successful career as a stage actress and nightclub singer. She also took on a much needed role of educator about transsexual issues. Her biography was published in 1967 and a film adaptation followed a few years later. Though engaged twice, she never married and died of lung cancer in 1989 at the age of 62. The words 'dignity' and 'eloquence' were prominent in her obituary notices.

Transsexuality is not a very common condition. In Ireland there are perhaps 100 to 150 adult men and 30 to 50 adult women who feel 'trapped in the wrong body.' For most of them, the realisation that something fundamental is awry takes place early in childhood. The provision of hormone treatment, gender reassignment surgery and other services such as counselling, electrolysis and speech therapy are now standard practice in most civilised countries. Not so in Ireland. Health Boards and Insurance Companies have paid for isolated cases to be treated abroad, but for most Irish transsexuals who opt for 'reassignment', they must pay their own way. Charing Cross Hospital in London is the principal destination for Irish people who wish to access transsexual health care.

What is particularly sad about the lot of the Irish transsexual, is that their own country does not even recognise a right to amend birth certificates. The head of the Equality Authority didn't mince his words when he said that 'transsexual people endure mockery, derision and abuse on the basis of their condition.' It appears that the Irish state doesn't do much better. Most of you will never be able even to imagine the trauma of sensing that you were born in the wrong shoes. The Irish transsexual is not asking for this. Just a modicum of respect and a miniscule level of resourcing would go a very long way.

THEATRE MUSIC
June 2006

These days patients have an inalienable right to know everything, even when they are asleep. So today I am going to tell you exactly what music doctors listen to as they fiddle with your bits. American surgeons have been spilling their iPod playlists in recent weeks telling the world precisely what they whistle to as they chop.

Dr Bill Inabnet, an endocrine (glands and stuff) surgeon at the New York Presbyterian Hospital likes Verdi's *La Traviata* when dissecting necks for thyroids, but shuffles off to the Red Hot Chili Peppers for more difficult operations. According to Dr Bill the Peppers provide 'good pancreas music', and who are we to argue with such firmly held clinical opinions. An ongoing survey of British surgeons has also been looking at the type of music they prefer in their theatrical domain. Classical ranks first with 24%, followed by 1980s Stuff at 21%, Popular and Jazz are close behind at 20%, then Rock at 13% with Dance Music, thankfully I think, bringing up the rear at 7%. A low 15% requested none at all, preferring the sound of silence (not Simon & Garfunkel) as they suture.

Some years ago the Irish Music Rights Organisation (IMRO) got wind of medical music and began to target doctors so that they might reclaim royalties for Bono, the Edge and other hard pressed buskers on this musical island. Fresh from their success in getting licensed vintners to cough up thousands each year, IMRO targeted

GP surgeries up and down the country and asked them to fork out cash for playing music in their waiting rooms. Many doctors simply chucked out the transistor and reverted to out-of-date National Geographics, cloudy goldfish bowls and deceased rubber plants to create that yawning ambience which sick patients are dying to queue in. Whether IMRO went after operating rooms in anyone's guess but if their inspectors can get past the scalpels and hacksaws, a treasure trove might indeed await therm.

Some studies show that surgeons perform better operations to music, but only if they get to choose the tracks themselves. Should Theatre Sister hold sway and Daniel O'Donnell's Greatest Hits for Irish Mammies is played from dusk to dawn, varicose veins mightn't be the only things stripped from exposed flesh. Surgeons who operate with their own favourite music have lower blood pressure, slower pulses and react better to stress. Most doctors agree that music interspersed with news or sports bulletins is not a good idea, as the temptation to close up early and watch the end of a match or breaking news could prove irresistible. One American surgeon who was scrubbed up during the Challenger Space Disaster admitted that all he could think about was escaping to watch it on video. Other doctors to come out of the music closet recently include a somewhat less than reassuring general surgeon who says that only Deep Purple's *Smoke on the Water* can calm him down when he is 'hyped up' and a stomach stapling specialist who says he 'gets more work done' when U2 are on the radio. As I write, the National Treatment Purchase Fund are probably negotiating fees with their manager.

There is however another breed of doctor in theatre-land who is very much more cautious about the effect of music during operations. In a survey of 200 Scottish anaesthetists, half of them said music was distracting when something goes wrong. And a quarter of them claimed that music made them less vigilant. Considering that a major part of their brief is to listen out for buzzers, beeps and the screams of patients, they might be worth listening to. The real pet hate of anaesthetists are those surgeons who insist on singing along to their favourite tracks. Surgeons retort in kind by suggesting that if anaesthetists (affectionately known as gas men) were to choose the play list, country and western would be the musak of choice and mortality rates would soar. They cite award-winning research from a University in Alabama linking country music with depression and higher rates of suicide.

So there you have it. Your opinion or musical taste, as the person at the sharp end of the knife, probably doesn't count. But if your doctor ever insists on doing a rectal examination while you are awake (and he may well do should you bring your prostate gland to his attention) - there are three pre-requisites to insist upon. A strong glove of the single-use variety, plenty of lubrication and I'm told that *The Girl from Ipanema* is the perfect musical accompaniment.

PACEMAKERS
February 2011

St Thomas' Hospital in London is a fine institution. It houses the Florence Nightingale Museum and was the very first hospital in the UK to organise a training school for nurses. They set it up with public money that was sent to the matron, in recognition of her work during the Crimean war. The hospital had a very significant Irish patient admitted for two days last month. Following 'exemplary' treatment by 'parliamentary paramedics' at the House of Lords, Lord Bannside (aka Dr Ian Paisley) was rushed to the hospital's Emergency Department. According to his family's account, a diagnosis was made within 40 minutes and the 84 year old politician was whisked off to theatre for a cardiac pacemaker insertion under local anaesthetic. The precise diagnosis was not made available, but it is likely that he had a sick sinus node setting the heart beat too slow, or indeed a heart block where travel of electrical signals through his heart's chambers was disrupted. His son, Ian junior, joked that his Dad was now 'turbo-charged' and that the pacemaker's 15 year life would see him through to his centenary. As with so many of today's political utterances, we take that one with a pinch of salt. But we never doubted that his old man had a big heart.

Some years ago I began to research the history of pacemakers in Ireland. I had thought that the first one was inserted in my old alma mater, the Royal City of Dublin Hospital on Baggot Street. However I was put right by an anaesthetist who wrote to tell me it had in fact taken place in the late 1960s in the Mater Hospital. The patient was a deaf lady in her late thirties who had a rather serious underlying disease in which her immune system was attacking her own organs. She had a number of cardiac arrests in the intensive care unit, and a junior doctor, who went on to become a very celebrated cardiac surgeon, suggested that a pacemaker might be the answer. The device, by today's standards, was fairly simple. A metal ring was placed under the skin at her collar bone from which two electrodes were attached to the right side of her heart. A second ring was then strapped to the skin overlying the embedded ring. This was connected to a machine that sent out an electric impulse every second or so - inducing a current in the embedded ring which was connected to her heart. The pacemaker was the size and shape of an 1980s mobile phone, and was attached to the lady's belt. The batteries had to be changed every three days. The operation was hailed in the hospital as a great success though the lady, because of her underlying illness, did not live as long as was hoped. The world's first pacemaker was inserted into a Swedish man called Larson in 1960. He died just a few years ago at the grand old age of 88.

CELEBRITY DOCTORS
June 2009

The death of Michael Jackson has taught me two valuable lessons. 1) Global warming could well be caused by all the hot air at Sky News and 2) the life of a celebrity doctor is not for me.

One minute it's pig's back time. Handsome retainer of 150k per month, perks, parties and a posh bedroom once occupied by Bubbles the chimp. Then the walls come tumbling down. Your family boasted that you were doctor to the stars, when you were just one cardiac arrest away from being pilloried as a greedy drug-pushing quack with faulty resuscitation techniques. It's almost as risky as working for the Health Service Executive.

Funny thing, in all my years of practice I don't think I treated a single luminary. A location thing perhaps. Had I put the plate up on a faux-Italian road in Dalkey, I could be eating scallops off the haemorrhoids of style icons three nights a week. Instead I chose a nice urban backwater, devoid of whims and pimms, and very pleasant people they were too. One day a well-known entertainer did wander when the surgery was deserted. We chatted for ages about life and his career in show business. When I enquired as to what the problem was, he pointed to a tooth that was almost completely enveloped by a swollen red gum. I asked if he had considered going to a dentist. It was at this stage he realised that he had entered the wrong door. He was gone like a rabbit down a burrow. I didn't even have time to give him a wave.

On another occasion I treated an insurance man and he asked me on the way out if I might be interested in doing independent medical examinations on some 'A list' life assurance clients. I agreed and a few days later had an urgent call to go to RTE studios at a very particular time to conduct an examination on one of his famous policyholders. The fact that the appointment made by the broker was bang in the middle of open surgery did not occur to him and he didn't think it funny when I suggested it would be more appropriate for his minor comedian to come to medical Mammon rather than the other way around. Needless to say there were no more medicals from Donnybrook, Hollywood or Bollywood after that.

Back in my casualty doctor days, many of us juniors moonlighted as joy-ride medics with the after-hours Doctor on Duty service. You saw much of life and where the two halves of the world lived it. I remember one night being driven from a fatal asthmatic attack in a block of tough inner city flats straight to the dressing room of an actor in the Abbey Theatre whose throat was itchy an hour before show-time. By the time I left, it was curtains for both of them. All in a evening's work. There was £20 cash from the Abbey. Not a penny from the call in the flats - as there was nobody left alive to sign the form. The two tiers of Dublin healthcare were alive and kicking.

Elvis had one. Marilyn had one. Adolf had two - and they frequently differed as doctors do. The concept of a personal physician is nothing new. Emperors and Popes, Dictators and

Queens - they have been domesticating their doctors for centuries. Any study of personal physicians reveals that too high a value is put on accessibility, and we all know that over-familiarity breeds medical contempt. If you want to hire a doctor to live with you, perhaps you should first ask what sort of doctor would want to live with you. Celebrity medical arrangements have not been particularly good for the health of the doctors either. Royal courts of Europe have been littered for centuries with the severed heads of well-meaning medical soothsayers.

Dr Theodor Morell, Hitler's favourite GP, was a strange man indeed. He had one medical mantra - if it came in a liquid, he would inject it. He prescribed widely for his Führer. He had his own pharmaceutical company which experimented with extracts from bull testicles and hyped-up multivitamins, as useless today as they were then. No surprise that he was also big fan of loading friendly bacteria into stomachs that didn't need them. Arrested by the Americans after the war, Morell was found to be unfit to attend testify in court. He suffered strokes, was hospitalised for many months. He died, in the words of his faithful assistant, like a stray dog.

Elvis Presley's physician, Dr George Nichopoulos was a run-of-the-mill family doctor who happened to work in a group practice in Memphis. Presley's legendary drug abuse went on long before Nichopoulos took over his care. His fatal error was to chose a patient who would end his medical career. With his master's death in 1977, the doc's life took a turn for the worse. He began to receive death threats, he became embroiled in the What Killed Elvis hysteria and his legal bills crippled him. He was eventually struck off the medical register in Tennessee for what was termed unethical behaviour and irresponsible prescribing. Nichopoulos organised a touring exhibition called 'Memories of Elvis' featuring his old black medical bag and an empty bottle of morphine with the singer's name on it. The show was pulled after allegations of poor taste were made. A benefit night for the doctor was planned featuring a performance of another of his patients, Jerry Lee Lewis. But the singer didn't show. Nichopoulos is 81 as I write this and a book called *The True Story of Elvis and Doctor Nick* is planned. On his new elvisdoctor.com website you can bid for a gold chain that Elvis once placed around his daughter's neck. Minimum bid is 15,000 dollars and it comes with the doctor's signature of authenticity. The same signature that wrote nearly 200 prescriptions during the last eight months of Elvis's life.

Doctors can be as enthralled as anyone else by the hairy chest and breath sounds of celebrity at the end of their stethoscopes. George Bernard Shaw wrote of the delusion that every doctor is a man of science, just as every organ-grinder is a Beethoven and every pigeon-dealer is a Darwin. Shaw claimed that a large majority of doctors are not interested in medicine or science, they practice only to earn their bread. Very true. Some of us even write for a crust.

A CONTRACEPTIVE HISTORY
February 2010

Dr Jukes de Styrap was a nineteenth century medic of considerable importance in his day. As his name might suggest, he wasn't conceived in Ireland, but he did spend time here and won a Licentiate from our own Royal College of Physicians. His main interest was in medical ethics, and he published many codes of Victorian manners that fellow doctors were encouraged to follow. He advised them on such things as how best they might consult with quacks like homeopaths. And on the sort of etiquette they might adopt if administering treatment in railway waiting rooms. But he counselled on serious medical matters too. One of his many chapters was devoted to handling patients who were slow payers. Styrap was wary of 'self-important sickroom critics', a code phrase perhaps for difficult relatives or nurses, and he urged medical colleagues to keep patients in ignorance of their exact prescriptions. Especially if there were other ears in the room. On contraception, Dr de Styrap was decidedly puritanical. In his widely read publication *The Young Practitioner*, which nowadays might be titled *Entering General Practice for Dummies*, he declared that the practice of advising on contraceptive matters was 'derogatory and degrading to the medical profession' and worse still, was 'a gross abuse of professional knowledge.'

Of course contraceptive pills did not exist at the time. The nineteenth century was the epoch of the condom. In 1844 Charles Goodyear patented a process that 'cured' rubber to make it more durable, and the motor, footwear and french letter industries never looked back. Sexually transmitted diseases were rife at the time, and though the medical profession knew that the devices could have an important preventative role, clinical thinking of the age was that nasty infections were deserved reward for immoral behaviour. The mass provision of sheaths to the great unwashed might add further temptation to already vulnerable bodies and souls. Only when armies were on the move, and the monetary and manpower implications of poxed soldiers was calculated, did governments suddenly become interested in shielding their members.

A post-treaty holy Ireland was spared from such revolutionary behaviour by heavy taps from croziers. In 1934, the very reverend John C. McQuaid, a doctor's son, school principal and careerist cleric, took it upon himself to write to an alumnus of his establishment at Blackrock College, Éamon De Valera. In his missive he expressed discontent about a new government bill that might allow condoms in through the back door, provided they were not for sale. McQuaid wanted the post office to be given the automatic power of search so that no citizen could have condoms mailed to him from unholy jurisdictions across the water. McQuaid's biographer, John Cooney, makes the interesting point that the young priest was so prolific in his letter writing to the Taoiseach, he acted more like a backbench Dáil deputy than a schoolmaster.

In the 1940s McQuaid had his heavenly reward for his endless networking and toadying. Happily ensconced in his palace, he saw to it that the 1944 Easter Meeting of Bishops would seek a similar ban on new-fangled sanitary items known as tampons. His widely read and worldly men of the cloth declared that tampons might 'stimulate' impressionable girls and lead them into contraceptive use. Health minister of the day, Dr Conor Ward, kissed the rings and obligingly instituted a ban. In 1957 a Tennessee Williams play *The Rose Tattoo* was taken off stage at the small Pike Theatre in Dublin for the crime of having the word contraceptive in its text. On this occasion Archbishop McQuaid used his contacts in the

Irish constabulary to have the director of the play imprisoned for a short period.

In 1960, exactly fifty years ago this June, the world's first oral contraceptive was approved by the FDA in the United States. It had been successfully trialled in the slums of Puerto Rico. By 1963, Enavid was available for Irish doctors to prescribe, not for birth control, but it was listed in the MIMS prescription manual as a pink tablet to treat abnormal uterine bleeding, endometriosis, painful periods and premenstrual tension. The dubious phrase 'cycle regulator' rode into the lexicon of Irish medicine, and for many years afterwards, ladies learned to present to surgeries complaining of irregular or heavy periods in order to obtain an often necessary contraceptive fix. Enavid was manufactured and marketed by G.D. Searle & Co who had their Dublin headquarters at 56 Harcourt Street. It stayed on the formulary until the early 1980s by which time Irish doctors had a wider range of safer alternatives with a far lower whack of oestrogen.

Mechanical barriers however still proved troublesome. In May 1971, fifty stalwarts of the Irish Women's Liberation Movement took the 'contraceptive train' to Belfast and in a very public and important milestone, imported condoms and spermicides illegally into the 'free state'. In the Seanad, a young Mary Robinson, later to be Ireland's first woman President, was meeting great resistance to even debating contraceptive issues. Her private members Family Planning Bill was refused a second reading. Conscientious objectors in the medical profession then began to wonder if they might lose out financially if patients flocked to more liberal-minded colleagues. By the end of the decade, Charles Haughey had contrived his infamous 'Irish solution to an Irish problem'. Condoms were legalised, but only on the prescription of a doctor. Thankfully, a Labour health minister, Barry Desmond, rescued copulating couples from the indignity of state, church and medical control of condoms. Half a century on from the first contraceptive pill, only doctors remain in control of the nation's fertility. Maybe the next fifty years will see control of sexuality returned to the people.

ORTHODONTICS
February 2006

Once every five years, my stomping ground in the capital city gets a makeover and is renamed Dublin South Central. Courtesy of political aspirants, the telegraph poles get festooned with giant-sized photographs of the great, the grim and the grinning. Name and face recognition is everything, especially when four of the five elected TDs don't even live in the constituency. Once the votes are counted, and free city centre car spaces for life have been claimed, all the combatants go remarkably quiet. Dublin South Central is not a patch renowned for production of ministers. Local family doctor and businessman Dr John O'Connell was the last complete article but his term in health office was noteworthy mainly for its brevity.

From time to time a glossy brochure pops through the door. This might be Mr Mitchell's latest research on the dastardly price of funerals. Or Mr Mulcahy telling us how wonderful the Luas light rail line is (he lives beside it, miles away in Ranelagh). Last week it was Dr Upton asking us to phone her in the Dáil if we'd like to avail of free twice yearly cleaning of and polishing of our teeth. (Telephone 01 6183756 if you are interested). I don't think Dr Upton's Doctorate is the sort that allows her look down your throat and prescribe antibiotics. Nor do I think it's the sort that allows her fill cavities or bore out root canals with a drill. But hey, it's good to know that our TDs and Doctors, despite all that important time spent at committees, meetings, debates, conferences and important fact-finding missions abroad, still have time to take our calls about tooth polishing.

Tooth polishing isn't the only life-saving dental procedure discussed in Dáil Éireann. The other one is Orthodontics - or tooth straightening to give it a real name. It even has its own Committee - The Special Orthodontics Sub-Committee of the Joint Oireachtas Committee for Health & Children. Orthodontics is a high priority in Government. Put the word Orthodontic into the search engine of the government website and you will find it is dealt with on seven hundred and ninety nine government websites putting it just behind breast cancer (1,252) but well ahead of prostate cancer (265), testicular cancer (71) and haemorrhoids (17) which trailed in at the bottom of my survey. So why do your elected representatives judge this to be a such an important issue? Was it De Valera's vision to have the laughter of happy maidens with straightened teeth and heavily wired jaws at every crossroads whilst their athletic men folk waited years up the trees to have their cancers diagnosed late?

Those of us who cut our teeth in Ireland of the 1960s and 1970s had little to smile about. None of us had even heard of orthodontics. There might have been the odd girl on the bus who was called metal mouth and couldn't speak clearly enough to abuse us back. A teenage rumour went around that rock singer Chris Rea coudn't break into the American market because some of his teeth were crooked. Then Pogue front-man Shane McGowan and Halloween fangs appeared on television and we all felt fine about ourselves again. Today this orthodontic obsession is everywhere. I've heard of children having their jaws broken and reset to accommodate perfectly perpendicular gnashers. Families are taking out second mortgages to get all their kids straightened out when it's quite clear they have simply inherited a slight tendency to dental overcrowding from their parents. Yes, there are isolated cases where orthodontics will correct and prevent serious dental abnormalities and chewing difficulties in the future. But there is a valid viewpoint that much of the orthodontics performed today is little more than window dressing, hugely expensive cosmetic surgery for kids.

Head down to Donnybrook any afternoon this month - joint home to Leinster Schoolboy Rugby and Schoolgirl Speed Dating. In the chattering terraces, you'll catch a glimpse of a terrifying beauty being born. A bewildering array of mouths opening and closing together, housing thousands of clean pearly teeth bound together in unison by enough wire to construct a few new prisons. Synchronised smiling. Galvanised grinning. The smirk of our Celtic Tiger.

A KICK IN THE BALLS
February 2004

A young man found a lump on one of his testicles. He had it checked by his family doctor who gave him a referral letter to see a urology specialist so that the nature of the lump could be ascertained. He waited many months for the appointment and when he did make it to the top of the waiting list, cancer was confirmed. And he began treatment much later than he should have done. Delayed diagnosis adversely affects survival statistics, but I'm happy to report that he is doing well. This case is not isolated, our health service has long left men (and their scrotal contents) very much out in the cold.

In January of this year, a minister at the Department of Health alerted camera crews to the fact that he was going to launch a report on *Men's Health in Ireland*. Buswells Hotel, next door to our parliament, was the venue where the minister confirmed that Irish men are dying on average six years before women. He followed this truth with waffle about the wonderful investment of half a billion euro that his department had put into cancer services since 1997. There was idle talk of working with stakeholders, developing a national policy on men's health promotion and formulation of a national plan. But not a single meaningful intervention was announced that might make a difference today or tomorrow to a young man who finds a lump on his liathróidí.

It is young men who succumb to testicular cancer. Most patients are in their teens, twenties and thirties - the prime of life generation. I should say here that there are many causes of lumps in or around the scrotum, and they certainly do not always signify cancer. Infections, hernias, varicose veins and cysts account for many swellings in this area. A GP will have suspicions, but needs the hospital system to step up to the mark with timely investigation and diagnosis.

When it comes to lumps, our health service practices a shameless apartheid system. Male ones have never been prioritised like female ones. There are dedicated breast units all over the country, staffed by specialist surgeons and liaison nurses whose job is to co-ordinate early diagnosis and appropriate timely treatment of all breast lumps - cancerous and benign. Family doctors are equipped with special early referral forms that can be faxed directly to the breast nurse who ensures immediate screening and access to specialist services. Irish society decrees that no anxious woman with a breast lump should wait more than a day or so to have her fears allayed.

Rules for men are different. Long patronised about being too macho to talk about health or too cowardly to present symptoms, those that do, are put to the back of the queue.

Swellings in Irish testicles are lumped in with enlarged prostates, irritable bladders, wonky kidneys and troublesome foreskins and referred to a urology service so hopelessly under-developed it would put a third world nation to shame. Speaking in the Dáil last year, a medical TD said that men in his area with waterworks problems had to wait up to five years for appointments because of the lack of a single urologist in his county hospital. Men need to make noise. Next time you get fobbed off with a delayed appointment, ring the private secretaries of the Taoiseach and the Minister for Health. If they don't intervene, write them a legal letter. Even men with lumps can move mountains.

HEALTH FASCISM
July 2009

The appetite of Governments for the control of lives that should really have nothing to do with them is quite insatiable. But what's particularly worrying about the torrent of health fascism sweeping Europe is that there is so little dissent. As I write, the Food Standards Agency across the pond has just called for the urgent downsizing of chocolate bars. Her Majesty's ministers, including those who have claimed Mars Bars as expenses, will gleefully fall into line and ponder wrapper sizes. A draft consultation document aimed at tackling the 'obesity epidemic' wants the size of plain bars set at forty grams and snack bars, whatever they are, set at fifty grams.

This new doomsday cult of climate change alarmists are at it too. Sandal-wearers in winter, writing in the *International Journal of*

Epidemiology, have declared that fat people are over-contributing to the warming of the planet. For those of you with a fetish for figures, a new paper in the journal claims that obese people contribute one billion extra tonnes of greenhouse gas emissions every year. Compared with what? Oh, probably size zero catwalk models or starving masses in Africa. Last year the climate nutters advocated a mass cull of cows, urging us to save lives and the planet by eating meat no more than once a week. Won't be long now before they advocate fish on Fridays.

Here in Ireland, freshly cleared in the last parliamentary session of religious blasphemy, Nero-like ministers continue to fiddle and issue edicts on their golden harps. We have a preposterous situation this summer where our police force has gone to tender (in both Irish and English languages) for the supply of twelve Glass Tint Meters. Your ministers, fired up by their successful regulation of bankers and developers, have decided to make the shadiness of car windows conform to new standards, and your police force, as if they haven't enough to be doing, are going to police it. They will share one Glass Tint Meter between fifty Garda stations, and will I reckon have to spend most of their crime-busting day transporting it from one jurisdiction to another.

Bertrand Russell wrote too about how the love of power was camouflaged as the love of doing good. The late Professor Petr Skrabanek of Trinity College wrote extensively about the rise of coercion in society - particularly in the fields of health and safety. Petr worried that our common human aspiration for wellbeing was being hijacked by a new class of 'experts' on safety and happiness who feed from a 'bottomless spring of dubious truths' and use 'statistical sleight-of-hand' to convert their theories into scientific certainties. Petr wrote about the strangely oppressive city of Singapore where a state initiative against child obesity meant children were given marks for their weights in monthly school reports. As with history and maths, children were given grades for both fitness and body shape which parents were then asked to monitor strictly. A decade and a half on, Petr's prophecies have arrived on these shores. Last year there was call for schools to reward children who lose weight with money or coupons. There have been demands for schoolchildren to be labelled as obese within the school setting at regular weigh-ins by teachers. Some schools have already provided kids with pedometers to measure precisely how far they walk or run on any day. We are told that after four weeks, children increased the number of steps taken each day by 76%. Talk about walking away from happiness. Not all educators are happy with the advance of health alarmism into childhood. The weight of young people can fluctuate substantially in pre-pubescent and adolescent years and worries about body image rarely help children. The 'experts' who manage obesity propaganda rarely speak to the experts who manage the obsessional traits and worries of young patients with anorexia nervosa.

A study of the rising intensity of language used by obesity alarmists is interesting. One Irish commentator was recently quoted as saying that 'it must stop, there is no cure. It just gets darker and darker from here on'. We are told that it one of the most 'devastating of diseases' and a 'ticking time-bomb'. Then there is the 'first generation of children to die before their parents' quote, widely bandied about by journalists with cerebral obesity. This laughable prediction is often attributed to Jamie Oliver, the cheeky chappy cook. But in fact it originated from a bunch of overfed MPs in a House of Commons health committee report five years ago. Not happy with landing teenagers and children with a burden they could do without, toddlers and pre-schoolers are now a target. The latest unsubstantiated statistic to dribble from the newswires is that 22 million under-fives are estimated to be overweight worldwide.

Good to see that the independent *Social Issues Research Centre* in Oxford has criticised both sensationalist claims and the unjustified use of terms such as 'exponential rise' and 'epidemic'. They claim that no service is done by 'hyping the plight' of heavy people, exaggerating their numbers or diverting limited resources away from where problems really lie. They point out that the bulk of society's weight gain starts after children leave school and become less active in adulthood.

Cast a cool eye on any playground next time you pass by. Do you see any evidence of an epidemic? Pandemic perhaps? Undertakers advertising in the school magazine? No. There were plump children on the margins when you and I went to school and they are still there today. What has widened are the goalposts - the norms are labelled overweight, the big children are termed obese and the very fat kids are now bullied by society as well as their peers. When it comes to weighty matters, a supersize portion of common sense is required. I fear the alarmists among us devoured that commodity long ago.

25 YEARS OF AIDS
May 2006

Early in June 1981, the Center for Disease Control in the United States published its weekly bulletin on infectious diseases. It included a report on five previously healthy young men in Los Angeles who had all come down with a rare form of pneumonia. All were homosexual and two had died. AIDS was born, and within 18 months we all knew quite a bit about it. Cases surfaced almost immediately in other American cities, then in France, Belgium and then it seems, we all had it.

So-called risk factors quickly emerged. In September 1982 I began medical studies in Trinity College and AIDS was already moving from medical news to public news. In June 1983, Minister for Health Barry Desmond informed the Dáil during the health estimates that the syndrome was probably not caused by a single new virus but was 'induced by multiple factors'. French and American researchers made claims and counterclaims about who had discovered the cause. By 1984 a virus had been well and truly identified. It was the Human Immunodeficiency Virus, known as HIV. It acted by destroying the immune system of its host, leaving the body vulnerable to all manner of opportunistic infections.

My recollection is of initially being told that all the major risk factor groups began with the letter H. AIDS was of course devastating the homosexual community, but the other H's were heroin addicts, haemophiliacs and Haitians. Later heterosexuals were added to the list and it was then that the whole country sat up and began to take notice. Theories and speculation abounded. Homosexuals who holidayed in Haiti were blamed for importing the virus to the West Coast of America. Freddie Laker's cheap flights aboard Skytrain were blamed for spreading AIDS from San Francisco to the wider world. Then somebody claimed that the disease was endemic in Zaire, a country of Central Africa. That was puzzling but it helped explain why Belgium had so many cases.

What I remember most about the whole arrival of AIDS, and the accompanying hysteria, was that misinformation was every bit as commonplace as good information. There was endless scandalising and scare-mongering. The media didn't care, as long as it was generating tomorrow's headlines. We were treated to the spectacle of celebrity AIDS deaths - beginning with Rock Hudson in October 1985 and followed by Liberace, Freddie Mercury, Arthur Ashe and Rudolf Nureyev. Ireland had its own share of well-known AIDS patients and those who worked or studied in Dublin's hospitals at the time knew the names well. In those days, the Irish press tended to respect personal and family privacy at times of personal despair.

Twenty five years on, it's interesting to reflect on what has happened with AIDS. There are now 65 million people living with HIV infection. 25 million people have died from the disease. One million every year. The medications we now have in the western world are phenomenally good at keeping the disease at bay. But most HIV infection is in sub-saharan Africa where the tablets are simply unaffordable. Some years ago the World Health Organisation launched a scheme with a catchy title - the '3 by 5' campaign to get 3 million Africans on anti-retroviral drugs by the end of 2005. It failed to meet even half of its modest target.

In Switzerland, home to the World Health Organisation, the Federal Health Office has just launched a million euro AIDS poster prevention campaign featuring motorcyclists, olympic fencers and ice hockey players - all competing nude without a stitch of clothing. *No Action Without Protection* is the slogan. This follows a campaign which encouraged all Swiss hotels to put free condoms next to the bibles on bedside tables. Less than half of one per cent of the Swiss adult population is infected with HIV and the infection rate has been falling for many years. Switzerland records about one death per week due to AIDS / HIV Infection. Every day in Africa, eight thousand new people get infected with HIV and more than six thousand die from AIDS.

Perhaps we should mark the 25th anniversary of AIDS by requesting that thousands of World Health Organisation head office staff move from their luxurious high rise accommodation in Geneva to the rural villages, shanty towns and refugee camps of sub-Saharan Africa. Decentralisation I believe it is called.

THE WORST DISEASE
IN THE WORLD
September 2004

Last month, the world watched on television as Pope John Paul II presided over Mass for 300,000 pilgrims in Lourdes. Some say this may be his last trip abroad. Others talk of a second trip to Ireland, oblivious to the cruelty of inflicting further non-essential travel on a dying man. Unlike American Presidents, the Roman Catholic Church does not subject leaders to public check-ups or allow the faithful access to his medical records.

But you don't need a medical qualification to spot that this pope is not a well man. Under a tented altar at Lourdes, it was pitiful to watch a frame that once powered down the snow capped Beskidy mountains now hunched forward, helpless, as if in a straitjacket. His arms rigid, motionless by his side, save for the resting 'pill-rolling' tremor of the fingers, give away diagnostic feature of parkinson's disease. Once expressive facial features stare mask-like, dolefully back at his flock. Saliva flows freely down his chin and what little energy he could summon was used to dispose of it on a white handkerchief. The service lasted a ridiculous two and a half hours in sizzling heat and at times you could see the pontiff gasping for composure, and for breath. The 84-year-old gasped, trembled and regularly asked aides for help. On the previous night he had asked to visit St Bernadette's famous craggy grotto to pray. Hoisted by his aides onto a kneeler, the pope slipped heavily and had to be lifted back into his chair. When his ordeal was over on Sunday, he was whisked away in his bullet-proof pope-mobile to the airport. Bullets are the least of this Pope's worries.

Doctors differ about lots of things, including the disease they would least like to get. Strong contenders through the years include leprosy, schizophrenia, alzheimer's disease, motor neurone disease and huntington's chorea. But parkinson's disease is never far from the top. It's interesting that when doctors vote on diseases they would least like to get, it is conditions that principally affect the brain and central nervous system that predominate. This reflects not just the deep interest doctors have in these diseases, but perhaps the knowledge that successful treatments and long-lasting cures are few and far between.

Last month, the pope was bringing his disease back to the country where it was first described. In the mid 19th century, Jean-Marie Charcot, a professor of neurology at the Salpêtriére in Paris first named this disease after Dr James Parkinson, a London-based doctor who had published a pioneering essay on 'shaking palsy' in 1817. It took another hundred years before the malfunction was traced to a layer of grey matter in the brain called the substantia nigra. Despite all the treatment advances since the 1960s and access to the finest medical attention in the world, one glance at the pontiff tell us that parkinson's usually wins in the end. The only miracle in sight looks dependent on stem cell research and experimentation on human embryos. A price no pope will pay.

SUPER SPECIALISTS
March 2006

There's a joke in medical circles that is so old, it has an awful whiff of decomposition. It was bound to escape sooner or later from the Christmas cracker.

An elderly spinster on a cruise trip is invited to the captain's table for dinner. She is seated next to the ship's doctor whom she politely engages in conversation. "And what do you do?" she enquires of the uniformed medic. "I'm a naval surgeon" came the reply. "My, how you doctors specialise these days." exclaimed the lady. "Have you a cure for one that keeps filling up with fluff?"

There is a grain of truth that lies behind this jest. In just a few decades medicine has specialised, sub-specialised and super-specialised beyond belief. Whether these changes have been to the advantage of doctors or their patients, is rarely discussed. It's fair to say that doctors made most of the running in the move to specialisation. Patients were never consulted either before, during or after this medical metamorphosis.

Specialisations took place rather arbitrarily. Initially there was the barber pole divide between those who cured with pills and potions and those who preferred the scissors and saw. Then another significant divide between mind doctors and body doctors followed - a demarcation that can still short-change patients today. A further group of doctors preferred office hours with weekends off so they took over care of the skin. Then we had a rash of body part pioneers who claimed whole organs to themselves - heart men, lung lads, joint docs, bone setters, stomach settlers, liver squatters and marrow medics. There followed squadrons of testing doctors, often on fee-per-item, who had all the advantages of billing patients without ever having to greet them. Enter the bug testers, blood letters, photographers of the living and dissectors of the dead. I could continue, but I feel a parable coming on.

A portly doctor is enjoying a few days of semi-inebriated rest over Christmas. It's the coldest festive season in years. His roof is white with powdery snow and icicles dangle from every window. Bang! His central heating breaks down. Not the nightmare you imagine. There's always one indebted plumber in the practice - eternally grateful that the doctor certified his bad back as one that would never withstand the hard benches of jury service. The plumber arrives in jig time with a plan of action. Firstly he will need a computer specialist to check the programmer setting. Then he needs a thermal engineer to check the thermostats. He asks a general electrician to check the power supply and then calls in another electrician who has a special interest in fuses. Next to arrive at the house is the motorised valve specialist. He finds some resistance so a motor dynamic engineer is called to assess the possibility of a burned out motor. The motor transplant team are placed on standby just in case. Meanwhile the plumber assembles a separate team to assess the pump. These include specialists in pump opening, manual starting, case-tapping, mallet-knocking and should all these efforts fail, the pump removal team who will prepare things for the pump transplant specialists. If the pump is working, the plumber will phone a gas supply assessor or oil well checker depending on what fuel system the good doctor uses.

This will be followed by a consultation with a filter specialist, a consultant in pilot light technology, a team of pressure assessment specialists, senior cisternologists, upper house radiator bleeders and lower house radiator bleeders. All fluids bled from the system need to be checked, double-checked and billed by very different specialists. Hydrologists will assess water content. Closed system biospherologists will assess for signs of life. Grease assessors will be required to make sure all is going smoothly. Meanwhile radiator endoscopists will bring in their own telescopic equipment to assess and record (on DVD for a small extra charge) every inch of tubing covered by the doctor's central heating. If further areas of doubt are thrown up, these can of course be checked by a multi-disciplinary team of radiator imagers - including those who can take x-rays, ultrasounds and magnetic scans, those who can read x-rays, ultrasounds and magnetic scans and those who can infiltrate radiators and piping with contrast dyes, heavy metals and biohazardous nuclear materials so that even more x-rays, ultrasounds and magnetic scans can be taken and read.

Now the plumber is very near restoring the doctor's heating. He just needs to call his insurers, his risk assessors, his risk advisors, his health and safety monitors and of course, his lawyers. After a final flourish of activity, heat is restored to the mansion. The doctor is ever so grateful. Private heating insurance will take care of everything on the itemised bill. He offers his plumber friend a glass of malt and the two recline in front of a nice hot radiator. "My, how you plumbers specialise these days." says the doctor. "Indeed and we do doctor. Did you never think of specialising yourself?"

CRYOGENICS
April 2006

The warm-hearted Madame G never fails to surprise me. Standing over the family freezer the other day, looking to rescue some tender petits pois from their plastic body bag, she promised to have me deep frozen after death. I was touched.

'You adore me so much that you will freeze my body until such a time as medical science can bring me back to cherish you all over again?' I wittered. 'No' she thundered. 'You'll be stored under the sacks of oven chips for eternity so that nobody finds out precisely how I murdered you.'

We tend to get hot and bothered in the Irish kitchen about euthanasia, terminations, the life cycle of spermatozoa and all manner of conjugal relations in between. But cryonics, the technology of preserving remains in frozen suspension for future revival, rarely gets a mention. Not so in America, where frosting Mammy over is as legitimate a business as psychiatric hospitals for pets or paying to have Granny spied upon in her own home by doctors trained in alzheimer spotting.

Now don't get the idea that cryonics practice is limited to cowboy country. Earlier this year there was an extraordinary case in France where a court intervened to have a husband and wife defrosted, and cremated for the public good. The two bodies weren't just any old pair of deep frozen corpses. One was Dr Raymond Martinot, an 80 year old medical doctor and cryonics enthusiast who died four years ago. The other body in the freezer bag was his wife Monique who passed on to her icy mausoleum in 1984. Dr Martinot lived in a country chateau in the village of Nueil-sur-Layon deep in the Loire valley. Well to do French squires, and belt-tightening former Taoisigh of our own, like to wear the Charvets under their knits and keep bottles of best vintage tiddlies in the cellar below stairs. Not so with Dr Martinot. When his dear Monique gave her final orders, he had her head immediately immersed in crushed ice, injected her with anticoagulant drugs and transported the corpse to a special crypt with a stainless steel freezer unit ready for her reception. Like any dutiful French husband he opened it at least once every five years to check on her progress. When he started running up some rather extreme electricity bills, he sold viewing tickets to the general public who by all accounts were quite happy pay for the privilege. Dr Martinot also had an alarm fitted to alert him if the temperature ever fell below the critical minus sixty five degrees centigrade.

Following a severe stroke in 2002, Martinot joined his wife in cold matrimonial storage. But their hapless son Remy immediately ran into trouble with the local gendarmes. They were insistent on upholding an old French law that demands all bodies must be either buried, burned or donated to drunken medical students in the Sorbonne. Following the best legal accountancy traditions, the case was delayed for a number of years as it ascended through various courts. It was due to graduate to the European Court later this year, but last month Remy gave up the ghost - not because of legal or financial pressures, but because his Dad's freezer broke down and the temperature soared to minus 20 degrees. After an appropriate period of defrosting (and mourning), the good doctor and his wife were cremated. Remy was rather philosophical about the whole affair. "Maybe the future will show that my father was right and that he was a pioneer" he told the French media.

Dr Martinot may well be a hero in his own fridge-time, but the truth is that most of the good work and crude business of the cryonics world is transacted in the United States. The field is populated by an eclectic mix of well meaning scientists, dreamy science fictionists and financial sharks who will relieve punters of enormous sums of money in hope rather than expectation. Advanced techniques for deep freeze embalming are not taught in Irish medical schools but I am led to believe they involve the use of heart-lung machines, lowering of temperature using ice-packs, blood draining, posthumous perfusion of multiple additives and preservatives before a final dip into a vat of liquid nitrogen. Sounds a bit like modern food production. If you wish to read more about cryonics there are two or three avenues I would suggest you tread. The so-called high priest of the cryonics movement is Professor Robert Ettinger, an academic from Michigan who wrote the seminal *Prospect of Immortality* in 1964. The animal most studied by scientists in this field is the grey wood frog which can drop its own body temperature for winter, line its blood vessels with ice, stop its own heart and jump-start the whole lot back to life when the weather improves. In Ireland, such slimy beasts are usually called winter golfers and have apartments on the Algarve.

As for beloved Madame G. The good news is that I accidentally broke her freezer the other day whilst defrosting it. I didn't know you weren't suppose to use a lump hammer. The bad news is that she had it replaced immediately with an upright model - that has three rather small drawers. Garda Commissioner please note.

PROBIOTIC LIFE-SAVERS
March 2005

As I was walking down Henry Street the other day, a young lady was handing out leaflets and free drinks. All around me shoppers young and old were gladly accepting this freebie, opening their mini-bottles and gleefully swallowing the contents. Most drank the pink liquid before they even read the label or accompanying leaflet. They were in fact guzzling a bottle containing skimmed milk and germs - bacteria in this case. To my knowledge nobody died on Henry Street that day. They were imbibing what the marketers call 'a once a day friendly bacteria drink.' I have never been sure what the food industry means by 'friendly bacteria'. They don't jump out of the bottle and embrace you in a bear hug. Nor do they perk up in a chirpy voice to ask 'How's your Father?' as you pass legions of them on the supermarket shelves. Youthful as I try to be, I am long enough in the world to know that nutritional health claims can't be taken too seriously. But old-fashioned sceptics in a gimmick-happy world are few. Let's get down to some bald facts about the 'friendly bacteria' probiotic industry. In the UK, consumers last year spent a phenomenal €300 million a year on yogurt-type 'health' drinks. Tesco says sales have doubled in less than a year and women are buying most of them. What manufacturers are lacking in scientific proof, they certainly make up for on marketing, and I fear this whole probiotic caper is spiralling out of control.

The sales patter is simple. First, tell the punter that the most vicious enemies to fight in your life are antibiotics, natural ageing, stress, late nights, booze, hectic work and travel. Then tell them that these horrors of modern life cause the vaguest symptoms imaginable - feeling sluggish, rundown, out of sorts - that sort of thing. This is followed by the final coup de grace - the mandatory health advice beloved of promoters of life extension - eat well, exercise a lot , oh and whilst you are at it . . . fill your stomach very day with a jar of invisible friendly beasties.

Bacteria pots are being sold as hangover cures, stress-busters, travel tonics, big night out rescuers, boozy night improvers. The latest gimmick is to emphasize the importance of 'digestive health' as a daily habit. The wheeze is that staying fit, eating healthily and including germs in your daily diet, somehow stacks your lucky cards up against something vague called 'bad digestive health' !

There are a growing number of scientists and medics who are raising concerns at how health science is being hijacked by the food industry. One study in the *British Medical Journal* expressed serious concerns about misleading labels on probiotic products. Scientists at the Royal Free Hospital in London examined the contents of 13 brands and found that only two matched their descriptions on their labels in terms of microbiological content. A well-respected professor of microbiology from the hospital wrote at the time that probiotic supplements do not always contain the stated species and quantitatively are often woefully defective. He claimed that some of these so-called 'life-giving products' showed no signs of life at all, and were in fact entirely sterile.

Draw your own conclusions. Probiotics may well be a harmless fad. If less was spent on marketing, and more on properly validated scientific research, someday they might turn up the occasional product that doctors could endorse without being paid to do so. But general medical wisdom at the current time says that many so-called health-giving foods are little more than quackery. When a professor of nutrition says that there is a serious lack of regulation in the marketplace and that not enough research is being done to identify effective ingredients and substantiate their efficacy and safety, it's time to take notice. Bring back cheap and cheerful full fat fruity yoghurts that fill you up and don't harp on about how many lives they save. Old friends are usually the best ones to trust.

THE ABSURDITY OF JOGGING
January 2005

Alastair Cooke, late commentator on all things American, described them as 'panting, slanting figures in shorts and T-shirts'. From the comfort of his 15th storey apartment, each morning he watched these 'earnest ideologues' in New York's Central Park jogging, jogging, jogging around the long circumference of the reservoir below. In sleet, biting wind and Arctic cold. In the brisk fall and in summer furnace. At one time they made him feel pangs of guilt, but as he grew older, and wiser, such feelings vanished. Mr Cooke lived a happy and privileged 96 years 15 stops up in an elevator, without ever joining them. He chose instead a life of golf club bonhomie, jazz soirees, evening tipples and tapping on his favourite typewriter. The ever-present cigarette in hand.

Cooke once wrote about three 'doctor friends' of his. The one in San Francisco told him that jogging over the age of 50 is madness, too much of a strain for the heart. The doctor from Baltimore (a man who advocated closed windows at all times) told him that more people have died of fresh air than any other noxious gas. And his medical friend in New York told him that two martinis will cure almost anything. Cooke chose to live in the latter city, the Big Apple that keeps doctors away.

The origins of jogging are interesting, and all too often ignored by those who promote it. Taking a lead from Herr Hitler who obsessed on the fitness of his master race, it was President John Fitzgerald Kennedy who declared that America's growing softness and lack of physical fitness was 'a menace to our security'. His US army badly needed draft fodder for their war efforts. Military chiefs were unhappy with the fare on offer. It's no secret that that country's National Committee on Physical Fitness was developed within the US Defence Office. By the 1970s and early 1980s jogging had become a big business in the sports industry. It was helped along in 1977 by a man called Jim Fixx, who decided to write about his favourite hobby. His *Complete Book of Running* was credited with igniting a jogging craze and went on to sell over a million copies. Fixx himself was jogging ten miles a day. He happily declared that qualities which are important in running have a radiating power that subtly influence other aspects of life. The Fixx qualities were will-power, the ability to apply effort during extreme fatigue, and the acceptance of pain. In 1980 he published his *Second Book of Running* to great applause and followed it the same year with an hour long film. This was set in beautiful locations across America giving advice on special dietary plans, the right clothes to wear and how to improve personal performance with tips from the master. In 1984, whilst running through the beautiful state of Vermont, Jim Fixx suffered a cardiac arrest, collapsed and died. He was fifty two years old. The post mortem revealed three major coronary artery blockages. A major setback for a most odd human endeavour? Not a bit of it. Like human torture and drugs of addiction, jogging became more popular than ever.

MORE MALAPROPISMS
February 2007

My recent column on medical malapropisms (or the funny things patients say to their Doctors) drew a pulsating postbag from readers. One was almost *incontinental* (ahem) with rage.

"Cold Limerick City. 14th January 2007. We parents group read your article every Sunday and appreciate your old cures and herbal remedies etc. etc. but today is an all low - a skit on the mistakes of patients. As a teacher I hear such every day, when a kind word can put many right in this age of bullying and low self-esteem often leading to suicide. We are amazed at your writing picking out the mistakes of your illiteral patients - all so sad, sick, desperate. Just how could you? Never again are we going to buy your paper or read you - for now you are nothing to us - a caring person but no words are low enough to describe you."

How and ever, I was greatly cheered by the rest of your postbag. It tells me that a sense of humour is alive and well, outside the walls of Limerick anyhow. It's also good to know that medicine isn't the only guild in which a sense of the ridiculous is actively encouraged. A Ban Garda wrote a lovely letter listing a 'few howlers' she had heard of late. At an accident she attended, the injured party spoke of *serious reconcussions* for the other driver. She once overheard a woman speaking about the drugs threat to Irish schools. 'They're all using them *amphibians*.' she declared (Amphetamines). The same informant also told me that when the Central Lunatic Asylum in Dundrum changed its name it was not uncommonly referred to as the *sentimental* (central mental) hospital.

A gentleman wrote to tell me that a good friend once advised him to laugh more often as it releases *embryos* from the brain (endorphins perhaps). And a delightful hospital receptionist told me of a friend of hers who has lovely *salad skin* (sallow) and a neighbour who purchased *magnesia blinds* (venetian). Another reader of the column sent me a ten-year old newsletter which contained some malapropisms recounted by an inner city Parish Priest. It confirmed my long-held view that Dublin is a world capital of puns and witticisms - intended and unintended. A visitor who was caught short on a visit to a convent asked the nun for permission to use the *piscility*. And a man told his wife that his memory loss was a sure sign that he was going *sea lion* (senile). One day, on a visit to a flats complex the parish priest met a caretaker who didn't want to cast *cistercians* at anyone but he did mention his concern about the unmarried couple upstairs who were *co-rabbiting*. The same parish priest once met a Dublin man who kept an alsatian dog in the back yard as a *detergent to frighten burglars*. He also recalled a hard-pressed wife once told him that her husband was like the pope - *he thinks he's inflammable*. Isn't it interesting that the three occupations who deal front-line with some of the most difficult work in Irish society - namely medics, guards and clergy, also like to let off a bit of steam and have a giggle at some funny things that are said to them in the course of their work.

So there you have it. Sick, low and desperate, not to mention a major contributor to suicide , but at least I'm not alone. Best-selling author, mathematician and defender of political incorrectness, Professor Des McHale of University College Cork wrote to say how much he enjoyed the piece and kindly sent me a signed copy of his most recent book 'A Decapitated Coffee, Please and other great malapropisms.' Mercier Press has allowed him put together a wonderful collection of over 700 authentic bloopers. All of Irish life is there, medical specimens too. From the lady who works as a doctor's *deceptionist*, to the *locust* doctor (locum) who takes over practices when the main man is on holiday. There is the confirmed *septic* when it comes to alternative medicine (sceptic), *consternation* when the bowels don't open (constipation) and the patient who was sent to an *eye and rear* specialist at the *Iron throat* hospital. There are children with *Crickets* (fragile bones of rickets) and expectant mothers avoiding tablets so as they don't damage their *faeces* (foetus).

And I have two true stories of my own. A house officer in obstetrics (delivering babies) overheard a conversation between a consultant and lady whose dates didn't correspond with her size. He asked her if she had a long cycle, to which she replied "No doctor, I just live around the corner. " And in paediatrics (children - not feet) the consultant was beginning to suspect that a child had a urinary tract infection so he asked mum 'Does his urine burn?' The mother was firstly astonished at the question, then she took umbrage and replied quite reasonably 'Well doctor, I never tried lightin' it.'

FAT BOTTOMED GIRLS & BICYCLES
December 2006

One advantage of a medical training is that it allows you to undertake all sorts of exciting research - in the interest of scientific advancement of course. So before penning this seminal paper, I dusted off my extensive archive of Queen videos from the 1970s and soon located a track called *Fat Bottomed Girls*. Fellow glam-rock buffs will know that this was released as a double A sided track, with *Bicycle Race* on the rear. FBG, if you will allow my acronym, was written by lead guitarist Brian May and concerns a young man who happened upon an appreciation of the finer qualities of the pear shaped human figure. For the video, Freddie Mercury hired Wimbledon stadium to stage a bicycle race. It was the middle of September in 1978 and all 65 contestants just happened to be naked members of the fair sex. The rest, as they say is history, and as in most good histories there are interesting footnotes. For instance, the company which rented out the bicycles refused to take them back when they realised what they had been used for.

I make the above observations for no other reason than to illustrate how strangely the human race, and doctors are worst offenders of all, regard the very ordinary practice of ladies riding bicycles. Take the current edition of the *Journal of Sexual Medicine* - it contains some distinctly bumpy-looking research on the health hazards facing female cyclists. A team of gynaecologists at Yale University and the Albert Einstein College of Medicine persuaded 48 ladies who cycle 10 miles a week to join a study that compared the sensitivity of their nether regions with 22 ladies who shunned two wheels and ran five miles a week for their constitutional exercise. The results didn't exactly move the earth. Using 'non invasive techniques' the eminent specialists ascertained that women cyclists do have a decrease in genital sensation compared with female runners. The lead author, the nicely named Professor Marsha Guess, happily reported no negative effects on either sexual function or quality of life. Professor Guess went on to praise her own study as the first ever to evaluate the effects of prolonged or frequent bicycling on neurological and sexual function in women and expressed impressive knowledge of the female anatomy. "While seated on a bicycle, the external genital nerve and artery are directly compressed. It is possible that chronic compression of the female genital area may lead to compromised blood flow and nerve injury due to disruption of the blood-nerve barrier."

It's good that these matters are receiving attention, because doctors, without the back-up of any research whatsoever, have long pontificated on the adverse effects of cycling. One of my professors at medical school had a special interest in the quack pontifications of doctors from yesteryear and provided us with a useful list. In Victorian times, a Professor See warned of the dangers of children under twelve using bicycles. Another professor by the name of Hammond went on to warn about abnormally developed thighs in habitual cyclists whilst rural doctors warned of a 'curiously distressed look' on younger cyclists and proclaimed that cycling causes 'too great a strain on heart and lungs which may result in immediate death or lingering illness.' Then, as happens in medical science, the moral minority entered the room and bellowed louder than anyone else. Dr Theresa Bannan writing in the *New York Medical Record* of 1895 described the saddle as being 'physically and morally injurious to women as the sensitive tissues are subjected to a pressure.' 'Moreover' she warned, 'the impingement and vibration of the saddle can act as a sexual excitant.' Any mention of sex, and the moral men jump in head first. Dr H.MacNaughton Jones, a well-known gynaecologist wrote an article on *The Special Dangers to Women of Cycling* in which he warned of irregularity of the heart action, anaemia and menstrual disturbances. He expressed 'little doubt that the saddle with the falcon pommel may prove a serious source of sexual excitation.'

Thankfully there were some strong women around who wouldn't

93

listen to such poppycock. Mrs Frances Willard, a social reformer took up bicycling in the 1890s at the age of 53 and encouraged friends to do likewise. "It's just as good company as most husbands. And when it gets old and shabby, a woman can dispose of it and get a new one without shocking the entire community". The men tut-tutted. Dr Joseph Price read a paper to a medical society in which he claimed to have spotted 'an enormous increase in appendicitis' in women who cycle. (He also spotted the exact same increase in lady golfers and cricketers). Even in the late 1980s, the doctors were still at it. Now it was the dangers of cycling in shorts. The *Journal of the Royal Colleges of Physicians* in London described a handful of cases of malignant melanoma on the legs of lady cyclists. Now, one hundred and something years after the invention of the affordable bicycle, doctors are back advising women to get out on their wheels hail, rain or shine. And it's in a good moral cause - the battle against obesity. Which brings me neatly back to the specimens with fat bottoms.

I must rewind that tape and study it again.

JOHN SPENCER RIP
August 2006

Those of us who further darkened the ambience of snooker halls in our youth, were saddened to hear of the death of John Spencer, doyen of Pot Black and three-times world champion in 1969, 1971 and 1977. He may not have had the transylvanian looks of Ray Riordan, the duty-free lifestyle of Alex Higgins or indeed the natural flair of Jimmy White, but Spencer had guts. Much of his courage was reserved for battles with medical problems that dogged the second half of his life. His story is ordinary and extraordinary in equal measure. Born, bred and buttered in Lancashire, Spencer hailed from a small coal and cotton town called Radcliffe, outside Manchester. His father lost an arm in the trenches of the first world war but somehow learned to play snooker, improvising a clothes brush as a bridge to hold his cue. Just after the second world war, Spencer senior introduced his teenage son to the joys of a full size snooker table. Within a year, young John was scoring century breaks.

Snooker was far from a sexy sport, not to mention a career opportunity in the 1950s. Indeed young Spencer abandoned the game for a decade when he entered national service. But a chance match for cash in the early sixties caused him to return to the baize and within a very short space of time he was English amateur champion. He plied his skills intermittently for various charities until Pontin's holiday camp in Blackpool offered him a regular wage to become their resident professional for a summer season. He borrowed one hundred pounds to enter his first world championship in 1969 and lifted the trophy plus twenty times his borrowings in cash.

In 1974, the snooker lifestyle of long nights and even longer drives back home took a cruel toll on Spencer. He fell asleep at the wheel of his car and was lucky to survive the accident. His beloved world championship snooker cue wasn't as fortunate as its owner. It shattered into multiple pieces and though expertly pinned like a fractured bone by a well known cue doctor of the day, Spencer knew life was never going to be as it was. In 1982 he suffered the indignity of watching his opponent Steve Davis score the first ever televised 147 break. I say indignity, because three years earlier Spencer had achieved the same feat only to discover that the television company had sent its camera crew on a tea break to avoid overtime payments.

Myasthenia gravis is a relatively rare medical condition that you may not be familiar with. It hinders the flow of electrical impulses between the ends of your nerves as they enter the muscles. It particularly affects the face and the eyes causing double vision and drooping of the eyelids. Not usually a lethal condition, it's probably the last disease a snooker enthusiast wants to battle, particularly one who plays the sport for a living. John Spencer awoke one morning in May 1985 with double vision and within jig time his doctors were relating bad news. He battled on in the professional ranks, assisted by prolonged and large doses of corticosteroid medication, but their side effects took a cruel toll on a gentlemanly nature. In a recent tribute to his friend and colleague, snooker commentator Clive Everton described the 'hellish' side of his treatment, the 'deep depressions, ungovernable spasms of aggression and obsession with suicide'. In the 1990s Spencer worked intermittently for the BBC in the commentary box and served as head of the World Professional Billiards and Snooker Association for six years. Everton records that his demeanour in later years was in stark contrast to his sunny good-natured self, a man who loved practical jokes, golfing and horse-racing.

Three years ago John Spencer received an even worse diagnosis - stomach cancer. Surgery wasn't an option but he agreed to undergo aggressive bouts of radiotherapy and chemotherapy. He responded well to treatment for two years but last year, John decided that enough was enough. He said it was getting to the point that the treatment was making him so miserable that he was upsetting everyone around him. 'I realised that I could have another 10 years but be miserable with the treatment or take my chances without it. Even if I have only 12 months left to live, at least I'll die happy.' John Spencer survived just over the year. He died in Bury hospice on the 11th of July and his final break was in front of many old friends from his sporting days at a crematorium in Bolton. Snooker players, perhaps more other sportsmen, are accustomed, when things look bleak, to throwing in the towel. There's always another frame. Another match. Another championship. John Spencer's decision to end treatment was particularly brave. Sometimes it just doesn't matter how many snookers you need to escape. The crucible awaits us all.

GLOBAL WARMING
April 2007

Across the pond, a royal battle looms in the British Labour Party as contenders jostle each other in succession stakes for the Blair grin. Lumbering Gordon Brown has spent two month's wages having ivory-coloured veneers glued to his teeth to make him look less Scottish on television. And the young pretender, environment minister David Miliband, has jumped aboard the climate change bandwagon, the political fad for politicians who tire of exaggerating child obesity epidemics or the dangers of passive smoking. Miliband, whose curriculum vitae lists philosophy, politics and economics qualifications from Oxford, has about as much training in scientific matters as a bluebottle on a dog-turd. So when he announced that 'the debate on climate change was well and truly over' my nose pricked up and I sniffed a nasty odour. In fact young David went even further and made some silly remark about another nail being driven into the 'coffin of climate change deniers'.

Now I am no weatherman, climatologist or expert in the gaseous emissions of cows, jeeps or greenhouses. But what I do know is that the day any branch of science closes itself to debate is the day our flat earth might as well stop turning.

Now I've always had a warm spot for Duncan Stewart. His softly-softly emissions on architecture and eco-friendly lifestyles on RTE television would melt the coldest of ice-caps. But on a recent radio interview with Ryan Tubridy, he came across like a man possessed. His rising dogma and intolerance of opposing views on climate change was astonishing, so much so that his host, a rising star of skepticism, gently teased him on more than one occasion about the high priestly fanaticism of those, who like Miliband, say all debate on the issue is over.

Miliband's statements were made in the wake of a conference of well-chosen weathermen and weathergirls. In February of this year, one hundred and thirty governments from around the world gathered in Paris to approve a collegiate statement on climate change. They announced that failure to cut greenhouse gas emissions would bring devastating problems - inland droughts, seaside flooding, failed crops and ruined ski holidays. Sympathetic newspapers waded. A correspondent for *The Guardian* said that there 'was no longer any place for climate change deniers' and said that such a position was the 'exclusive preserve of the deluded and the breath-takingly cynical.'

The major prediction from the Inter-Governmental Panel on Climate Change was that the earth would warm by four degrees by the turn of the next century. Cleverly, the authors know that most of us won't be around to see if they are correct. But it is worth noting that the previous dire warning of climate watchers, issued only six years ago, warned of a six degree rise by the same year. That's some climb down already from their lofty pulpit.

As I write, Al Gore, a one-time vice to the Clinton Presidency, is touring the world promoting himself as an expert on global warming and energy conservation. His film on the subject 'An Inconvenient Truth', recently won him a Hollywood Oscar. Gore then found himself slightly inconvenienced by the truth when it was announced that his family house is so big that it uses 221,000 kilowatts of electricity each year - with gas and electric bills running to €2,000 a month, 20 times the US national average .

Another mouthpiece on eco-matters is HRH Prince Charles. Last month he was presented with a 'Global Environmental Citizen Award' for his campaigning work. So what did he do? He flew himself and no fewer than fourteen staff first class to Harvard Medical School to pick up the award. The entourage for the overnight trip included two private secretaries, a doctor, a butler, four security staff and a handful of logistics and luggage people. One small award for a man, thirty giant carbon footprints for mankind.

CLIMATE CHANGE
January 2010

Just before the midnight news on BBC Radio 4 runs *Today in Parliament*, a thirty minute programme dedicated to what's happening in our old ruling house at Westminster. For insomniacs, it is highly recommended by medics, inducing precisely the same numbing effect as ten milligrams of Mogadon. But a particularly exciting show the other night kept me awake until five to twelve when an interesting exchange took place between right wing Tory MP John Redwood (often drawn as Mr Spock by cartoonists) and Ed Miliband, the younger of the bland Miliband brothers and now the minister for climate change (usually drawn as a schoolboy).

Mr Redwood asked Mr Miliband which climate model predicted the extremely cold winter in Northern Europe this year? The reply he got was telling. The young Miliband got stuck for words. The best reply he could muster was that 'the weather fluctuates as anyone knows' and he then bumbled on to criticise those who might use isolated climate fluctuations as any kind of evidence against global warming. It was an interesting altercation, because every tremor, every puddle, every early daffodil and every late barbecue is consistently linked with this dreaded 'climate change'. But when a scintilla of evidence to the contrary is raised, it is not allowed in the debate and promptly put outside the back door to freeze its nuts off. I get worried when politicians, and the scientists they sponsor, say the time for debate is over - particularly on a delicate matter for which few have any scientific credentials to begin with.

There are just two infallible rules in the whole science of meteorology. The first is Christophorus Henricus Diedericus Buys Ballot's Law which states that if you stand with your back to the wind in the northern hemisphere, the pressure is always lower on your left side than on your right. The other infallible rule is that if you stand in front of the television when the weather forecast is on, you run a high risk of being misinformed.

We are consistently told that thousands of 'climate scientists' agree on this vital issue and that the future of our four and a half thousand million year old planet is suddenly under threat. The data being used to create this hunch, has been collected over just a few decades. The story about e mail hacking at a UK university alleging that scientists may have colluded in retaining data from public view, is the least of worries. There are deeper questions about the exact credentials of climate science. What exactly is it? Who are these people who secretly e mail each other about the end of the world and delight in whipping themselves into the eye of a media storm whilst jetting around to conferences? My personal opinion is that the emperors of climatology wear very few clothes indeed. Climate science and its new brand of scientists are very much in nappies. As a discipline, it has not got a strong hand of history on its shoulder. Few scientists have left an indelible mark on the study of climate, and the current crop are unlikely to add to the medals table. Was it not climate scientists who predicted an Indian summer in 2009? Wasn't it climate scientists who predicted this current ice age season would be the mildest of winters? Isn't it climate science that gives meteorological forecast each evening and admits they cannot predict beyond the end of the week?

What particularly worries me about this whole climate change business is the absolute intolerance of any contrary opinion. Any community that closes itself off from debate and attacks dissenting voices is in my book unworthy of a scientific title. A lifetime in medicine teaches doctors to be as wary as they are knowledgeable about the use of statistics. Any public relations expert will tell you they can be massaged and moulded to blow a wind in any direction of your choosing. Modern climate science is built almost entirely on the analysis of statistics by computers that have been told by human hands what to do. Global warming is just one of their hypotheses - an interesting one that is worthy of debate - but unworthy of the attentions of people who will not tolerate dissent. Climate scientists may be right about recent global warming. But equally they could be wrong about its cause, its significance and its longevity.

Many of those who have been recruited to the cause of global warming, choose to pontificate in newspaper columns about its significance. There is one who writes weekly in the *Guardian* and another in the *Irish Times*. Qualifications in the field of climate science are not listed under their articles. They are believers who attack the integrity of disbelievers. David Bellamy the Botanist has been attacked, as has Pat Kenny for simply doing his job and asking questions. My own professional expertise, should any of it persist, is in sore throats, haemorrhoids, referral of the very sick and removal of ear wax. Limited proficiency on climate science is based on a lifetime of weather observation, a few years grounding in university sciences and close study of evolving scare stories. What I find is that the more I inform myself of the science and non-science invoked by global warmists and hot-under-the-collar politicians, the more sceptical I become.

As a medic, I am all too well aware of the power of the scare. Frighten too often and too loudly, and your audience loses trust. We spend too much time pretending to save lives, and not enough on retaining patients' ears. We saw this with mad cow disease when all sorts of dire predictions were made about beefy prions whisking millions of brains into sponge trifle. Then we had SARS - here today, gone tomorrow, and in between we had state cars chasing Chinese people with sniffles around Dun Laoghaire. As I write, the dreaded swine flu has been frozen off the news agenda. Press conferences at Hawkins House could be held in a telephone box, if you could find one. If the world is still here next week, I'd like to return to this subject with a closer look at the credentials of climate scientists and their supporting politicians. I'd like to know what's fuelling their bandwagon.

MORE CLIMATE CHANGE
January 2010

I made a threat last week to return to this strangely consensual planet of Global Warming, a recently explored land where debate is not tolerated, naysayers are accused of being in the pay of oilmen and ordinary decent doubters are abused from high pulpits. The appropriation and misappropriation of language by climate alarmists is very interesting. It would appear that even the term Global Warming is no longer kosher, for in recent months, official mention has begun to recede like waters down a pothole. With a minimum of subtlety, the nomenclature has been diluted to an all-encompassing and thoroughly meaningless phrase - Climate Change. You can deny all you like that the world is heating up, but it takes a particularly brave soul to deny that our weather actually fluctuates.

What first began to ring my cynical buttons was a letter to Time magazine a few years ago from an American Professor of Psychiatry. Using his undoubted expertise on anxiety, he wrote in to suggest that the title 'Global Warming' simply wasn't scary enough. He explained, in the convincing patter psychiatrists use, that the idea of a warm planet was far too benign and perhaps even enticing for the general populace. Without a hint of a smile he suggested that that the title of this latest in a long line of looming catastrophes should be changed to 'Global Boiling'. Injecting a modicum of science into his view he stated that the human brain is 'hardwired to respond to immediate dangers, not ones that are years or decades away'. The psychiatrist polished off his letter with some reference to famous medical experiments on frogs. I won't bore or alarm you with the details - suffice to say that Kermit reacts rather differently to a dip in warmed water than he does on immersion in a boiling cauldron.

The learned author of this astonishing letter was a convert to the church of latter day humidity. This scion of American psychiatry had developed a sudden interest in climate change, in his own words, 'on the last Earth Day following the birth of his granddaughter.' He has since written extensively on the 'projected health and mental health risks' of global warming suggesting that it will cause new infections, increase the incidence of all sorts of diseases, create more violence, more depression and more post-traumatic stress disorders. Perhaps it will keep him so busy he can cease writing scare-mongering letters about boiling frogs.

I pointed out last week how climate change gurus have been quick to attack those who question their theories, hunches and computer-modelled predictions. When I went to school, and it's not that long ago, there was a big geography class scare about a return to the ice age. In fact some of the very same climate boffins who are now part of the polar opposite consensus were at the forefront of that very scare. Just a decade ago, the big frightener was in the computer class. The Y2K bug, a semi-mythical computer glitch, was going to turn off life support machines and send aircraft tumbling from the sky. Multiple billions were spent around the world on all manner of new-fangled computer and software upgrades. Then nothing happened. Industries told us this was because we had purchased all their new stuff. But those who ignored the scare and continued to run homes and businesses on old tried and trusted frameworks knew otherwise.

Nobody listens to British Prime Minister Gordon Brown any more. Perhaps just as well, as in October last, he said we had fifty days to save the planet. Well I'm still here and able to listen to his latest warnings that we shouldn't become distracted by 'behind-the-times, anti-science, flat earth climate sceptics.' Ed Miliband, Brown's minister for weather warnings, is now a conspiracy theorist claiming that there are 'climate saboteurs' at work. Tory leader David Cameron went to Norway to have his photo taken on a sledge whilst leader of the Liberal party Simon Clegg castigated doubters are 'ideological dinosaurs'.

The UK's political leaders are proudly supported by the tree-hugging, flower-conversing homeopath known as HRH - the one who hopes not to be too old to inherit some of Mummy's palaces. As part of a green economy drive, bonny Prince Charles has cut personal spending by a quarter, down to a tidy £1.7 million a year. This wasn't too difficult to achieve as canny developer Charles sold £40 million of brick and mortar assets just before the property slump. His Aston Martin is running very nicely on wine and Camilla has no great vertical extravagances. HRH's personal carbon footprint is coming in at a very neat 2,601 tonnes of carbon dioxide per annum. So who would deny his Highness the luxury of a built-in shower in the £300,000 hired jet that took him to research the Amazonian rainforest? Or the retinue of 20 staff that filled another jet so that he might collect his Global Environmental Citizen Prize in New York from Al Gore? Yes, the same Mr Gore whose eight-bathroomed Tennessee home was rumoured to consume twenty times more electricity than the average American dwelling. Before the 'green refit' that took three years and goodness know how many dollars to accomplish.

There are a growing number of inconvenient truths that are ignored by those who present us with the fait-accompli of climate change and imminent catastrophe. They have every right to question the motives of those who attack them, but they risk adding more assumptions to the ones they have already inserted in their theories. Even doubting Thomas's like myself worry about the sort of world our children and grandchildren stand to inherit. But an ideal future is one in which young minds are encouraged to stay open, dogma is open to regular challenge, and the freedom to think and express contrary opinion is valued . It would take quite a change in the current scientific climate to give us that kind of world.

HEAD THE BALL
April 2004

Back in my old school yard, Head the Ball was an oft used term of mild abuse, reserved for that classmate considered a goal or two short of a hat trick. It was a label for boys whose behaviour was off the wall, unpredictable or wild even. We didn't know who imported the term into our limited vernacular, but the expression didn't come about by accident. Scientists have long wondered whether heading a football is dangerous to health. Ten years ago, a series of experiments, cruel ones probably, were conducted on laboratory animals, They were subjected to repeated concussions every five minutes for two hours. Scientists were able to gleefully report that no residual damage was caused and the Head the Ball hypothesis was laid to rest.

Much of this work was turned on its head recently when an inquest on former England soccer international Jeff Astle concluded that the death of the demented 59 year old was due to an occupational disease. Namely that he spent much of his professional life applying his head to heavy leather footballs. Astle's mental and physical deterioration was painful to watch. You may recall those cringe-worthy weekly performances as the end of show buffoon on the Baddiel & Skinner Fantasy Football programme. Prior to his 'discovery' by ITV he had been working out his post-football days as a window cleaner. By the time he died, Astle no longer even recognised his own family. The coroner's verdict was very clear. But it was very much at odds with the case of former Celtic player Billy McPhail who in 1998 lost a legal claim that his deteriorating mental health was caused by heading the ball.

Doctors have given conflicting evidence about the existence of a Head the Ball Syndrome, or to give it its proper medical title, Chronic Traumatic Brain Injury. In 1989, 37 former Norwegian internationals underwent neurological examination and tests to investigate header-induced brain damage. Sixteen of them had been complaining of symptoms like headache, irritability, lack of concentration and poor memory. Tests showed these players were significantly more likely to have abnormalities when the electrical activity of the brain was measured on an EEG machine. A further

WHAT THE DOCTOR SAW

study of Dutch footballers in 2001 hinted that both amateur and professional players may suffer from mental impairment due to the heading of footballs.

Before parents start red carding junior strikers and removing them from penalty boxes, it should be stated that the modern leather football weighs in at a much lighter half a kilogram. It also now has a waterproof coating that prevents it becoming the leaden mass nodded about by players of the Astle and McPhail generation.

To end on an optimistic note, a Brazilian neurologist, Dr Celio Levyman wrote recently to the *British Medical Journal*, with words of comfort from a country where football is the national religion. With millions of players plying their skills everywhere from giant stadia to small parking lots, the specialist says that in his entire career he has yet to see ball contact cause brain alterations of any kind in footballers. He suggests that head to head contact in today's game is a much more real danger for Head the Balls.

LOVER OF THE RARE
March 2005

Many doctors suffer from a not-so-rare condition called Spanophilia. For the most part we hide it well from patients, though a bout of ill-disguised yawning during your ten minute consultation might alert you to its presence. Spanophilia was described by Dr Richard Asher as one of the seven deadly sins of medicine - the others being obscurity, cruelty, bad manners, over-specialisation, stupidity and sloth. It is the illicit love of unusual and rare diagnoses above all others. It is a disease that is rampant and usually first caught in medical schools. I have long suspected that it is transmitted by text books which are too large to be read comfortably on the bus.

The late aforementioned Dr Asher, whose daughter Jane became an actress of repute, practised as a specialist at the Central Middlesex hospital during the London blitz. He noticed with some astuteness that a growing number of medical students were becoming so well read on medicine that they kept failing their exams. A student who examined a man with a nosebleed might incline to impress his professor with a diagnosis of multiple hereditary haemorrhagic telangiectasia when the real culprit is simply some over-rigorous picking of the nostrils. I once trained with a student whose first question to any patient with a cough was to ascertain whether they or not they kept pigeons. Twenty years on now, he is probably still searching for his first case of pigeon fancier's lung and has yet to spot that most barkers are simply self-polluters of breathing tubes with cigarette smoke.

There is something about the education of doctors and the aspergian culture of medical schools that encourages its apprentices to focus on the rare and unusual. We are quick to criticise journalists and newspapers for concentrating on atypical and unusual stories, but the truth is that doctors are no more immune to such temptations as anyone else. In a lifetime of practice we might see hundreds of patients with passionate delusions. But we tend to remember the one with delusions of passion.

In the 1920s, a beautifully named French psychiatrist, Dr Gaetan de Clérambault, invented a diagnosis peculiar to ladies. It's called erotomania. The patient typically believes that a famous or exalted person, whom she has never met, is passionately in love with her. According to the *Oxford Textbook of Psychiatry* the supposed lover is often married, of higher social status, and is commonly some sort of entertainer, television celebrity or politician. Most of the documented case histories of this erotic delusion originate in Italy or France. Another giant textbook of medical literature, *The Hypochondriac's Handbook* is informative on Erotomania. It mentions that the patient may well follow her object home. She may embrace him in public or send sexually explicit singing telegrams to his workplace. It alludes to the fact that the condition is difficult to cure and suggests that the cost in human lives and laddered tights is incalculable. However further examination of De Clerambault's syndrome by modern psychiatrists reveals that the diagnosis, though exceptionally rare in either sex, is also found in men if you bother to look for it. One study of a hundred men charged with violent offences found evidence of the syndrome in at least four of them. One problem with this syndrome is that the patient can make considerable nuisance for the object of their affections.

The irrational belief remains unshakeable, even when lawyers or police come knocking at the door. And a delusion of love may quickly change into a delusion of persecution. The patient may begin to make public complaints about the innocent object of their erotomania.

In 1997 the celebrated British author, Ian McEwan, wrote a tragic novel based on a man with erotomania. *Enduring Love* was subsequently made into a much lauded yet disturbing film. It describes the trials and tribulations of a science writer who is stalked by a man suffering from De Clerambault's syndrome. The appendix to McEwan's book mentioned that the story was based on a case report in the *British Review of Psychiatry* written by Dr Wenn and Dr Camia. It took two years before it emerged that there is no such journal and that the surnames of the doctors were simply an anagram of Ian McEwan. Psychiatrists and critics, some of whom panned his book for not being imaginative enough, fell for the trickery hook line and sinker. Proving perhaps, that fiction is very often stranger than fact.

IN THE PSYCHIATRIST'S CHAIR
July 2007

Just as anglers collect volumes about fishing, many doctors take pride in reeling in a good collection of medical books. I've always been a bit of a magpie in this regard, collecting far more literature than I could possibly read in a lifetime. If a first edition of a favourite title comes my way, I'll gladly double up and hand the paperback on to somebody else. Amongst the best stomping grounds for first editions in Dublin are the growing chain of dedicated Oxfam book shops. The only disappointment is that the staff who run them tend to be of the knowledgeable sort so you are unlikely to find a first edition of Harry Potter and the Philosopher's Stone for a euro, that Sotheby's auction house might flog for £15,000 sterling.

Just the other day I bagged a bargain. I came across a first edition of *In The Psychiatrist's Chair* by Professor Anthony Clare, the first of three books to accompany his famous radio series. Its original price tag from Fred Hanna in 1992 was £18.20. The book was relatively clean with a good jacket and its new price of six euro was a very fair trade. For the amateur psychiatrist in all of us, this book is priceless.

Professor Clare was ahead of his time in many ways. His BBC radio series in the 1980s was an early recognition of the allure of celebrity. He conducted insightful interviews with over sixty leading lights of the day in a manner that was far removed from the modern trend of 'dumbing down'. What Anthony Clare managed to achieve with a combination of forensic hunting skills, careful excavation of childhood memories and a relaxed interview style, was the demystification of many well known personalities, complete with foibles, warts and prejudices that are common to us all.

Whenever I see Sir Jimmy Savile, I think of Anthony Clare's description of him as a champion boxer, always wary and edgy, dancing on his toes, dodging punched questions, and constantly on the lookout for a blow below the belt. As Savile devoted much of his life to charity fundraising, Clare was fascinated by his emphasis on money and his denial of feelings. He suggested to Savile that a key feature of his life was his control of it, exemplified by his refusal to marry and refusal to have children because of the demands this might put on him. Savile nodded and replied. 'One of the great problems of human relationships is that either one or the other wants the other party to change, not compromise, I mean change'. Clare's final diagnosis does not appear in too many psychiatric textbooks, but is nonetheless of great interest. 'If he is to be believed then he is a calculating materialist . . . he can cope with people who need him for things he is prepared to give, mainly material things, in no instance himself.' But Clare confesses that he found 'something chilling about this 20th century saint' and he wonders how much an emotionally indifferent and materially deprived childhood might have made the man.

Professor Clare also introduced listeners and readers to Dr Ronald Laing, an extraordinary figure in the recent history of psychiatry. The diminutive Glaswegian doctor pioneered the idea that for many people, mental illness is a journey of exploration that is both misunderstood and fuelled by their families. He also believed mental illness was often misdiagnosed and worsened by doctors. Irish television viewers might recall Laing as the doctor who had the temerity to have a few drinks before going on Gay Byrne's *Late Late Show*. He received the Annie Murphy treatment from our foremost broadcaster and many still cringe at the memory. Funnily enough, Laing was also mildly inebriated when Professor Clare interviewed him for his radio programme, and whilst much of the content was edited, the psychiatrist elicited a story of childhood that would make the hardest of grown-ups weep. Can you imagine being the son of a mother who would burn any toys she believed you were getting too attached to? Laing told Clare that relatives would only give him money for birthdays, such was his mother's passion for disposing of anything which he loved. Ronald Laing succumbed to the elements of life and withdrew his name voluntarily from the medical register late in his career. He died on a tennis court in St Tropez in 1989 whilst leading a set by four game to one. Had he lived longer, he would be just 80 this year.

Another interviewee of Professor Clare was a familiar figure on the tennis court. The late Wimbledon champion, Arthur Ashe succumbed to AIDS in 1993 at the age of just 49, a consequence of HIV infection contracted during a coronary bypass operation. His surgery was made necessary by a massive heart attack which almost claimed his life at the age of 36. The most poignant parts of Clare's interview focused on death, principally the effect on young children when death visits their family. Ashe was just six when he lost both his grandfather and mother in quick succession. The final question asked of him in the psychiatrist's chair was what he might say if he ever met his mother again. Ashe answered 'I don't think I'd say anything. I'd probably just let her hold me for a while, for a long time. Yes, that's because I can't recall that ever having happened.'

It's a position of extraordinary privilege to be asked by fellow beings to doctor them. To be invited to probe the mind, the memories and the thoughts of fellow human beings, as psychiatrists do, is perhaps the greatest privilege of all. Arthur Ashe, a man of insight both off-court and on, once said that for every hour spent on the playing field, two should be spent with a book. Fifteen years after publication, this book as comforting and riveting as it ever was. I wonder what might tempt Professor Clare to come back for In an Irish Psychiatrist's Chair. I have the guest list drawn up and waiting.

Postscript: *Professor Anthony Clare died from a massive heart attack in a Paris hotel just a few months after this article was published. He was just sixty four years of age.*

DEPARTMENT OF SECOND OPINION
July 2011

The recent foetal ultrasound scandal has done serious harm to the trust which generations of expectant mothers have placed in the everyday machinery of obstetrics. A pregnant lady from North Dublin was told after a scan in hospital that the baby she was carrying had no heart beat. She was given an appointment for a D&C womb-clearance operation and prescribed medication to assist the evacuation. In great distress, having previously had four miscarriages, she presented to her family doctor in great distress for a second opinion. A subsequent scan that he arranged showed that the baby was very much alive. The human cost and wider repercussions of this fiasco are immeasurable. Our blood contamination disaster, unmasked in the 1990s, was a crisis of international proportions. But the ultrasound heartbeat scandal is very much local and we need to ask major questions about standards in a range of hospital disciplines in small and big town Ireland.

One always looks for positives that can result from these tragedies. As happened in haematology following the contamination of blood products, we can expect major investment over the next decade in obstetric care. But the money will come from somewhere else, perhaps from social, disability or mental health budgets, areas of care where mistakes are less noticeable and where patients may be less vociferous and informed. One laudable principal, now being espoused by the HSE for the first time, is that of Second Opinion. In a health service where a single first opinion can still be so difficult to access, there is some irony in the fact that our bureaucratic masters now advocate 'shopping around'. They also hint at the importance of trusting maternal instinct and asking for a second doctor.

Second opinion is an important but undervalued branch of medicine. Patients invest far more of their faith and money in them than their state does. Many patients in Ireland have two or more doctors and they use them for their own advantage. One might look after illnesses whilst another is used solely for something like tranquilliser supply. They may use one doctor for major illnesses and another for minor ailments. Or one doctor for the kids and another for the grown-ups. The advantage of these sorts of arrangement may only be apparent to those who regularly take out mortgages, health protection or life assurance policies. If a company looks for a medical report, they might be referred only to the doctor who has information about sinus infections, ankle sprains and tummy bugs. The doctor who has clinical notes about adverse family history, cancers, a dodgy back or mental illness may find that his existence is not reported to the insurance company on application.

In a utopian health service, every hospital would have an easily accessible department of second opinion. It would be staffed by the most experienced clinicians, preferably those whose skills and interests span across a range of specialities. And they might have access to the rarest and most precious medical commodity of all - time.

The true home of second medical opinion is the Mayo Clinic in Rochester, Minnesota. The story of how this extraordinary institution with an Irish sounding name was founded begins not far from here, in the industrial town of Salford near Manchester. William Mayo, son of a carpenter, was born there in 1819. He studied chemistry and emigrated to the United States in 1845 to take up a pharmacy position in a New York hospital. Within a few years he had migrated westwards, followed a number of medical courses, and was practising as a 'horse-back doctor' on the edge of the prairie. He got married, and to supplement irregular medical work, worked as a tailor, census-taker, publisher and draft examiner for the army. He settled in the small frontier town of Rochester and developed a busy practice, working long hours seven days a week. He re-mortgaged his farmstead to finance a microscope for his practice and took his young sons Will and Charlie with him on house calls to apprentice them to his new family trade. Busy periods in his surgery included treating the wounded from a local Sioux rebellion and tending to victims of a tornado that rippled through the town of Rochester in 1883. William Mayo amassed a huge collection of medical and surgical literature and he wrote his most important prescription for the sons he idolised, He insisted that they read books for at least two hours every day. Will and Charlie were packed off to medical schools of a higher calibre than the ones their father attended, Michigan and Chicago respectively. They both became surgeons of the highest renown and with their father, developed a small nun's hospital, St Mary's, into the most talked-about and admired medical institution in the world. Once Will was asked by a patient if he was the 'head surgeon' and he replied "No, that's my brother Charlie, I look after the abdomens."

What set les frères Mayo apart was their single-minded capacity for new learning. Between them, they visited Europe over eighty times, to meet contemporaries who were seen as progressive in a variety of surgical fields. They pioneered live teaching in operating theatres and soon the world came to visit them to see what they were up to. Alastair Cook described their achievement as one of the most impressive and romantic stories ever to come out of America - particularly as they hailed from an area once thought only to grow corn and bigotry. He loved the tale of two farm boys in the prairies with their horseback doctor of a father, developing the capital city of world medicine, right in the middle of their small home town.

Today the Mayo Clinic in Rochester has 30,000 staff. It's an extraordinary industry when you consider that the town's next biggest employer has one tenth of this number. Patients flock to it from all over the world. Its annual revenue is about half of the entire Irish healthcare budget. Doctors are paid a fixed marketplace salary and its founding ethos is to spend as much time as possible with patients. Everything about the hospital's design and method is about maximising the doctor-patient relationship. Waiting weeks, or even days, for test results is unheard of. The Mayo has a long tradition of being 'cutting-edge' with patient files, test results and care plans that make the journey home with you a day or two later. And putting Irish hospitals to shame, I believe they are so advanced in the Mayo Clinic, they even reply to letters.

PETR SKRABANEK
June 2010

I often mention the late Petr Skrabanek, a one-time professor of mine at Trinity College. And I have been remiss in not explaining who exactly he was. This is his story. When Russian troops invaded Prague in 1968, Petr was a young Bohemian who was holidaying in Dublin with his wife Vera. They opted to stay and continue their studies here, rather than return to watch repressive tanks thundering through Czechoslovakia. Petr was a toxicologist by training and he added medicine to a sparkling curriculum vitae by completing his Licentiate at Dublin's Royal College of Surgeons. It was while working at the Mater Misericordiae Hospital that he began to make noise. Young Dr Skrabanek was a prolific writer of interesting letters and papers, showing himself to be an erudite and well-studied critic of authoritarianism in medicine. Later he took a professorial position at the Department of Community Health at Trinity College and it was from his base in one of the University's Pearse Street tenements that he began to ruffle feathers. He would question medical fashions, the spinning of health promotion and the less than libertarian ideas of some medical colleagues. The free-thinkers of the international medical community, especially those in academia and journal land , began to sit up and take note. Petr was often invited to visit their towers, ivory and otherwise.

The editor of the distinguished medical journal *The Lancet* was particularly smitten. He described Professor Skrabanek as a gentle, humorous man of immense culture and learning and appointed him to his international team of editors. He later portrayed Petr as a 'gadfly who roamed the world adding zip and controversy to otherwise anodyne meetings.' His role as a learned challenger to new-fangled dogma was an important one and it's sad to report

113

that few in today's money-based medical world are willing to play that adversarial role.

Not only was Petr Skrabanek well-read in the dark arts of medicine, he was also an authority of much renown on James Joyce. In particular, the impenetrable *Finnegan's Wake*. He very much cherished his role as an outsider - not for him the gowns, parchments and processions of cosy medical hierarchy. I have a fond memory of students sipping pints and discussing medical morality with him in Dublin's Nassau Hotel whilst across the road in the august College of Physicians (of which he was a Fellow) the teetotallers were dusting down robes, polishing their maces and admiring the length of each other's qualifications.

In many ways, detachment was his greatest asset for it allowed him the freedom to challenge without fear of offending friend, foe or self-appointed authority. Petr would rarely attend meetings without challenging the dogma on offer for the day. I have heard it said once, in Trinity, that he could be 'rude' to visiting speakers. But these allegations are made by those who would consider it an affront to challenge anybody whose reputation surpasses their scientific credentials. A scientist who disapproves of challenge is not a scientist at all.

Getting to the truth was for Petr more important than meeting half-way in dull or ignorant consensus. If he occasionally pricked bubbles of pomposity, so much the better. Petr confronted and contested many statistics that doctors used to advocate screening for hidden disease. He argued that the dangers of screening - faulty results, missed diagnoses and false reassurance - were usually hidden from the very people screening was supposed to help. The language Petr used in his lectures and writings was telling. It was from somebody who took refuge on the other side of an iron curtain. He warned against totalitarian medicine, lifestyle surveillance, big brotherism and coercion towards better health. He began to see elements of the very oppression that forced his exile creep into everyday healthcare. He wrote movingly about the 'utopian nature of the health promotion movement' and the onward march of health fads and doctrines that sacrifice personal liberties for the 'health of the nation'. He despaired that many 'meddlesome cranks', who in other eras were ridiculed for their eccentricities, follies and soap-box preaching had assumed centre-stage in a new medical world, He worried that public relations was the new trump card, replacing scientific debate. He scoffed at one-time UK health minister Virginia Bottomley whose greatest contribution to the NHS (and perhaps humanity) was to ban biscuits at coffee breaks and replace them with a piece of fruit.

He wrote about health obsessives at the White House where it became an absolute requirement that presidents were photographed jogging, whilst their loyal first ladies issued press releases about how they had removed ash-trays from the oval office. Petr liked to poke fun at the Kellogg family whose carbohydrate droppings continue to promise myriads of unusual health benefits. The latest appears to be heart shaped bottoms when you wear skinny jeans. It was Dr John Harvey Kellogg who became medical superintendent of a Seventh Day Adventist funny farm in Battle Creek, Michigan. His twin specialities were sexual hygiene and healthy lifestyle. In his book, *Man, the Masterpiece, or Plain Truths about Boyhood, Youth and Manhood,* Dr Kellogg lists his 39 suspicious signs of solitary vice (masturbation) in young men. Sign 28, Petr's favourite, was the use of tobacco.

The anniversary of Petr Skrabanek's untimely death in 1994 falls today on the 21st of June. He was just 53. He didn't live to see statistics on passive smoking manufactured out of thin air to enforce smoking bans all over the western world. He missed those homespun comedy programmes where fat people are abused and cajoled into shedding pounds for 'life transformation'. And those using messianic TV medics with laptop computers that supposedly tell 'unhealthy' people how long they had left on planet earth. Petr didn't live to see Green Party Ministers sideline parental choice by advocating a ban on children's toys in children's restaurants. Nor did he witness a Labour MEP advocate new laws to prevent 'facebook addiction', something she termed a 'danger' and a 'clear and present mental health threat to millions of European citizens'. Petr may not have seen them, but he certainly saw them coming and warned us. Before he died, Petr completed the manuscript of his final and fitting work *The Death of Humane Medicine*. It is one of the most fascinating books that I have ever read. Sad to say, much humane medicine seems to have died with him.

115

THE HEALTH OF TRAVELLERS
September 2009

The health needs of the travelling community weren't on the curriculum as I hurdled through medical school in the 1980s. Our only exposure to their plight came during secondment to the lovely old National Children's Hospital on Harcourt Street. There we saw a lot of chronically ill children who had rare inherited conditions called metabolic diseases. They were mainly the progeny of first cousin marriages, most were very small for their age and the sickest ones had large protruding bellies of the kind we were used to seeing on collection boxes for Africa. Many died before or shortly after they reached their teens. My abiding memory is of mischief-loving brothers and sisters, mini-adults before their time, laughing and dying in front of us. Visiting time was noteworthy for the sheer volume of family members that came to the bedside and the chaos that all too often resulted in red-faced nurses. Many of the sickest children had lived most of their lives on the wards in Harcourt Street, too ill to be let back to a home where loving parents weren't enough to sustain them.

I think it was 1987 before Ireland sat up and took note of the plight of our own home-bred ethnic community. In that year, the Health Research Board published a shocking study showing that traveller children had twice the risk of dying in infancy. They also found that the life expectancy of adults was more than a decade shorter than was the case for settled people. Genetics was only a small part of it. Atrocious living conditions, poorly provided education, inadequate healthcare and families too large to feed well were at the heart of these statistics.

After qualifying in medicine, many of us worked the wards during the day and moonlighted at night with the locum doctor services in Dublin. Nocturnal visits to caravans and sites were not infrequent and it was on one of my winter shifts that I first encountered a great grandmother gypsy over the age of 80. For once, I had no list of calls to go to, so she made tea and related the story of her life - a childhood on snow-lined bóithrins of County Wexford, her half-dozen dead children and her late husband's skill at mending pots. It hadn't dawned on me until then that the reason we see so few older travellers, is that they die long before the rest of us. It's a true and sobering statistic that just over one in a hundred travellers are over the age of 65, compared with twelve in a hundred for the rest of us.

In the intervening two decades since traveller health first pricked the national conscience, not much has changed on the ground for nomadic families. Some have done well, and have the new registrations of their cars noted by the same snobs who note them on settled people too. But for most travelling families, a grinding poverty of opportunity persists. Some of the larger halting sites, in Dublin particularly, are in a worse state than shanty towns. Many traveller children still have no access to clean running water and some continue to manage without electricity.

Whilst their parents left school at an average age of thirteen, traveller children now leave at an average age of just thirteen and a half. A study from the North Dublin area shows that half of all traveller children do not attend school. Over eighty per cent of traveller children have no safe play area on the sites where they live. Their acute medical needs are met by emergency departments and a few stalwart GPs who are happy to have traveller families on their medical card lists. Travellers are generally happy with the doctors that they have, but are used to the sinking feeling that some medical card lists suddenly become full when they knock on the door

A family doctor who works with travellers wrote a fascinating piece this month in the GP magazine *Forum*. She describes their heightened fear and worry about cancer - for travellers, even the most minor symptom is often attributed the start of cancer. Whilst health anxiety is pervasive, paradoxically they are not great users of our health service. Traditional cures and healers still abound. Mothers of asthmatics place three hairs from the tail of an ass into an envelope, under the pillow of the sick child. If the hairs are gone by morning, the asthma would be cured. Whooping cough has many cures, including the leavings where a ferret is fed bread and milk and whatever is left behind is fed to the sick child. There is a belief that conventional medicine can break cures and a strong reliance on using healers and priests for hands-on therapy.

The article notes that a strong sense of nihilism about health matters prevails in traveller men. Their traditional occupation, the tinsmith, never recovered from the advent of plastic. They tend not to listen to their wives on health matters and a stoical 'it's my business' position can deter them from seeking medical attention.

The Irish state postures, press releases and throws the odd few bob at the problems of Irish travellers. Since that seminal HRB report of 1987, there have been more studies, followed by strategies which usually recommend even more studies. Many university and HSE researchers, well meaning as they are, sustain themselves and their departments on the study of travellers. In 2002, when I sat on the board of the Eastern Regional Health Authority, we were presented with a big glossy hundred page manifesto called the *National Traveller Health Strategy*. Full of pious plans, few have been followed through - and all it seems to have spawned are further studies. The next one we are waiting on is the *All Ireland Traveller Health Study*.

There have been programmes to train travellers to become health care workers in their own communities, and this has helped with the provision of healthcare advice and appointments. As is often the case, women are open to change, men much less so. To date we have failed to make a difference. Perhaps the key to failure is the fact that all approaches have been made through the women and children. Notable for his absence from all discussions is the all-powerful enigma that is the travelling man. Until we shake his worn hand, and seek to create a mutual understanding, little looks set to change.

BELLY OF EVIDENCE
October 2003

New research has been looking at how women appraise the anatomy of men when they first meet. If we exclude the obvious facial features that make the initial impression, the next most popular destination for lady's eyes is shoulders with 30%, followed by 23% for legs and hands at 19%. Tummies tuck in well behind at just 9% which may be good news for optimistic men who struggle to conceal a paunch. In fact when women were further asked about how they view beer-bellied men with short legs, they were quite happy to overlook these traits if he had big firm hands to compensate.

Just how correct is this term Beer Belly? Scientists divide on the issue but research in this month's *European Journal of Clinical Nutrition* suggests that beer intake has little to do with the size of your belly. The study was conducted on Czech drinkers, amongst the biggest consumers of beer in Europe. Contradicting many preconceptions, they found that the beer-swilling population of Prague actually weighed less than those who abstained.

More light is thrown on this finding by a further American study which suggests the term Binge Belly is more appropriate. Researchers at the University of New York in Buffalo found that tipplers who imbibe small amounts of alcohol regularly had the smallest bellies, whilst those who had four or more drinks on irregular boozing sessions had the biggest guts. Interestingly they also found that consumers of strong spirits were more likely to display midriff spread than beer drinkers.

A myriad of health research is thrown at us every day, and it's important to remember one golden rule - association does not mean proof. Just because 50% of heart attack victims eat marmalade for their breakfast does not mean that their toast spread blocks arteries. The human condition depends on many factors, and the strongest one that determines your shape may well be carried in your genes.

A study was conducted last year on a thousand male employees of Olivetti, the Italian electronic company and created headlines around the world about the discovery of the 'Beer Belly Gene'. A team from the University of Naples reported in the *Annals of Internal Medicine* that they had found a genetic variant known as DD which was linked to excessive abdominal fat, high blood pressure and mid-life obesity.

To confuse further, another study suggests that waist size increases as testosterone levels decrease, and that testosterone replacement therapy may 'cure' your beer belly.

The truth about pot bellies is likely to be a mishmash of all of the above. Men blessed with genetic washboards may continue to do as they please. Those born with a tendency to swell may want to modify their diet and swim regularly. In a world that demands Abs of Steel, many of us are happy to wear braces and tie our own laces. Ladies know a good cushion when they see one.

HOMEOPATHY - THE TROUBLE WITH SAM
November 2005

Make what you will of tourists who visit graveyards on their holidays. It's an old hobby of mine, forged many moons ago in the long Summer days of childhood. It was in the North Dublin seaside town of Skerries that an aunt introduced me to the pleasures of slab-spotting and I've been scouting ever since. In Paris, such behaviour is readily excused. With the delights of the Père Lachaise cemetery on your doorstep, there is no more invigorating and life-affirming way to spend an autumn walk than ogling the headstones for your favourite decomposers. For those who take issue with frequent heresies expressed in my columns, it might comfort you to note that this burial ground contains more deceased Guérets than anywhere else in Europe.

Alas my humble ancestors from the suburbs of Paris don't even merit a full stop in the guidebooks to the Père Lachaise. The maps are more likely to direct you to the lipstick coated international tombstones of Wilde, Morisson and Callas or noteworthy French nationals like Seurat, Noir and Proust. On my last trip to Paris, I bypassed the celebrity trail and set about finding the grave of one of the greatest medical fraudsters of all time. Samuel Hahnemann was the so-called 'father of homeopathy'. Born in Germany he qualified as a doctor but soon became disillusioned with the quackery practiced by his contemporaries. He devoted himself to the translation of classical medical texts into his native tongue. And his idle studies of ancient remedies led him to three remarkable delusions.

1. Diseases can be cured by drugs that cause the same symptoms as the disease.

2. The tinier the dose, the more effect it would have in stimulating the body's vital force.

3. A remedy has to be struck many times with a leather pad to excite its medicinal properties.

In effect, Hahnemann was stating that the cure for poverty is poverty itself, and the less money you have, the wealthier you are. As for his leather fetish, that is beyond this simple enquiring mind.

Hahnemann returned to general practice fired up by his newfound dogma and found that his treatment was far more popular than the traditional medical practices of the day. You see mainstream medicine was no less of a con job - its repertoire amounted to little more than unproven lifestyle advice, blood-letting and chemical evacuation of the bowels. There is little surprise that patients found Hahnemann's remedies more tolerable. His medicines, as with all of today's homeopathic 'remedies' contained nothing more than water. In sharp contrast to his contemporaries, Hahnemann was unwittingly following an age-old dictum of medicine - *Primum, Non Nocere* translated as First, do no harm.

Hahnemann's daft ideas did not stop there. His 'new science' was heavily criticised by medical colleagues who disowned him. In response, he made another sweeping generalisation by declaring deafness, asthma and insanity as iatrogenic diseases - meaning that they were all caused by doctors themselves. In 1843 Samuel Hahnemann died in his adopted home of Paris. The city of a thousand neuroses had taken to his medicines like ducks to water. To judge from his burial crypt, it is also clear that his quackery created enormous wealth for his descendants.

That homeopathy still survives today bears testament to the twin capacities of the human race for mass delusion and being easily parted from their cash. Homeopaths delight in telling us that their cures are the treatment of choice for members of the British royal family - though strangely few of them relying on shaken water remedies when faced with acute appendicitis, ectopic pregnancies or jug ears that needs taming.

Musing on homeopathy and the fact that it still captures the fancy of some conventionally trained doctors, TCD Professors McCormick and Skrabanek suggest two possible reasons. Either it is an indictment of the education provided in medical schools or evidence that some minds are congenitally incapable of developing critical faculties. If Hahnemann was still around, he'd probably have a cure and pour water on that particular ailment too. From his elaborate resting place in the Père Lachaise, he continues to pull the wool over far too many eyes with the nonsense they still call homeopathy.

GENITAL RETRACTION SYNDROME
June 2004

I've woken up in some odd places in my time, but a decrepit mental hospital on the outskirts of town on Christmas morning was probably the worst. The short straw meant that I had a family-free feast day with only a phone, a few unlucky nurses and even more unfortunate patients for company.

And my troubles were only starting. At 10.30am a call came through from a man who had 'cold-called' the hospital seeking admission. Medics have an extra sense to know they are in for an interesting consultation, especially when the opening gambit is "It's my penis, Doctor".

This particularly applies when the doctor is an acting psychiatrist.

"It's my penis, Doctor, it has begun to disappear."

My first inclination was to consider the matter a cruel hoax. Such deceptions had long been practised by gangs of deranged junior doctors, a breed whose sense of humour makes black look pale. But surely colleagues had more to be doing on Christmas morning than annoying the poor bugger who drew the nightmare shift. If it was a prank, I had to play along. So as the rest of the country unwrapped presents and up-ended their stockings, my patient and I discussed the matter of a shrinking penis for the best part of an hour.

As far as I can recollect, the gentleman was already an outpatient of the hospital and was prone to odd delusions that over the years had proven difficult to treat. I was able to ascertain that he posed no particular danger either to himself or others and advised him to attend the next outpatients, and to contact his family doctor if anything else untoward arose. The rest of my Christmas day was the quietest I had ever experienced, so much so that I regretted not inviting this most interesting of patients to come in for admission, or even Christmas lunch.

This strange belief that the male sexual organ is going to vanish up into the abdomen is nothing new and has been described in the annals of psychiatry for more than a hundred years. Doctors know the condition as koro, signalling its far eastern origins. Yanks have tried to replace this excellent title by foisting their own americanism on colleagues, but thankfully GRS, Genital Retraction Syndrome, is not catching on. Much of the literature on koro focuses on Chinese patients in whom it is said to be most common. Men with the condition can suffer extreme anxiety, not just because they wrongly believe that their penis is shrinking inside them, but because they also believe they will curl up and die when the retraction is complete. Some men go so far as to tie their friend to a hanging stone to arrest their perceived loss. Others have gone so far as to build small wooden enclosures for their threatened manhoods.

Western psychiatrists report that koro, though relatively rare, is becoming more common in this part of the world. Even stranger are reported cases of epidemics where groups of people have become multi-delusional about their penises at the same time. Presenting on its own in a new patient, koro may herald a more serious psychiatric illness. So it's a wise doctor who takes the complaint seriously and never laughs the patient out of surgery.

Talking psychiatrists go to great lengths to explain this phenomenon. Freudians have pondered whether these men have subconscious sexual desires for their mothers but consciously fear that their fathers will punish them by castration. Eminently more sensible behaviourists argue that men are innately anxious about both genital size and sexual performance and that some may take organ checking to obsessive lengths. Considering that anxiety and exposure to cold shrink the healthiest of penises, those who take penis-checking to new heights may assume that their prize possession is shrinking inside them when in fact it's the cold weather doing what nature intended. Whatever the psychology or

123

psychiatry of Koro, it is not a diagnosis men easily forget. Medical men anyhow.

IVEAGH BATHS
September 2009

The speed with which forty 'bicycle for hire' bays were installed around Dublin city last month surprised many, particularly those involved in the day to day needs of homeless people. A quick look at the location map will show you that the more salubrious parts of the city have far more than their fair share of the 450 bikes available, whilst the poorer quarters have been studiously neglected. I know very few homeless people who have on-line access and even fewer who can pay the 150 euro deposit by credit card along with annual and daily fees. I don't wish to be a killjoy. This is a great scheme for visa card holders, native and visiting. But it would have been nice to see the same public spirit and speed of response to the simple washing and showering needs of the less fortunate pedestrians in our capital. For many years now, human rights campaigner and friend to many homeless people, Nurse Alice Leahy has been crying out for the installation of very basic washing facilities in our inner city.

A hundred years ago, Dublin's poorest citizens were given the Iveagh Baths by the Guinness family. Built in 1905 during a welcome fit of Edwardian urban renewal, architects from London cleared an area of slums on Bride Street and gave Dubliners an art nouveau bathing and showering facility to be proud of. Generations of Dublin children from the south inner city learned how to swim in the baths. Admission was just a few pence, often overlooked in time of need, and the tiled walls and high glazed roof ensured a boisterous atmosphere with an eye-watering whiff of chlorine. For those who had pennies to spare afterwards, the fish and chips or 'wan and wan' at Burdochs gave them a good feed before the walk, bus or tram-ride home. By 1955, more than 30,000 people visited the Iveagh baths each year. The larger baths on Tara Street which were run by Dublin Corporation had three times as many clients, but they had a murky reputation for not changing the water quite so frequently. This was once mentioned in a parliamentary debate when Deputy James Dillon created an unedifying picture with his analogy to pea soup.

There were no such problems at the Iveagh. The baths had a name for spotlessness and the gleaming white tiles were visible whether you jumped into the deep or shallow end. In the 1940s, a TD remarked in the Dáil that it was a useful place for anyone who wished to emigrate to England - they could be de-loused in the Iveagh before taking the boat. Visitors described the Iveagh Baths as being steam-filled and resembling a washhouse. Which is apt, for that is exactly the part it played in the lives of many less fortunate citizens. Sadly, the Iveagh Baths closed in the 1990s. The beautiful listed building that purified generations of Dubliners now boasts an exclusive private gym which encourages corporate membership and offers personal trainers, pilates and yoga classes. Those unfortunate men and women who sleep rough now rely on canals and charity for the human need to bathe and wash.

Alice Leahy has done more than simply call for public showering facilities. With the assistance of young civic-minded architects, she has submitted wonderful plans to counsellors and ministers. Three years ago she highlighted the urgency of this measure, suggesting that it might prevent people becoming homeless by making it easier to overcome temporary difficulties. They would help out people in emergency accommodation, newly arrived visitors or back-packers to our city as they find their feet, people living in overcrowded accommodation with poor washing facilities. Public showering facilities would help isolated elderly people who are afraid to bathe at home in case they fall and are not found. A very serious and thoughtful proposal for glowing cubes, advertising drums and shower shelters was made to those who have the power to change. Lots of potential sites all around the city were identified.

At the time that these plans were submitted, the *British Medical Journal* asked doctors to look back over the last 150 years and decide what the greatest advancement in modern healthcare has been on these islands. Readers were given an extensive choice ranging from open heart surgery to transplant operations, antibiotics to vaccines, control of fertility to anaesthetics. The clear winner of the poll was none of the above. It was plain and exceptionally simple - the

125

sanitary revolution. Clean water, bathing and toilet facilities for all. It's something we continue to deny to our most vulnerable citizens. Yet Alice's heartfelt call for this most basic public health measure has been met with that old authoritarian Dublin response. On yer bike.

MEDICAL SENATORS
May 2007

Summer has arrived and normal people are looking forward to trips to the beach, eating undercooked sausages from the barbecue and queuing up to buy September's schoolbooks. Not so for your scribe. With the conclusion of elections to the 30th Dáil, hundreds of would-be politicians - the disappointed, the ambitious and the downright mad will be clambering up and down the country to fill sixty comfy chairs in the Irish senate. I belong firmly to the final constituency - mad as the March hare. Despite great efforts to eradicate a political bug that bit me as a youngster - I am entering the race for one of the three seats at Trinity College. It's not a maiden voyage. In 2002 I survived until the 9th count when my transfers helped secure the seat of Dr Mary Henry, who has been one of the senate's most eloquent humanitarians for the last decade. Mary is retiring this time out and there will be an almighty scramble to succeed to the blue seat with a harp on it.

The Irish Seanad, the second house of our Parliament, was established to ensure that 'vocational interests' influence legislation for the public good. The great pity is members of the public do not get a chance to vote for senators. Eleven are nominated by the Taoiseach, forty three are elected by the combined vote of sitting TDs, senators and county councillors, and the remaining six, traditionally independents, are elected by graduates of Trinity and NUI Colleges. In 2002, less than 47,000 votes were cast nationwide in the Seanad election. What can be said for the university seats is that at least they have some semblance of democracy, 46,000 of the votes were cast by graduates of Trinity and NUI. Candidates generally set out a manifesto that reads like a laundry list. On this occasion my campaign focuses on three main issues - the importance of science in education, the plight of the outsider in Irish society, and the provision of services that will make Ireland a safer place to grow old.

Down the years there have been some very distinguished medical senators. Dr James Ryan, a native of Taghmon in County Wexford served as a medical officer in the GPO during the Easter Rising. For his bandaging skills and expert field surgery he was rewarded by His Majesty of the day with life imprisonment. However the 1917 amnesty, nothing to do with tax in those days, was kinder to him and he went on to have a long and distinguished career holding ministries in agriculture, health and finance. Dr Ryan sat in Seanad Éireann towards the end of his political career and died in 1970.

Dr Oliver St John Gogarty was another extraordinary senator, a real renaissance man, poet, surgeon and bon viveur. Like Oscar Wilde's dad, Gogarty was an eminent ear, nose and throat man in Dublin. He was renowned at Trinity medical school for his quick wit and I remember during my time there we were encouraged by enlightened seniors to read his literary output such as *Tumbling in the Hay* and his infamous autobiography *As I was going down Sackville Street*. First editions of Gogarty's work are going up in value, and his fame is assisted in that he was the model for James Joyce's stately plump Buck Mulligan in the opening instalment of *Ulysses*. Gogarty was a free state supporter and once escaped from unhappy Republicans by swimming up the river Liffey. He died in New York in 1957.

Another Trinity medical graduate to sit in the Seanad was the legendary Dr Noel Browne. A native of Waterford, Browne had a childhood that easily rivalled Frank McCourt's miserable one in Limerick. Both of his parents succumbed to TB when he was a child and Noel relied on his own scholarship and financial assistance from the well to do Chance family to complete his education. He himself contracted the disease in his youth and his autobiography *Against the Tide* describes in heartrending detail an extraordinary tale of triumph against adversity. Dr Browne's place in Irish history is assured. Appointed minister for health on his first day in the Dáil he sold off buildings and lands owned by his department and used the money to introduce free screening for TB. He also saw the value of investing in public information services about health matters and is credited with revolutionising tuberculosis services that were hugely underfunded. Browne was a somewhat prickly character though. He walked in and out of many political parties and some commentators suggest that bitterness against former colleagues clouded much of his later life and took away from his good work towards a fairer health service and a more secular Irish society. But his Seanad term in the 1970s was an important one as Ireland was at last beginning to free itself from religious shackles and Browne made an important contribution to debates on freedom and liberalisation. Back in 1949 Noel Browne was the only minister with the humanity, gumption and good sense to go inside St Patrick's Cathedral for the funeral of former Irish president Douglas Hyde. The rest of his cabinet colleagues followed the petty line dictated by their Catholic bishops and stayed outside in the grounds while the Protestant church service took place. For that alone, Browne is a hero in my book.

Postscript: *Professor Ivana Bacik finished in 3rd place in the 2007 Seanad Election at Trinity and took the senate seat vacated by her Labour Party colleague Dr Mary Henry. The independent Dr Gueret finished fourth.*

MR AND MRS LINCOLN
February 2010

In an early career speech, the man who was to become 16th President of the United States, Abraham Lincoln, declared that the ballot is stronger than the bullet. Some years later, his theory was sorely tested by a constituent who dispatched the contents of a .44 caliber Derringer behind the president's left ear. The fact that Lincoln was attending a theatre performance of *Our American Cousin* is well recorded. A lesser known fact, is that the president took nine hours to succumb. He was taken by doctors in the audience to a nearby boarding house and laid diagonally across a bed. He was too tall to fit head to toe. Lincoln's life ebbed slowly away and he never regained consciousness.

This year is the 150th anniversary of Lincoln's republican nomination to run for the White House and he is back in the news. Steven Spielberg has embarked on a movie and there is speculation that Liam Neeson might play the leading role. The tallest man in Ballymena, a studious actor, is on record as saying that he has read about 22 books on Lincoln. No mean feat, just 1,800 left to go. My school history books were kind to Abraham Lincoln. We got a line about his address at Gettysburg, another about the abolition of slavery. And of course his tragic demise at Ford's theatre in April 1865, when the last line in his life was delivered by a young actor called Booth.

Our pen-pictures show a tall gaunt man, high-hatted and hirsute-chinned, poor boy, woodcutter, small town lawyer come good for the people. But always only half the tale, for Lincoln was a man of great contradictions. In his early legal practice, he defended railroad interests as often and as vigorously as the common man. His opinion of black Americans was not as revisionist as America might like us to believe. His commitment to slavery abolition was partial, and didn't apply to southern parishes where a key vote might be obtained. Lincoln did not want emancipation or americanisation of slaves. His plan was to rail them out of the country to lands in South America and beyond.

Gore Vidal, our greatest living exponent of pen warfare, has been prominent in calling for the truth about Lincoln to be acknowledged. He accused one biographer of 'reducing one of the most interesting and subtle men in world history to a cornball Disneyland waxwork'. Vidal says that official Lincoln is cast as warm, gentle, shy and modest, with Shirley Temple curled up on his lap. Yet opponents of the day saw him as intellectually arrogant, cunning as a fox and possessed of an unconscious assumption of superiority.

Vidal rose academic historians from their reverent presidential slumbers some years ago when he stated matter of factly that Lincoln had syphilis and passed the condition on to his wife. This was no idle claim - the evidence is on parchment, in the ink of Lincoln's trusted law partner. Lincoln told him of the town in which he had become infected, the lady from whom the germs were retrieved, and the name of the doctor who treated the young lawyer for his embarrassing ailment. The claim that Lincoln subsequently infected his wife, and that tertiary syphilis caused her later life madness, and perhaps even the death of three of their four children before adulthood, is not the sort of thing west-wingers like to include in the lyrics of Barack Obama speeches.

The President's wife, Mary Todd was directly descended on her father's side from a native of County Longford, who exchanged life in the Slashers County for Presbyterian Kentucky. Mary had chronic headaches all her life and was not renowned for an even temper. She became quite eccentric, paranoid, believing herself to be poverty-stricken when this was plainly not the case. Her high spending in the White House was a source of both gossip and disapproval. Towards the end of her days she attempted suicide at least twice and was known to sew large amounts of money and bonds into her undergarments. When her only surviving child Robert attempted to sign asylum papers for her, mother and son fell out seriously. She managed to escape from one mental institution and ended up in the care of her sister and doing a great deal of travel in Europe.

Gore Vidal declares that Mrs Lincoln's many symptoms, the manner of her demise, and her partial post mortem (only the head was dissected) show ample evidence that she had presidentially-acquired third stage syphilis, otherwise known as general paralysis of the insane. Like Clinton's penis, it is not the saintly image a self-sanitising America likes to chisel into Mount Rushmore. American physicians of historical bent, continue to dissect Abraham Lincoln, Mary Todd and the skeletons of their extended families for clues as to their medical make-up. Lincoln's height (nine inches taller than the average mid 19th century American), his long fingers and unusual visage have led some to speculate that he may have had marfan syndrome. Fifty years ago, the genetic condition that affects connective tissue, was found in a distant blood relative, and the theory gathered fresh momentum. Others speculate that Lincoln was actually suffering from cancer at the time he was shot, citing weight loss in office, chronic constipation and a particularly gaunt appearance in his last photograph as supporting evidence. Two years ago a book proposed that the Lincolns suffered from a hereditary cancer syndrome called multiple endocrine neoplasia. The type postulated is an extremely rare, one in a million. Many doctors love the rare to the detriment of the common. We call it spanophilia and this may be a case in point.

In centuries to come there may well be medical musings, learned textbooks and academic conferences on this bright generation of Irish politicians. Why did high office turn Brian Cowen's brain to offal? Was John Gormley a victim of rapid recycling disorder? And what tourette-like public speaking tic curtailed the career of Enda Kenny?

Postscript: *Daniel Day Lewis eventually played the part of Lincoln, not Liam Neeson. Gore Vidal died in July 2012.*

THEM BONES
October 2006

Them Bones Them Bones need Calcium. And that's a Natural Law. Or is it? The heretofore grassy world of the milk industry is being seriously challenged by medical scientists with calls for the immediate modification of guidelines on calcium intake. Last month, the *British Medical Journal* published a review study which threatens to churn one of the most sacred cows of human nutrition. A team of Australian researchers has found that calcium supplementation in healthy children has little or no effect on the density of their bones and does little if anything to prevent bone fractures. For decades, most consumers have swallowed the marketing line that any amount of cow's milk is good for you. This new study, if it receives the attention it deserves, will force a rethink. In an accompanying editorial by Professor Amy Joy Lanou, a well-respected Ph.D. nutritionist with an interest in children, it is pointed out that populations which consume the most cow's milk and other dairy products have the highest rates of osteoporosis and later-life hip fracture in the world. She also points out that in a western world that increasingly frets about childhood obesity, dairy products are a growing contributor to the intake of fat and sugar in children. She also suggests that three quarters of the world's population are lactose intolerant after the age of weaning and do not tolerate the consumption of milk and dairy products well. She challenges western governments to think seriously about their nutrition policies which as I write, still encourage a very high intake of calcium and dairy products in childhood and adolescence. No surprise that health officialdom in this land of dairy saints and pint-sized scholars has yet to respond in any meaningful way.

There are no public relations companies employed to spin out this latest research. So it probably comes as news to many of you. Indeed, it is also quite possible that the research will drift past many doctors in their busy workplaces. Professor Lanou believes that the research strengthens previously discerned evidence that calcium or dairy products do not have any meaningful impact on the bone health of young people. For decades now, most of the information doctors and consumers receive on dairy products comes straight from the industry themselves. Teams of well-qualified and well-paid nutritionists are directly employed to do their public relations. Their primary duty is to shareholders and producers whose ultimate aim is to sell the general public more dairy produce. Independent research of a contrary nature tends to be conveniently ignored.

Since the research and editorial was published, there has been some interesting support for Professor Lanou in the on-line version of the *British Medical Journal*. Dr Roberta Gray, an American paediatrician with 20 years experience has written about the detrimental effects of over-consumption of milk and cheese in her patients. She describes how she has to try and dispel myths about cow's milk nearly every day as she is faced with a growing number of children with 'calcium derangement'. She says it is not uncommon to see pre-pubertal youngsters consuming up to 60 ounces of cow's milk daily (much more in teenagers) often with cheese in the daily diet as well. Dr Gray claims that the detrimental effects of a dairy-loaded diet far outweigh any benefits. Negative effects she lists as significant obesity, osteopenia and later life osteoporosis, kidney stones and bladder dysfunction.

Modern medical thinking on the milk trade and bone health may be about to change. Instead of raising kids on litres of white liquid, pink yogurts and cheese dippers, you might in future be asked to let them out in the sunlight so that they can manufacture their own vitamin D. And perhaps indulge in some bone-protecting exercise while they are at it.

All good scientists declare their interests, something to look out for whenever you read health-related matter. So here is mine. I have never owned or had unlawful carnal knowledge of a bovine creature in my life. I was raised on cow's milk and took to it like a calf to a clean udder. In the good old days before supermarkets killed kindness, twelve glass bottles landed on the family doorstep at four thirty each morning and twelve empties were removed. (No extra charge from the dairy for the clattering alarm call.) At least a third of these bottles lined the stomach of your scribe each day and the calcium never did him any harm. Never had so much as piece of grit in the kidney and I've tumbled down the highest slopes in the Kilternan Alps, skis akimbo, and never had a fracture. My back is as straight as the next man's and the bladder, though weakening in middle age, is up there with the best in the golf club. So what harm has the dairy industry ever done to me? Besides making a handsome contribution to a well upholstered but beautifully maintained 19 stone frame, divil a bit.

HABEMUS HEALTH PROBLEMS
April 2005

Let's muse this week on the health of a male superstar. His strange face has barely been off the news bulletins in recent months. His court appearances are made in robes and pyjamas. He waves to photographers. Adoring children hang out below his balcony. He has a voice of great innocence and lives in a timeless wonderland surrounded by phenomenal wealth. The rich, the famous and the powerful all want to be his friend and will testify to his goodness. He is a man with a long track record in popular music - in his time he has criticised the Beatles, the Rolling Stones, Led Zeppelin and Queen. Yes, I'm talking about gentle Ben. Pope Benedict XVI.

Now before we begin this dissection, let me declare a personal interest. As soon as the world's media began talking down his chances of winning the papal stakes, I backed Cardinal Ratzinger at rather generous odds to win the conclave handicap chase. Bavarian Benny didn't disappoint - his red racing cap was in front all the way. He was the runner with form - not afraid to use the whip and the favourite of the thinking man's Catholic punter. Despite all the hot air that went up the Sistine chimney about saxophone-playing South American smoothies and smiling pasta-gobbling Italians, there was only ever going to be one result from the 6.10 at St Peter's. In male clubs the world over, from Portmarnock golf club to the IRA army council, the outgoing captain gets to choose his successor. Benny's good fortune was that for three decades he was firmly stitched to the hemline of his buddy JP2.

So what do we know about this new pope's health? Well as the oldest man to be elected pontiff in almost 300 years, Benny XVI is no spring chicken. At 78 he has outlived the age at which both his parents passed away. If he chose to drive his own car he would have to get his medical fitness assessed every three years and might even attract loading on the insurance. Indeed if he went on holidays he may have difficulty getting insurance to drive at all.

What we do know is that he suffered what we term a 'haemorrhagic stroke' in 1991 that temporarily affected his vision. In lay terms this means that a blood vessel in one sector of his brain burst - possibly its elastic wall was weak or blood pressure had reached a dangerous level and something had to give. Either way, his recovery seems to have been excellent. It was also reported that he had a nasty fall whilst on holidays in the Italian alps thirteen years ago. He clipped his head off a radiator, went unconscious temporarily and apparently bled profusely. It's possible that he was taking medication like aspirin or warfarin to thin his blood, but given a history of a haemorrhagic stroke this could be risky. A young German priest told the media soon after his election that the new pope has a 'delicate constitution' and is a poor sleeper, but neither trait is unusual as the years advance. I have also heard some medical comments here in Ireland about high colour and blotchy complexion, something that was not apparent during his first balcony appearance. This is much more obvious when he filmed in side profile however there is no proven correlation between having a high colour and automatically having an illness. It is a myth, peddled in much the same fashion as the nonsense that all red noses belong to boozers.

On a positive note, Pope Benedict is reputed to have a fondness for cats. Protection Leagues the world over tell us that life assurers are keen on moggy-lovers. Like avid gardeners and enclosed nuns, cat lovers may be a better than average risk if gambling on a long life. Benny is also reported to be fond of cookies so the nuns at St Peter's had better lock up their cupboards at night-time or they could find telltale crumbs under the papal duvet each morning.

So how long might Pope Benedict 16 be with us? Well that's the six million dollar question. Nobody on this earth knows the answer. But the betting man will know that the average time left for a 78 year old man is another seven or eight years. But then, when did Mr average ever get to be Pope?

Postscript: *The papacy of Benedict XVI lasted exactly seven years and ten months. He retired in early 2013 citing poor health.*

JAMMETS
January 2012

Your papers this month are full of stuff, bluff and guff about how Irish families can produce little Einstein offspring by getting mammies-in-waiting to eat more fish. The research is nothing new - it's early, it's ongoing and the bit you read about this January is already a few months old. The European commission office in Dublin sent out a waffling press release titled 'Fish boosts unborn babies' brainpower' and the scientific slaves of the media did their wedding of Cana bit, miraculously turning one piece of paper into hundreds of news headlines. The small study this 'news' was based on was German and was published last year in the American Journal of Clinical Nutrition. Don't get me wrong. I'd rather you supported your local trawler and fishmonger than your hawker of fish oil capsules at wildly inflated prices. But I'd also rather that selective and preliminary results were pondered and debated, with appropriate input from independent experts, rather than gift wrapped by EU public relations people as fodder for the indebted masses.

One Dublin restaurant that knew how to prepare fish, as opposed to fishy stories, was the legendary Restaurant Jammet, which closed its doors in the late 1960s. Its Filet de Sole Jammet (20 shillings in 1967), served on a silver salver coated with the finest fish velouté and garnished with a finger-sized fleuron of pastry was the stuff of ladys' dreams. I know this, not from personal experience, though family lore has it that the Guérets of Sandymount and the Jammets were once well acquainted in Dublin. I know it because Santa Claus left a wonderful book in my stocking last month titled *Jammet's of Dublin 1901 to 1967*. It is written by Alison Maxwell and the late Shay Harpur. There can surely be no other Dublin restaurant that deserves such a book, and there is no book currently on the shelves that is more deserving of a read. The wine lists alone are worth their own volume.

Jammet's of Dublin says on its jacket that it was the resort of actors, politicians, artists, literati, film stars, judges, journalists, doctors, chancers and characters. I think they got the running order just about correct, though the cast of medical characters mentioned inside is very bare indeed. The real stars of the show were the ordinary folk who cooked the food, waited at tables, decanted the wine and prepared the large bills. These were the staff who gave loyal service to the Jammet family for two generations and deservedly they top the bill. What struck my roving clinical eye was how young many of the staff were when they died, and how many died from heart disease. Perhaps the difficult working hours, perhaps the fine food, perhaps the smoke, perhaps none of the above and just an observation of chance.

I particularly enjoyed the story of Victor Hurding, the elegant man on the cover of the book who met his future wife in Restaurant Jammet. He was a waiter, king of the cutlery, Mary was the cashier. Their eldest daughter Irene developed kidney failure (in the era before transplantation) and he would cheer her by asking visiting international celebrities to autograph and wish her well on Jammet postcards. Bing Crosby, Sean Connery, Elizabeth Taylor and Rod Steiger were among the many who obliged and their good wishes to the ailing Irene are recorded in the book. Victor died young of a massive heart attack a year after Restaurant Jammet closed and his daughter Irene died a year later, aged 23.

My relations in Paris may well disown me, but I have long believed that the principal difference between a good French restaurant and a good Italian one, is that you will never get a free drink in the French one. One contributor to the book, the late Patrick Campbell, described Louis Jammet as 'the hardest man he ever met' and suggested that a mean story circulated about him in Dublin. It hinted that Jammet had made a bet with himself - the stake being one year's profit - that he would never stand anyone a free drink. And being French, he'd have stuck to his guns .

DR DOG
April 2007

The three year old heiress to the Guéret fortune is already a great fan of doctors. Her main interaction with the medical profession is through an expanding library of children's books and her favourite medic, Papa excluded, is the sublime creation that is *Dr Dog* Cleverly written and gloriously illustrated by Babette Cole, Dr Dog was first published thirteen years ago, but is still very much in print. Some months ago, I contacted the author through her website asking if it might be possible to purchase some original drawings of Dr Dog. But Ms Cole, in a lovely reply, said that these were being retained for a rainy day and pension requirements. I suspect Sotheby's auction house on Bond Street may be the ultimate beneficiaries.

Dr Dog is a great role model for the medical fraternity. At the beginning of the tale, just when his owners, the Gumboyle family fall ill, he proves that old adage that the doctor is never there when you need him. Dr Dog is off with umpteen other medically qualified mutts, sunning himself at a bone marrow conference in Brazil. He is summoned back by telemessage to the untidy terraced house of his masters. Now the Gumboyles are a family who enjoy all the vices of life. They don't have time to get bogged down in pompous doctrines of health promotion. Eldest son Kurt has a smoker's cough before he reaches his teens. Younger brother Kev swaps brushes and combs with wild abandon and gets infested with nits. Baby Gumboyle likes nothing more than a good suck of his own fingers, which is all very well except that his other pastime is to stick them in another part of the body where the sun doesn't shine. He gets a nasty infestation of intestinal worms. The Gumboyle girls don't fare much better. Gerty goes out socialising with too few clothes on and eventually needs a tonsillectomy for chronic throat infection whilst younger sister Fiona succumbs to earache and dizzy spells. Her parents put these symptoms down to cartwheels on the lawn, so by the time Dr Dog gets back from his junket, she is in a pretty bad way and needs a hefty dose of antibiotics. Dr Dog scolds his family for not taking better care of themselves, warning of serious repercussions for their health. 'So what' comes the reply, 'we've got you to look after us !' Meanwhile another patient is seriously ill in the family bathroom. Granddad's consumption of beer and baked beans seriously alters the delicate balance of gases in his bowels. With monumental consequences for the whole family, and for the roof of their house. The tale ends with our hero Dr Dog flat on his back, hogging the couch of a canine psychiatrist. Stress is diagnosed and the shrink prescribes a tropical holiday well away from pesky patients. Alas, for Dr Dog, the Gumboyles have other plans.

You may think medics are far too busy and serious-minded to bother about how they are portrayed in children's books. But you would be mistaken. Last year the *British Medical Journal* published a detailed scientific report on fourteen *Going to the Doctor* books written for children. Their findings were most interesting. They found three common factors in the portrayal of all doctors in childrens' books - a white coat, a stethoscope and a permanent smile. All but one of the male doctors wore a tie and medics were eight times more likely to wear spectacles than their patients. Most female doctors wore sensible flat shoes and long skirts. Middle-aged or elderly doctors were a rarity and young patients were actively encouraged to play with delicate medical instruments. Many doctors also carried out the jobs that would traditionally be carried out by nurses. Little gifts from grateful patients, a custom that is dying out almost as quickly as medical fees have risen, included thank-you cards and ice-cream. Researchers also found that doctors in children's literature are almost universally friendly and well-mannered. And they have infinite amounts of time to look at their patients. Perhaps something to do with the fact that none have computers on their desks? Most of them display an abundance of degrees and certificates on the wall to create that all important aura of cleverness. Body parts that are most examined are the ear, the mouth and the throat. All doctors appeared busy - medical hands never rest. Most complaints were of a minor nature, and half of all patients received a prescription. Oh, and all the patients left the doctor's surgery with a smile on their faces and ultimately get better. Nothing beats a bit of fiction.

DEMONISING BARBERS
February 2004

In medieval times, a Hobson's choice of healthcare provider was available to sick patients who had the money to pay for treatment. Surgeons, physicians and barbers touted for the custom of the poorly and the dying. Practitioners had little in common, save the complete disregard for the professionalism of their rivals. Physicians and Surgeons eventually coalesced into a united medical profession, a move that had much to do with mutual antipathy to 'ignorant' blood-letting barbers and anyone else perceived as a threat to their monopoly on medical knowledge. The battle for the hearts and guineas of patients was won by the medics who believed that the barbers' fingers were all thumbs. The truth however was that the barber-surgeon had more time to listen, and proffered understandable advice with a physical action aimed at curing. Even if cures failed, as they often did, barbers made patients feel that somebody cared about more than the fee. In France, the barber-surgeon ruled supreme - indeed every King had one of his own. One of the most famous was Ambroise Paré whose principled philosophy was to act always as an advocate for his patients and only to administer treatments when absolutely necessary. He was a barber who could have taught physicians and surgeons a thing or two.

Aside from the odd scalp treatment or facial massage, all that remains of the old tradition of barber shop consultation is the red and white striped pole. Today the men's barber shop is enjoying something of a renaissance, so I thought today we'd look at some modern medical hazards that might lurk around your vacuum-pumped chair. There is some interesting research doing the rounds about wash-basins and neck compression which suggests that some clients may be risking strokes by overextending their necks during their shampoo. Less serious but more painful is a new-fangled American diagnosis called salon sink radiculopathy, a kind of whiplash type ailment caused by overstretching the neck and damaging the nerve root. Sycosis barbae, otherwise known as barber's rash or sore beard, is a skin ailment that can sometimes follow a shave. The term is generally applied to an infection that enters the hair follicles causing a painful redness. Ugly boils or abscesses may ensue if it spreads. Improved hygiene makes this a rare gift from the barber shop of today. Clean towels are a must for any reputable barber shop as the second-hand use of towels is a well recognised source of infections such as impetigo, conjunctivitis, scabies, ringworm and other microbial nasties.

Slightly more worrying are suggestions that barber's equipment may be a heretofore under-reported source of infections with blood-borne hepatitis viruses. The *New England Journal of Medicine* has published a letter concerning retired US Army personnel at a Veteran's hospital, who had much higher than expected rate of hepatitis. The author, a Dr Colleen Kelly, observed communal use of an electric razor that was not disinfected between each use, a practice that is not uncommon in hospitals, prisons and indeed barber shops. So be careful out there. Don't get a closer shave than you bargain for.

THE PROMISCUOUS MALE
August 2004

I've just finished an extraordinary early life biography of the American president. Not the current GWB one who chokes on his pretzels. It's about his predecessor, the one with many policy positions on ladies. Nigel Hamilton's *Bill Clinton - An American Journey* charts the childhood crises, happier university years and rise to power of slick Willy. It's the real life fairy tale of the lumbering but likeable poor boy turned lawyer from the backwater southern state of Arkansas.

Hamilton is a historian, and a good one, and I expect his book will be rather different to the ex-president's own autobiography which we are told is in the pipeline. *Bill Clinton - An American Journey* is a book as much about the drive to have sex, as the drive to succeed in politics. No politician in America can have hungered for and received as much extra-marital sex as Bill Clinton. Miss Lewinsky was a mere late-comer in a long line of sexual consorts stretching back through the decades. There may be objections from hardcore fans of JFK, but Clinton surely wins the golden condom as the most promiscuous leader the modern democratic world has known.

There are a multitude of views on male promiscuity. Most are spoiled by moral overtone and contribute little to science on this topic. We can frown and peer down Victorian noses at a man who fails to fulfil his wedding vows. Or we can widen the blame game and make his life partner the real culprit. Bill's friends were happy to recall how much he enjoyed group sex games, casual petting and foreplay, but have been less kind to Hillary whose nickname was Sister Frigidaire and was not considered good 'date bait'. Even Bill called her Hilla the Hun.

Doctors, sometimes at the instigation of patients, or their lawyers, often seek to medicalise the idea of a man enjoying multiple sexual partners. They casually explain it away as some sort of addiction. This sort of nonsense is gaining currency in professional circles. Increasingly, a diagnosis of sex addiction is being used to excuse, lessen or ameliorate the horrors of rape, assault and other dark deeds.

Allied to this is a growing media trend to treat any form of sex outside marriage as promiscuity. A survey from a prominent medical school reported that men aged between 25 and 44 who are separated, divorced, or widowed are amongst the most 'promiscuous' groups in society. This grabbed plenty of tabloid headlines but examination of the small print revealed that it was based on the fact that under 40% of them reported having slept with two or more partners in the previous year. Hardly the stuff of Caligula.

This biography of Clinton is as much a treatise on the behaviour of the alpha male, as a politician in the making. It explores the twin

141

worlds of American politics and television evangelism, linked by their shared ability to gain converts, empty donor pockets, and reward ministers with daytime power and nocturnal sex. It tells the tale of the first son of a talented heavily made-up mother who herself had a penchant for weak men. Bill was a goody-goody at school who craved the friendship of every classmate. It was this lifelong battle for approval that packed him off for a double twist, or tryst, in the oval office.

One of Clinton's oldest friends, Jim Blair, is quoted as saying that what makes men promiscuous is their close relationship to primates, namely the chimpanzee whose legendary promiscuity is directly proportional to the size of their testicles. Blair opines that testosterone and genetics predestines humans to promiscuity and that men are genetically and innately licentious when it comes to sexual behaviour. That's perhaps a lot nearer the truth than some guff you'll heard from psychiatrists about sex addiction. Biologists confirm that sexual promiscuity is built into the genetic code of most living things, not so much for pleasure, but to ensure survival of an intact species.

So come again Bill, all is forgiven.

THE IRISH LOBOTOMY
January 2005

I looked up the word leucotomy on the Irish version of the Google search engine today and it returns only two references. This surgical procedure is perhaps one that the psychiatric and surgical professions would rather forget. Known as lobotomy in America, many fell hook, line and sinker for the medical sales patter. The operation was generally reserved for mentally ill patients who were unmanageable, unemployable or both. It involved severing the white nerve fibres that connect the frontal lobes to the rest of the brain. One writer of the time described it rather less clinically:

An icepick is hammered into the skull just above the tear duct on each side and then wiggled about.

The frontal leucotomy was championed by a Portuguese

neurologist and politician called Professor Egas Moniz. In 1949 he was even awarded a Nobel prize, one of a number of awards the Swedish Academy might wish us to forget. A speaker at the presentation banquet in Stockholm described the recipient as 'a notorious savant in various fields when, accidentally, he came to the conclusion that the surgeon's knife would bring relief or even recovery to patients suffering from certain serious psychic disturbances.'

Nobody knows precisely how many of these operations were carried out in Ireland, but more than 10,000 were carried out in Britain from the 1940s on. Irish surgeons and psychiatrists were no different to their international colleagues, quick to jump on the departing bandwagon. In 1946, procedures began at Dublin's Richmond Hospital under the direction of Ireland's leading brain surgeon of the day, Mr Adams Andrew McConnell. By the summer of 1947, twenty three operations had been carried out. Three patients recovered well enough for discharge from hospital, the rest were described as 'more managcable' by the bleak institutions that housed them. Most of these patients had what psychiatrists term schizophrenia. The operations continued well on into the 1950s so it is likely that there may still be some survivors alive.

In the United States the operation was championed by Dr Walter Freeman, who is credited with the idea of using an icepick-like instrument to carry it out. It was touted as a general cure for all sorts of mental ills, including badly misbehaved children. It's reckoned that as many as 40,000 operations were carried out. Mercenary surgeons went on the road with their newfound toy, hiring out hotel rooms in which to operate. One doctor drove himself around in a fully equipped van which he called his lobotomobile. Earlier this month, the death took place of Rosemary Kennedy in the United States. A younger sister of politicians JFK and Bobby, her father organised the operation for this 'pleasant but slow' girl in 1941. She spent the remaining 63 years of her life in a trance being cared for in an institution.

With the development of new drugs, the operation fell out of fashion, and the medical profession shows little interest now in researching the long term effects of the procedure. In Norway the Government ran a newspaper campaign asking surviving 'victims'

143

to get in touch as they may be entitled to claim compensation. This news was not greeted with universal acclaim. One UK based psychiatrist wrote that "what the Norwegian fiscal administration chooses to do with presumably surplus money is its own decision, but the use of the word 'victims' implies that patients who had a leucotomy in the past were the subjects of medical misjudgment, if not frank assault." This, he said, requires correction. Psychiatrists still argue that there was 'simply nothing better.' Had their patients not been experimental fodder for a procedure that robbed personality and blunted emotion, they might argue that there was simply nothing worse.

Postscript: *Following the publication of this piece, I received two letters. One was from an elderly man in the North West of Ireland who told me he successfully underwent this operation in his youth, for an obsessional condition, and never looked back. A retired physician also wrote to tell me about a female civil servant patient of his who also did well after the procedure. Lobotomy had some successes.*

MAN IN THE GARDEN
March 2005

It's ten years since the male boycott of Helen Dillon's suburban garden began. Allow me refresh your minds on the origins of the affair. One cold December morning in 1994, green-fingered gentlemen up and down the country were shocked out of their sheds by Ms Dillon's grievous insult to their masculinity. In her weekly gardening column for the *Sunday Tribune*, Ireland's foremost bucket wielder and wearer of denim romper suits, cast serious aspersions on man's dedication to the great outdoors. She poked fun at his boundless refusal tactics when offered 'little jobs' and callously referred to a man in the garden as 'a bit of a deadhead.' What most offended readers however were her cutting jibes about the physical prowess and libido of the male gardener. Allow me recap on her hurtful observations.

At 30, man's passion for motorbikes metamorphoses overnight to an

144

obsession with mowing machines. At 40 he adds extra virility to his image in the form of a compost shredder or leaf blowing machine. And at 50, he needs an extra boost, a ride on mower, he whizzes the lawns astride his toy tractor, all the thrill of an expensive steed, the vroom vroom, not to mention the quivering joystick.

Such remarks constituted a grave case of over pruning in deepest winter and did not go down well with the male gardening fraternity. The men's boycott of 45 Sandford Road began. A decade on, it's time to decommission wounded pride and call a truce with Ms Dillon's paradise in Ranelagh. This summer, I intend to return (minus the pitchfork) and shake dibbles with the lady who made male gardeners feel as low-life as a slugs on an adolescent Delphinium. I'm told by domestic channel hoppers that there is a new series on the goggle box called *Desperate Housewives* which features the weekly exploits of bareback male gardeners. This has aroused lady passions in ways not imagined since illicit copies of *Lady Chatterley's Lover* were hidden behind the begonia tubs. The Irish Male Gardener, 2005 XPeat model, has a newfound swagger, a confidence in his wellies and who knows, may soon be sporting an alluring aftershave called Monty Don. (Sorry Diarmuid, fragrance of rotting compost doesn't wash.) Whether it's all down to the rise in Viagra sales or the retirement of Alan Titchmarsh is open to debate. This year's male gardener is standing to attention and ready for action.

There is little in medical literature about the beneficial effects of gardening. That doesn't stop 'Good Lifers' heaping up countless new age platitudes about gardening being a therapy that will keep you alive until you are 100. If you want to believe that gardening lowers cholesterol, reduces blood pressure, arrests diabetes, slows osteoporosis or prevents strokes, then you are just as likely to survive them all because of excessive gullibility. On the other hand, the medical doomsday brigade have plenty of forewarnings about the perils of abandoning the armchair - heat stress, heat stroke, heat rash, heat cramps, heat exhaustion, heat illness and if you recover from these - hives, bites, stings, back ache, rat pee disease and lethal poisons lurking in the herbaceous borders.

Spring has sprung so ignore all those health warnings. Go tend to your garden for the absolute fun, the utter misery and the sheer dirtiness of it all. Ladies get your male feeds ready. Ten years ago I wrote down Helen's recipe - a daily watering can of flattery, a half bucket of compliments, one regular teaspoon of honey and a weekly massage, of the ego.

BEN'S GYM
November 2004

There is something odd about listening to a well-upholstered businessman like Ben Dunne promoting aerobic exercise, health & fitness and gym membership. It's a bit like Micheál Martin promoting hair restoration remedies or Bertie Ahern publicising a one day seminar on anti-dithering techniques. To be fair to Ben, I did hear him on a recent radio show saying that he was more of a stick than a carrot-man. He liked to warn punters that they too could have a body like his, if they didn't avail of the cut-price membership!

Now I live within snorting distance of Ben's new Dublin emporium, the Carlisle Club at Dublin's Kimmage Cross Roads. Whilst their owner exhibits stern resistance to viewing the campus, my dogs very much enjoy sniffing around the vicinity late in the evenings as they indulge their hind legs in their own particular form of exercise.

Ben's exhortation to physical fitness brought to mind a quotation from George Santayana, a Madrid-born philosopher.

He said "that the need for exercise is a modern superstition, invented by people who ate too much and had nothing to think about. Athletics doesn't make anybody either long-lived or useful." Exercise-mongers delighted in telling the famous thinker he was wrong but old George had the last laugh, outliving them all to celebrate his 89th birthday. Doubtless he got plenty of exercise carrying their coffins up the aisle. Santayana was by no means alone as an exercise cynic. Mark Twain described it as loathsome whilst Dr Jonathan Miller continues to bemoan the fact that people are so busy trying to lengthen their lives with exercise they don't have time to live them. The late Petr Skrabanek, a Professor who mentored a generation of medical students at Dublin's Trinity

College, liked to remind doctors-to-be that 40,000 Americans drop dead each year whilst exercising for their health. Every day in our surgeries, punters ask for their hearts to be checked out to see if they are fit to be members of gyms. The truth is more uncomfortable than doctors like to admit. We are no better than Madame Mystic's crystal ball at telling what your future has in store. Five seconds on the end of a stethoscope is about as useful a predictor as a single tarot card.

Now I have nothing against exercise. I regularly lose golf balls and have even been known to lift a leg over a snooker table to stretch for a difficult pink. But I find working-out a serious bore. Exploring dunes, dancing the tango or tending to a perfumed garden bring pleasurable rewards. But contracting other folk's warts and yeasts, inhaling armpit odours and having your ears deafened by the intellectual wasteland of 24 hour news is a new low in human endeavour. There is nowhere on earth quite as desolate or depressing as a gymnasium tightly packed with sticky-boned ladettes in lurid lycra leotards and reflection-obsessed nancy men pumped up like donkey-dumps.

In one dastardly moment of human weakness, impressed perhaps by the bounce on the indoor tennis courts, I once joined a fitness club near the Dublin mountains. It was so far away as to be thoroughly useless to me and for all the use it got, must have cost €500 a set. My abiding memory of the place was the nauseating and horribly repellent odour of its changing rooms.

Ben, you're a great chap. I'll eat a 24 ounce steak in Shanahan's with you any time. I'd even go out on a ledge for you. But you'll never catch me in a gym.

ALL CREATURES GREAT AND SMALL
June 2010

One of the joys of writing a homily each Sunday is the cohort of critics and supporters around the country who offer praise, dissent and advice in equal doses. I also receive plenty of 'requests' looking for columns on particular topics. These can range from the health advantages of brown bread over white to the questionable success rate of cessation therapies in smokers. One favourite correspondent is a very kind lady MRCVS who occasionally sends me a veterinary perspective on something I have scribbled about. A few weeks ago I questioned why we had seven medical schools on this small island when one or two would surely suffice. I felt it an apt moment to raise this issue because many professors from these same schools have been at the forefront of the campaign to close or 'rationalise' small county hospitals. My colleague from the animal world wrote to confirm that there is just one veterinary college on the whole island of Ireland (at University College Dublin) and it does very well, encouraging not only cross-border husbandry but also acting as career midwife for many overseas students in a wonderful new complex at Belfield. Such is the standard of work and education there, it is one of very few veterinary colleges in Europe that is accredited across the Atlantic. Since 2008, UCD graduates have been able to dehorn bulls or pop suppositories into sheep right across the United States, without anyone questioning their credentials.

One bee under my summer sou'wester is the fact that there is virtually no mingling between the related disciplines of human and animal medicine. Even within colleges that host both medical and veterinary courses, the former stick to their towers whilst the latter have to share lecture halls and smells with pig farmers, foodies and wellied agriculturalists. Surely it would make a lot more sense to educate vets and doctors together, in the interest of one learning from the other. There is a sense that medics view the animal world as a great field for experimentation or practising unnecessary operations, but rather less useful for real learning. This month's major press release from modern medicine decreed that a cure had been found for breast cancer in mice. I have a lingering suspicion that few mice will reap the benefits. And even fewer will be leaping from their traps to celebrate.

The first veterinary school in Ireland opened at UCD in 1800, at the instigation of the Royal Dublin Society. It's main mission was to service the burgeoning horse and cattle industries. In 1954, Trinity opened their own school to teach about Protestant husbandry, but by 1977 it had been subsumed into Belfield. There was an old joke doing the rounds in my undergraduate days about a country doctor who had to go to an important conference on golfing injuries in St Andrews but couldn't find a locum to look after his flock. In desperation, he phoned the veterinary member of his Wednesday fourball and asked if he wouldn't mind covering a few days for him. When they caught up on the first tee a week later the doc asked his colleague if there were any problems? 'Divil a bit,' said the vet, 'just one difficult birth all week - spot of trouble persuading Mrs Murphy to eat her placenta.'

And a colleague once related a lovely story of a house call she had undertaken in a piebald pony estate of west Dublin. When she had finished dealing with a sick child in the bedroom she was invited downstairs to the kitchen for a second patient who turned out to be a horse resting on the lino. I quite forget how she made her escape - 'not covered on the medical card scheme' perhaps, but it is perhaps not unreasonable of patients to assume that a qualification in one branch of medicine might impart a modicum of expertise in another.

The recent *Genius of Britain* series on Channel 4 celebrated Edward Jenner, an English country doctor who trained in London but came to know quite an amount about rural and animal life in Gloucestershire where he practised. He was particularly struck by the fact that dairy-maids (who had close daily contact with cattle), rarely succumbed to smallpox. He devised a dangerous experiment on an eight year old boy to prove that the milder disease of cowpox could offer protection against lethal smallpox infection. We owe to Dr Jenner many millions of lives (human and animal) saved over the past two hundred years by vaccination. Perhaps closer daily contact between doctors and vets could also work to mutual advantage. It could be a wonderful innovation to see our new primary care centres invite veterinary doctors in to share facilities and advance each other's knowledge. They might also teach us a thing or two about hygiene.

Aside from occasional visits to our excellent local veterinary team, my day to day knowledge of advances and controversies in the animal world is sadly limited. The complete DVD box set of *All Creatures Great and Small*, though life-affirming in many ways, is no substitute for a missed education on the medical foibles of creatures we have subjugated. I'd like to know what veterinarians think of voluntary human euthanasia. I'd like to hear more about the new discipline of veterinary psychiatry. Is it only mad dogs and English soccer fans that suffer from separation anxiety and nervous aggression? Do angry cats and children share a common aim when they scratch furniture and 'eliminate inappropriately'?

Do vets use rude acronyms like doctors do on their clinical charts? Like ROBO for Run Over By Owner or BSBF (Buy Small Bags of Food) when delivering a bad prognosis. And what exactly is the difference between Buiatrics and Ruminant Healthcare? I can feel joint conferences in Switzerland during the ski season coming on. Yes indeed, the Lord God made us all.

PASSIVE SMOKING – HYPE AND HYPERBOLE
February 2004

"The speculation and debate are over. It is now time to prepare for the successful implementation of a smoke-free workplace" The words of Ireland's health minister last month when he announced a start-up date for a crusade against second hand smoke. It might appear strange for a medic to denounce this whole prohibition lark, but there are grounds for at least some us to become conscientious objectors. Sure, our indoor air will be cleaner from March 29th. A night out will be easier on the eyes and those with sensitive lungs and noses will be able to dine out and drink in more comfort. You might even be able to wear the same clothes again the following day. There will be positive cosmetic benefits to this rushed ban on indoor smoking. But what makes me uncomfortable is that science is being used to elevate passive smoking to a public health hazard on a par with handling asbestos or unearthing the spores of anthrax.

With typical hyperbole, one anti-smoking group described the ban as the public health initiative of the century. Frankly it is nothing of the kind. The ban on passive smoking creates a neat smokescreen for a minister who inherited a discredited and dangerous health service and will pass a discredited and dangerous health service on to another publicity-hungry successor when his own public relations stint is up.

Anti-smoking campaigners are quite correct in their determination that personal smoking is a major risk factor for various cancers, lung illnesses and some cases of heart disease. But they persistently seek to extend the bounds of reasonable science by implying that passive smoking is a mass-killer, when clearly it is not. The editor of the respected *International Journal of Epidemiology* has written that the passive smoking literature is littered with inconclusive studies. He went on to say that there are occasional significant observations which hint at real effect, but that this may reflect the author's point of view or wishful thinking. Indeed most of the scientific studies in this field are conducted by vested interests, the anti-tobacco lobbies on one hand and profiteering tobacco companies on the other. Real science has been smothered by the warring factions in the passive smoking war. Perhaps a ban will encourage more smokers to quit, but equally it may encourage others to dine, drink and smoke their lungs out in sitting rooms, exposing spouses, infants and children to the very dangers the minister is so concerned about in adult workers.

The experts in risk to life and limb are those who work in life assurance underwriting. If you check your premiums you will know that they don't give a fiddler's curse about how many smokers you share your air with, as long as you don't smoke yourself.

Our minister is not the first political figure to declare a religious war on passive smoke. Pope Urban VIII issued an anti-tobacco bull in 1642 threatening instant excommunication should any priest soil the altar linen during mass or infect his church with noxious fumes. Perhaps an incense ban is next .

COCAINE - NOT TO BE SNORTED AT
April 2004

A perk traditionally enjoyed by the medical profession was the right to sample their own medicinal compounds, before pontificating to the great unwashed about their many dangers. So it was with cocaine, recreational drug by appointment to royal families, their wealthy friends and rising stars of the middle classes. Although the active chemical was only isolated in 1859 and synthetic manufacture did not begin until 1885, the pain-killing and stimulant effects of coca leaves were well known to the natives of South America who had harvested the plant for centuries.

In the days before he purchased his first couch, a young Viennese psychiatrist named Sigmund Freud experimented with cocaine. He remarked in a letter to his wife-to-be that a small dose temporarily cured his depression and 'lifted me to new heights in a wonderful fashion'. He went on to tell his betrothed that he was busy collecting literature 'for a song of praise to this magical substance.'

Another medic to take an interest in cocaine was an American surgeon named William Halsted who had also been studying in Vienna. Halsted went on to have a remarkable career as a pioneer in modern surgery, but his early experimentation with cocaine caused an addiction, which he then tried to cure by switching to morphine. His substitute proved unwise and necessitated months of convalescence in a mental institution for treatment of a 'nervous breakdown'.

And therein lies the mystery of cocaine. Despite what prophets of drug doom might have you believe, many users, like Freud, have found occasional use of cocaine to be a singularly positive experience. Yet others, like Halsted, find their lives descending into cycles of madness, addiction and sometimes destruction.

In the late 1980s, western countries panicked at the harrowing and lethal effects that an aberrant substance called crack-cocaine was having in the ghettos of New York. Whilst there have been seizures of this dangerous derivative by customs and the Gardaí, by and large these shores have been spared the doomsday scenario many at the time predicted.

Some years ago a team of Scottish academics issued a challenge to the medical establishment. They published a study suggesting that most users of cocaine were not addicts, but occasional users, and that for most of them their participation was not a particularly dangerous experience. They claimed that much of the research on the perils of cocaine use was derived from observation of 'deviant samples' of visible drug users, and not the preponderant upper crust that can afford to gamble their inheritances and high earnings on recreational cocaine use. The Cocaine Scottish Research Group published a book called *A Very Greedy Drug - Cocaine in Context* which challenged the anti-drugs hysteria that pervaded in public health circles. There is more than a grain of truth in their message. In fifteen years of hospital and general practice in Dublin, I must have met dozens of patients who have taken cocaine, yet I cannot recall even one whose consultation was as a result of this misdemeanour.

If a soccer pundit pronounced that each and every team he saw was equally bad, he'd bore the proverbial pants off listeners fairly quickly. Nobody would bother listening.

And that's precisely what crusaders of the anti-drugs movement are in danger of doing. None of us can afford to snort at fresh thinking.

SYPHILIS - A POX ON EUROPEAN UNION
July 2004

I was writing recently in *Medicine Weekly* about the strange things doctors hear in clinics that deal with sexually transmitted diseases. A retired family doctor from Dublin wrote to tell me of a merchant seaman he once treated for syphilis at the 'special clinic' in Dr Steeven's hospital. The sailor presented with the hallmark sore on his penis and asked somewhat anxiously:

Will this carry away me Bobstay Doctor?

In general, the answer is no. But this was not always the

case. Before the antibiotic era, syphilis reaped a toll of terrible deformities and death. Innocuous looking genital ulcers might come and go, but if left untreated, a dormant syphilis could resurface with a vengeance months or years later. Destroying bones, joints, faces and lives in its wake. Syphilitic deaths were not pretty. Less fortunate survivors often succumbed to its maddening effect, ended their grim lives away with the birds in lunatic asylums.

There has long been a great snobbery about syphilis - not just personal but geographic too. In these islands it was once known as 'the French Pox'. The Dutch called it Spanish Disease. The Turks knew it as Christian Disease. The Russians blamed the Poles. Everyone else knew it as Portuguese Disease.

Though the very first cases were described during the siege of Naples, by and large, Italians get off scot-free. In the 19th century syphilis became especially virulent and notable writers and thinkers such as Maupassant, Baudelaire and Nietzche all had firsthand knowledge of its vagaries. Our own Dr Steevens hospital had its fair share of patients who were treated with mercury, a fairly toxic substance that promoted saliva production. They sat around all day hocking spit into large pewter mugs whilst their doctors tailored the mercury dose according to the contents of their spittoons. Professor Davis Coakley's excellent book *Irish Masters of Medicine* records that doses were so large that side effects were often much worse than the disease. Patients lucky enough to leave the premises alive often had no teeth and badly scarred kidneys.

Next year will be the 100th anniversary of the discovery of treponema pallidum, the bug that causes syphilis. Just three years ago public health authorities in Dublin reported that the disease had once again reached epidemic proportions. Now the word epidemic is oft-abused in medicine but nevertheless there was serious cause for alarm. In the mid 1990s there were in the region of fifteen cases a year, and just a handful of these were infectious. But in 2001 there were 257 cases and a majority of these patients were able to pass their disease on.

So what has caused this sudden rise? According to recent research, nine out of ten cases are happening in men who have sex with men. It is not their sexual orientation that presents the problem, it is the fact that the average number of sexual partners in this group of patients is over ten times that of heterosexual men. Much of this sex is unprotected. Another major concern of treating doctors is that much of the sexual activity leading to syphilis is anonymous so it is not possible for infected patients or their doctors to alert past partners to the risks they may be facing. That's the bad news. The good news is that the number of new cases has begun to level off and that antibiotic treatment is quick, effective and far removed from the days of mercury. Nothing to salivate over.

HONEST CRISPS
July 2004

When a potato crisp you've never met before, decides to call itself Honest, it's time to delve deeper into the world of 'healthy' snack foods. If we don't cry halt now, soon they'll be tempting us with flavours like divine & holy, candid & virtuous or pious 'n chaste. As my expansive mass will testify, I'm no leaf-eating mullah of the church of latter day health promotionists. In fact I'm every bit as partial to a crisp as the man perched on the bar stool next to me.

But I do feel uncomfortable with food producers donning therapeutic mantles, promoting highly processed carbohydrates as sources of unbridled goodness or eternal life.

I'll deal with probiotic yoghurt nonsense and daily defence guff another time. Today I'd like to set the record a bit straighter on the multi-million euro potato snack industry. Manufacturers will tell you that their 'healthy treat' is a high energy natural food specially designed with balanced nutrition in mind. This is usually code in the business for 'packed with calories'. A product described as 'Light' usually means that the packet contains a lot than it did a decade ago. And while I'm at it, yes, 24 grams of crisps is exceedingly light indeed, less than an ounce by my reckoning.

Recently I saw one crisp bag advertising itself as 'sugar free' yet its own label plainly contradicted this. Sugar-free in industry seems to mean less sugar than before. Be wary also of claims about reductions in salt. The UK government's Food Commission found that the average level of salt in crisps doubled between 1978 and 2003. Any claim of a 20% or 30% reduction should be seen in that context and taken with a large pinch of the very stuff. Crisp packets conveniently mention sodium content on their label information, but omit the fact that a sodium content of 0.4 grams actually means that a packet contains about one full gram of salt.

'Naturally high in fibre' is another catchphrase designed to appeal to consumers who have bowel hang-ups. But when fibre makes up just 7% of the product, (assuming that you don't eat the bag), just how do they stand over this claim? High carbohydrate food would be an infinitely more appropriate title seeing as carbs make up roughly 60% of every bag of crisps, light, honest or otherwise. Fans of Dr Atkins diet revolution know exactly what over-consumption of high carbohydrate snack foods do to waistlines. Likewise, claims of being a natural source of vitamin E are of little relevance considering that this is probably the rarest vitamin deficiency of all, found principally in extremely premature babies.

The potato crisp industry is thriving and is particularly vibrant in Ireland and the UK. Across the water, British couch potatoes spend £250 million sterling annually on one leading brand alone. This new-fangled gimmick of promoting 'healthy crisps' has little to do with saving lives. It marks the opening skirmish of a brand war, a calculated response to fears that crisp munchers may give up their habit for health reasons. In America, one businessman has invented 'happy crisps', liberally sprinkled with a herb called St John's Wort which built up a cult following as a so-called 'natural' antidepressant for hippies. Hippocrates famously declared 'Let food be your medicine'. I don't think he meant crisps.

75 YEARS OF ELECTRO-CONVULSIVE THERAPY

August 2004

"This won't hurt, it'll be over in just a minute !"

The psychiatrist's comforting words to Randal P. McMurphy (Jack Nicholson) as he underwent electric shock treatment in *One Flew Over the Cuckoo's Nest*, the Oscar sweeping movie of 1975. A large rubber dog bone was stuffed into his mouth. A team of heavies held him down. And an enormous electric shock was delivered to his brain. What followed was as gruesome a scene as was ever etched on the silver screen.

For many, *Cuckoo's Nest* was the only depiction of Electroconvulsive Therapy they have ever seen - but ECT is still alive and kicking in modern psychiatry. A thousand patients in Irish mental hospitals still undergo the procedure every year. ECT has been sanitised over the years - fractured bones, bitten tongues, strokes and cardiac arrests have been virtually eliminated with the use of modern anaesthesia and powerful muscle relaxant medication. The range of disorders for which ECT is prescribed has also narrowed over the years, retained almost exclusively now for cases of severe suicidal depression where conventional treatments have failed.

The story of ECT has been long and controversial since it began 75 years ago in Italy. Dr Ugo Cerletti, a maverick neuropsychiatrist in Genoa, first developed the shock treatment for alleviating symptoms of mental illness. Following initial experimentation on pigs, he shocked his first human guinea-pig, a vagrant who had been found by police wandering around an Italian railway station. The man had symptoms of schizophrenia. Cerletti formulated a theory that electric shocks delivered to the brain created a vitalising bodily secretion, which he called acro-amines, a mythical compound that magically returned the patient to normality. No scientist, then or since, ever discovered Cerletti's magic potion. This didn't stop him claiming ECT as a cure for a myriad of afflictions ranging from paralysis to asthma, and psoriasis to baldness. At one time ECT was touted and used as a 'cure' for homosexuality.

Concerns about serious potential side effects like memory loss and brain damage have been studiously ignored over many years, despite the fact that data from psychiatric ranks indicate that side effects are more prevalent than first thought.

Concerns have also been raised about low standards in ECT clinics. In 1997 the *British Medical Journal* reported that 70% of clinics were either deficient in some area of practice or downright poor. Up to recently, the treatment was delivered mainly by unsupervised and untrained junior doctors, often using antiquated machines. Thanks mainly to the vigilance of our Inspector of Mental Hospitals, standards in Ireland have improved in recent years. His annual report has also commented on 'considerable variations' in its use from service to service. A quick glance at the most recent statistics would indicate that patients in the South East of the country are six times more likely to receive ECT treatment than their counterparts in Cork and Kerry. Similarly, psychiatrists in the Western Health Board are five times more likely to prescribe ECT than those in the Midlands. The Health Board area where most ECT is delivered is the region which covers South West Dublin, Kildare and West Wicklow. In private hospitals too, there are marked discrepancies in the use of ECT. I would have a major concern is that there is no mechanism to audit or follow-up the 20,000 patients who have had ECT and are still alive in Ireland. ECT can work, I have seen it get results. But I have also observed that giving a television an almighty kick can restore a clear picture. After 75 years usage, it's high time psychiatrists audited each and every patient they have treated with electro-convulsive therapy. Certainly the ones who are still alive.

Jack Nicholson in *Cuckoo's Nest* summed up his experience at a follow-up group therapy session.

"They've been giving me 10,000 volts a day - the next woman who takes me on is going to light up like a pinball machine and pay off in silver dollars."

BOOZE LIMITS
August 2004

Medical school professors drum a lot of facts and figures into their protégés. Not all have a well researched provenance. Safe alcohol limits as a good example. Every medic can rattle off the maximum 'safe' levels of weekly booze consumption - 21 units for men and 14 for women. But if you ask your doctor for the names and addresses of those who came up with these figures, he won't know. You could press him further by asking why a six foot seven inch female volley ball player of fourteen stone is only allowed two thirds of the allowance of a four foot tall male jockey who weighs half that amount? Or indeed quite reasonably ask if it's medically safe for a pint-sized man to consume ten and a half pints every Sunday night and stay teetotal the rest of the week?

Safe alcohol limits, though well intentioned, are meaningless. No more than quasi-religious moral guidelines. They were introduced in 1987 by three of Her Majesty's hallowed institutions - the Royal College of Physicians, the Royal College of Psychiatrists and the Royal College of General Practitioners. Members of these three august bodies would have alcoholism rates far higher than the general population. They should know what they are talking about.

In the mid 1990s, new research hinted that regular lubrication with alcohol may in fact be good for you. A Danish study reported that drinking more than the guidelines allowed could offer benefit the heart. The research was joyfully picked up by the tabloids whose headlines proclaimed that five pints a day keeps the doctor safely away.

These were unwelcome tidings for the moral guardians of public health medicine. The colleges reconvened a booze-free working party in 1995, which refused to relax the safe drinking limits imposed eight years earlier. It was not a matter of science winning out. The colleges were afraid that if they did not retain their original stance, the drinks industry would easily persuade governments to ease up on anti-alcohol campaigns. Truth is all too often the first casualty of public health prohibition.

You might think that with coronary heart disease our nation's number one killer, and non-drinkers statistically much more likely to die of heart attacks than drinkers, that our modern day Father Mathews might encourage pioneers to renege on their pledges.

Writing on the Rise of Coercive Healthism, the late Trinity Professor, Dr Peter Skrabanek called it accurately.

"If there is the slightest hint that something pleasurable may do harm, such evidence is immediately accepted, inflated and disseminated. If however the same pleasurable activity is shown to be beneficial in any respect, such evidence must be suppressed, ridiculed or dismissed."

It's a pity that so much attention is given to so-called safe limits for the occasional drinker because those at high risk of booze-related ill health are simply forgotten. These are the stormy husbands, legless wives and assorted bachelors, spinsters and teenagers who comprise 3% of the drinking public yet imbibe 30% of the booze. In Ireland, day to day services for the non fee-paying alcoholic are simply appalling. Facilities for drying out and treating delirium tremens (DTs) in supportive surroundings are virtually non-existent.

These are the real casualties of a booming drinks industry, the men and women who drink uncontrollably and put their families, their jobs and their personal health in daily peril.

They need better services far more than the rest of us need guidelines.

KLEPTOMANIA AND OTHER INVENTIONS
August 2004

Doctors are well used to standing in the dock, accused of over-medicalisation. It's a peculiarity to our trade. Plumbers are never accused of over-plumbing and politicians would laugh if you suggested that they tend to politicise everything.

With a few honourable exceptions in the realm of psychiatry, it's not as if patients are trussed up on the streets and bundled into our meddling care. More often than not, doctors are invited guests at a myriad of life events from delivery to deathbed. (We have yet to crack weddings.) We do get things wrong more than we own up to. But if major faults like lack of time and occasional profiteering are put to one side, the profession that prides itself on listening and caring remains a relatively honourable one.

A bad workman may blame his tools, and an even worse one blames his customers. But recently I have been wondering how much responsibility for the over-medicalisation of life is born by our patients, their families and their lawyers.

An e mail has arrived on my desk from a lady who is concerned about a male friend. She is wondering where she might go to find help for his 'addiction to stealing'. Had the good lady chosen to send her e mail to the minister for justice she might have been told that the diagnosis was one of chronic larceny syndrome and she would have been advised to turn her friend in at the local Garda station for follow-up treatment at the four courts. Instead, she chose to go down the medical route. I advised her to discuss the matter further with her family doctor.

Kleptomania is not something people boast about at dinner parties, but it is a useful excuse if three wooden serviette holders and a dozen after eights tumble from your pocket as you leave the house of your host. The condition was first described in 1816 and is known to order-loving psychiatrists as an impulse-control disorder. The diagnosis is more likely to be used when items of little value are taken on a whim. The great libertarian shrinks of 19th century France took kleptomania to heart, placing it alongside pyromania and nymphomania as the great 'monomanias' of flawed psychiatric thinking. Presumably these other manias refer to setting fire to or copulating with 'things of little value'. Kleptomania was seen very much as a disease of women 'victims' who were referred for moral and mental treatment at the very best sanitoria. Male thieves however had difficulty playing the innocent party calling card. They were more likely to be treated with a spell behind bars or finding sea legs on a jolly long transportation.

Sceptics have good reason to mock kleptomania. Like many of the French 'partial insanities', it was often viewed as a fraudulent condition that helped barristers get middle-class shoplifters off the hook.

And like so many medical diagnoses, the width of kleptomania's goalposts has increased over the years to let more folk in. Apologists and disease promoters claim, as they always do, that that their pet condition is not being recognised enough and is therefore greatly under diagnosed. Kleptomaniacs even have their own website. It's at shopliftersanonymous.com if you feel like nicking it.

The support group who run the site state quite brazenly that they cater not just for shoplifters, but people who embezzle, steal from others or from their workplace, or who are engaged in any other kind of repeated forms of fraud. That's another website bank executives won't be allowed view at work.

HEART SHOCKS
ON THE GOLF COURSE
August 2004

The favoured haunt for male doctors who wish to chill out from the stresses of killing rooms is the golf club. On Wednesday afternoons and Saturday mornings they throng tees and greens, merrily mingling with tooth-pullers, pill-counters and collarless men of the cloth. Health may well be on the conversation agenda, but the great unwritten rule is that a doctor is never asked for a diagnosis, the dentist doesn't bring his drill and the pharmacist keeps his suppository firmly in pocket. A clergyman may ask for divine intervention - but only for his own balls.

This serene world is about to change as a growing number of clubs are choosing to equip themselves like operating theatres. The latest gizmo is an expensive little machine called an external defibrillator. Now this device can be quite nifty at saving the odd life. Should you choose to be near one when your heart stops beating (what we call a cardiac arrest), there is an outside chance that when applied to your chest wall and switched on, the defib might jolt you back into the rhythm of life and allow you a few more double bogeys.

Most of the hype, and plenty of the encouragement behind the growing number of defibrillators in public places is coming, unsurprisingly, from those who manufacture them and their shareholders. What is beyond doubt is that early use of defibrillation improves survival in patients who have cardiac arrests outside of hospitals. If we place them in every public space imaginable, somebody, sometime, somewhere, will reap a benefit. But at what cost?

There is plenty of conflicting information about whether defibrillators are worth the financial cost to cash-strapped health services, let alone golf clubs. Five years ago, there was much fanfare in Dublin when a large shopping centre announced that it had installed such a device and had trained dozens of staff in its use. Shoppers were told they would be in good hands should they drop dead at the prices and shopkeepers were primed to keep an eye out for situations in which an electric shock might restore customers to buying mode. The machine has never been used.

A few months ago, public health doctors in Scotland calculated the cost of saving one life if defibrillators were placed in all major airports, railway and bus stations throughout the country. They found that the cost of adding just one year of good quality life to one single patient would be in the region of €60,000. In terms of health economics, this is very dodgy expenditure indeed.

A hidden aspect to the whole question of defibrillating outside of hospitals is the potential of lawsuits down the line.

What happens if shocks are administered to patients who don't need them? What happens if there are battery problems and product recalls? What happens if the only people around in the rare case of a cardiac arrest have no training or have forgotten the little they had years before? Will families of deceased patients start suing public places because they did not have defibrillators close to hand? Will clubs be sued for not having scalpels to hand to save the lives of chokers at the captain's dinner?

Golfing members of the fire brigade are not required to bring tenders and hoses to the clubhouse. Nor are handcuffs and truncheons stored in the locker rooms of golfing policeman. Doctors will gladly step into the breach for any situation that demands it, but turning our one sanctuary into a fully fledged emergency room? That's one shock we could do without.

EPO - THE ATHLETE WHO CAN'T SAY NO

August 2004

I have a modicum of pity for the Irish long distance runner who has admitted using EPO to improve his performance. Not only is his athletic career in tatters, it may not help his legal one either. Even an optimist would have to admit that becoming chief justice is a long shot now.

This week I thought we'd have a look at the substance that made this athlete draw such opprobrium from commentators. EPO, or Erythropoietin to give it its full name, was discovered fifty years ago by Allan Erlsev, a Danish haematologist. He showed it to be a naturally occurring kidney hormone which stimulated production of extra red blood cells that carry oxygen around the body. It took 35 years for Erslev's research to bear fruit. The EPO gene was not cloned until the late 1980s when mass production of the hormone began. Three population groups drew benefits from Dr Erlsev's work - patients with chronic kidney failure, middle to long distance athletes and professional cyclists. Erythopoietin was manna for patients on kidney dialysis, for whom living with anaemia was a tiring fact of life. It spared many of them the dangers of regular blood transfusions and gave back real quality of life. Runners and bikers were less deserving of its merits.

Like Marie Curie and other old-style pioneers in medicine, Erlsev never made a single cent from his discovery. Doctors of his generation were more interested in patients than patents. He died in 2003 in the United States at the age of 84. A recent obituary in the *British Medical Journal* said that he and his wife devoted much of their lives to civil rights, housing and social issues. One of Erslev's hobbies was mountaineering. He had a particular interest in people who lived at high altitude, a place that gave them naturally elevated levels of red blood cells and EPO to carry oxygen around in the blood. Watching the Ethiopians win Olympic medals all around them in Athens last month, it's easy to see the advantage they have. Maybe our disgraced Irish runner was just trying to level the playing field.

KILLING BILL
September 2004

There's nothing like a celebrity heart scare to send lifestyle preachers ascending into their pulpits. Bill Clinton's recent brief encounter with the next world was the perfect example. Within minutes of hearing that four bypasses would need to be constructed around his ailing coronary arteries, the 'I told you so' mullahs of modern medicine were out pontificating on the reasons why slick Willie's oxygenating vessels were failing his heart.

They blamed everything from big macs in his youth to his recent encounter with the low-fat low-carb south beach diet. Even his 'hefty' book-signing schedule was implicated. The media was hungry for explanation, truthful or otherwise, and so the gospel of heath faddists was rolled out and swallowed in one.

Let's get real about Bill Clinton. Here is a middle-aged man stripped of once onerous responsibilities four years ago. He now travels the world at his leisure and earns vast amounts of money for being himself. So why did he require major heart surgery at the age of 58? He doesn't smoke aside from occasional flirtation with cigars. He follows the new-fangled dogma of regular aerobic exercise and has jogged most of his life. As President, his weight once tipped the scales at sixteen stone but for most of his middle years he has held it comfortably between thirteen and fourteen stone. In fact he boasted that his recent fad, the widely publicised south beach thing dropped him a 'healthy' three stone. Clinton's cholesterol is perfectly normal although one presidential check-up did find an elevated LDL level which was corrected by a single course of lipid lowering drugs. Recorded blood pressure readings during presidential physicals varied between 122/68 and 138/84 - noteworthy only for normality in any doctor's book.

The truth about Bill's coronaries is quite unpalatable for cooks who dream up broths for longevity. His heart problems were probably pre-determined before he was born. The serious condition that affected his heart was probably no more preventable than the grey hair on his head. In fact his early onset of silver mane may have been the only external clue to the condition of his coronaries. Bill Clinton told an interviewer back in the 1980s that his mother's family had a bad track record when it came to hearts. His father's medical history is every bit as mysterious as the stories peddled about who exactly his father was. As the song goes - whatever will be, will be. Get well soon, Mr President.

CRACKING MEDICAL CODES
September 2004

When you snuff it, it's the folk at the General Registry Office, known to doctors as the GRO, who record your death for posterity. Recently, bureaucrats at the GRO issued a warning to doctors about using abbreviations on death certificates. They warned of confusion and said that using abbreviations for medical conditions gives rise to Grave Risks Of Error (known to doctors as GROE).

Acronyms and abbreviations are a fact of life in medicine, or were, until lawyers thought we were a good source of fees. We practice to make perfect in a trade that smothers us with endless forms, thankless repetition and mountains of paper. And that's just the bank lodgements.

This week I thought we'd run a short course in medical shorthand, to help you when your solicitor demands sight of your clinical records. Health Warning: If your suffer from a congenital absence of humour (CAOH), please do not read on, go straight to the next chapter.

First of all, I should say that medics are not alone in keeping secret codes. Next time you bring your mutt to the pet clinic keep an eye out for DIMITO on the outside of Fido's file. This means that your family vet has carefully checked your animal's IQ and is very pleased with the result. DIMITO alerts fellow chart users to the fact that the *Dog Is More Intelligent Than Owner*.

Casualty departments are the birthplaces of many medical abbreviations, particularly rude ones. The infamous *GOMER or Get Out of My Emergency Room* - originated, as do most abbreviations, in America. FOD means *Full of Drink*. FORD is *Found on Road Drunk*. Unfortunately it also means *Found on Road Dead*. This can result in confusion and successful lawsuits, so the acronym has fallen out of favour. PAFO is perhaps the most commonly recorded abbreviation in emergency rooms, especially after ten at night - it means *Pissed And Fell Over*. ADASTW is somewhat more serious signifying a distinct lack of medical success - *Arrived Dead And Stayed That Way* whilst LTBB may indicate that you survived the administration of the wrong drug - *Lucky To Be Breathing*. TTTL is a pejorative expression that will create mirth, excitement and flashing dollar signs in the eyes of discovery lawyers and may result in fitness to practice enquiries on the scribbling doctor- I have never seen it but am told it stands for *Too Thick To Live*. Similarly TBBUNDY means *Totally Banjaxed But Unfortunately Not Dead Yet* and TFBUNDY is similar to TBBUNDY only ruder. Hypochondriacs who are well known in a particular emergency department may find their charts branded with WOTAM - *Waste of Time and Money*.

Psychiatrists are wordy individuals and rather precise specialists on matters of diagnosis. My friends in the mental health industry tell me that CB means *completely bonkers*. A slightly lower dose of injectables may be required if you are NAFC - *nutty as a fruit cake* - whilst the outlook is infinitely brighter for those who are SN - *slightly nuts*. British-trained Psychiatrists use the acronym RADA to describe patients who are over-theatrical. It stands for *Royal Academy of Dramatic Arts*.

Maternity Hospitals provide rich pickings for acronym hunters. Your new baby's chart may have been christened with FLK - *Funny Looking Kid*, but FLKFLD means that the doctors aren't so worried - they think this strange little baby looks just like Dad, *Funny Looking Kid, Funny Looking Dad*.

Be vigilant if your wife has PM on her chart - this doesn't mean she is going for an autopsy but rather that junior (juvenile even) male medics have marked her down as a *Pretty Mum*. Such charts are likely to find their way to the top of the consultant's pile during a busy outpatients where she is likely to attract odious amounts of what he thinks is charm.

Midwives have their own secret codes and won't thank me for breaking one of them. You might be a little perplexed to see HIVI stamped on your wife's chart after you've mopped her brow for twelve hours labour and forced by modern mores to watch an event that for uninitiated men can be more disturbing than the Paul Daniels Magic Show. No it's not some virus she didn't tell you about - it's just that having observed your general demeanour around the delivery suite, the nurses have come to a conclusion. HIVI means *Husband is a Village Idiot.*

Postscript: *I should add here that these abbreviations have never, ever, ever been used on charts by the nice doctors, mannerly midwives or well-bred vets of Ireland.*

THE LIFE OF BRIAN
September 2004

Clinton Syndrome is big in New York this month. Cardiologists are reporting a 50% rise in business as thousands of chest-clutching baby boomers flop onto their couches demanding immediate attention. Private heart screening centres are reporting a threefold increase in activity. Proving, if nothing else, that celebrity health scares, particularly involving former presidents, are potent weapons in the battle for patients' wallets.

Across the minor pond, in the Kingdom of Her Majesty, there is little evidence to date of a Clough Syndrome. Drying out clinics in Nottingham, liver transplant units in Newcastle and nursing homes for superannuated footballers in Derby, report the usual steady trade. Brian Clough is dead, and his final two years were far from his finest. They were marked by an abstinence from booze, a ten hour liver transplant operation and a final submission to cancer of the stomach. Judging from photographs of Cloughie, his declining years were harrowing in the extreme. He had declared a wish for no great epitaph, but simply an acknowledgement that he contributed something, and that perhaps somebody out there liked him. Like many men of his generation, he had to pass away to discover just by how much.

When grown men start ringing live radio programmes to admit they haven't stopped crying since news of his demise broke, you know something momentous has happened. Clough didn't have the glamour of a Princess Diana, or the worldwide fan base of Elvis Presley. Brian Clough OBE - he said it stood for Old Big 'Ead - was the most cherished character ever to grace British football. He had his demons - the love-hate relationship with alcohol, a reported avariciousness for money, and a big mouth with matching head. But that's what made Brian Clough, and what made so many love him so much. His insights were cutting and his honesty was devastating. No dictionary of quotations is complete without a few pages devoted to Cloughie. Who else could remark "David Seaman is a handsome young man but he spends too much time looking in his mirror, rather than at the ball. You can't keep goal with hair like that."

Cloughie was unashamedly a man's man, no fan of female soccer

"I like women to be feminine, not sliding into tackles and covered in mud."

Clough's extraordinary legacy of success might dissuade some from pontificating about the loser mentality of drunks and drinkers. But as with all lives that descend into alcoholism, it's the nearest and dearest who know the full chapter and verse. The public life and private life of the problem drinker can be every bit as different as heaven and hell. Repeated studies of leaders, movers and shakers in all walks of life, medicine included, show greater rates of alcoholism. Clough's career highs were extraordinary. With meager resources, a small league club and a band of highly motivated Joe average players Clough managed to win two successive European Cups. In recent years he took to taunting another manager, Alex Ferguson.

"For all his horses, knighthoods and championships, he hasn't got two of what I've got. And I don't mean balls"

Brian Clough had plenty of falls on the hard-knock path of life. An early school-leaver from a three-in-a-bed Middlesborough council house, he thrived in professional football scoring an incredible 251 league goals in as many matches. His playing career was cut short in 1962 by a devastating leg injury, film of which was captured by an early TV camera. Those who have seen the footage of his collision with the goalkeeper can't be surprised that the damage was permanent. His horrific knee injury pre-dated today's cosseted orthopaedic world of telescopic joint surgery and round-the-clock physiotherapy. It wasn't long before the bottle took the place of his crutches and a life-long procession of depression, elation and lengthy boozing in between.

Clough's liver was weeks away from packing it in completely when he got the call for a transplant. At 67, Clough was relatively old for the operation although the world record for oldest transplant recipient has just been broken in the USA by an 85 year old who needed a new kidney to keep his pension fund alive. It was reported at the time of Clough's operation last year that his new organ came from Ireland. Another footballing recipient of a spare liver, George Best went back on the drink soon after his own operation. The surgeon who operated on Brian Clough was less than pleased. Mr Derek Manas of the Freeman Hospital in Newcastle said quite soberly that Best's post-transplant binge drinking would do nothing to encourage people to donate organs. Old Big 'Ead mightn't have been quite so diplomatic.

DYSMORPHOPHOBIA
November 2004

There's an ugly aspect of the cosmetic surgery industry that concerns many doctors. The thorny question of what is wrong with some of the people who look for it. There's an excellent article in the latest edition of *Irish Psychiatrist*. It was written by two plastic surgeons who conclude that a significant number of patients seeking cosmetic enhancement gain no long term benefit, and that procedures may actually cause their mental health to deteriorate.

35% of men have an aspect of their appearance that concerns them. That's the bad news. The good news is that this is half the level found in women. Preoccupation about appearance lasts in women until they reach the age of 60 and sometimes beyond. Male worries about appearance peak between the ages of 18 and 21 and then decline quickly with age. No surprise perhaps that concern about appearance is far less in men who have found life partners. But married women are just as concerned as their unattached female friends. Such vagaries of human frailty are the lifeblood of vampires in the cosmetic surgery industry.

One of the most interesting conditions I came across in psychiatric training was dysmorphophobia. This is an obsessional-delusional type illness where a person becomes preoccupied with one element of their outward appearance that they consider to be ugly. For instance a man may be convinced that his perfectly normal inherited family nose has the size, shape and appearance of a giant parsnip. he may also feel that passers-by, family and friends are constantly looking and commenting upon it. The condition was first described in the late 19th Century by Dr Enrique Morselli and was made famous by one of Siegmund Freud's patients - known as the Wolf Man. Another case was brought to public attention recently by London psychiatrist, Dr Raj Parsaud. He wrote about a German girl who wrongly believed she had a prominent pubic bone and that everybody was looking at it.

Recently psychiatrists tried to re-classify this illness but succeeded only in clouding waters further. Their new-fangled body dysmorphic disorder, abbreviated to BDD, is loosely defined as a 'preoccupation with an imagined defect in appearance, or a markedly excessive concern about a slight physical anomaly'.

What we do know is that dysmorphophobia can be a devastating condition. Patients subject themselves to a life of misery, self-torment and social isolation. 25% try to kill themselves. There is a tendency to constantly seek reassurance from others about the true state of the offending body part. It may be more prevalent in people whose traits include shyness, oversensitivity and perfectionism. Obsession with a facial feature tends to predominate.

For disturbed patients the flattering adverts of cosmetic surgery clinics may appear as manna from heaven. Medical opinion has long been that surgeons should avoid treating such patients at all costs. However some scientific papers do suggest that carefully selected patients with a single minor physical abnormality can do extraordinarily well. Dysmorphophobic patients are easy prey for increasingly aggressive marketers of private clinics. They don't tend to sue, and often return for more. If unhappy with one clinic's results, they may simply turn up on someone else's doorstep. If one body part is 'cured' the phobia may simply transfer to another. As a measure of how unhappy these patients can be, it's not unknown for them to conduct DIY surgery on themselves.

Psychiatrists agree that dysmorphophobic patients are 'difficult to treat' which in layman's terms means we don't know a lot about their condition and haven't a ready cure. Some patients can do well on anti-depressant medication, others are prescribed more powerful anti-psychotic medicines that are used in schizophrenia.

What this suggests is that there is considerable overlap with other psychiatric illnesses and symptoms.

Some textbooks condescend to suggest that patients should be told tactfully that there is no real deformity. But the fact remains that despite legions of 'talking therapies', many do not change. All in all, dysmorphophobia is a particularly miserable affliction. If ignored, it won't just simply go away.

HEALTHY HEARTS & BLISSFUL BOWELS
December 2004

This whole 'Right to Health' movement is going a bit far.

Last week the Irish Heart Foundation solemnly declared that 'all children born in the 21st century have the right to live to 65 years free of heart disease'.

It seems the encyclopaedia of health twaddle has a whopping new entry. Every day, children are born in this country with congenital heart disease, abnormalities of the heart's chambers and its blood vessels that challenge the normal function of this vital organ. Thankfully many are cured with pioneering surgery, feats that previous generations of doctors could only dream of. Conditions that up to a few decades ago meant certain death can now be remedied or improved by great advances in cardiac surgery. But on the other side of the chamber, there are those who are less fortunate. Congenital heart disease and the surgery used to remediate it, still claims many young lives every year.

The conferral of meaningless rights does nobody any favours.

You don't have the right to beautiful tonsils and sinuses at 16, the right to hale and hearty skin and bones at 41, the right to a vigorous brain and gall bladder at 63 and the right to a dynamic anus and fully functioning external genitalia at the age of 97.

Nobody has the right to good health, they have the right only to good treatment and care. Life's a lottery and health can be an unfair weekly game.

Another idiotic trend from the purveyors of long life theories is the allotment of a 'healthy' adjective to each body part to signify how well it must keep. The do-gooders are already out inspecting food halls and eating places around the country awarding 'happy heart' badges, merit awards and certificates to beat the band. Next thing we'll have canteens promising genial guts, blissful bowels, knock-out knees and laughing lungs.

A myth is enveloping this country that disease is an enemy that is easy to defeat. The idea that you can keep your heart content by eating particularly happy foods is one such nonsense. Just recently I heard of a poor man who dropped dead in his early forties from a massive coronary. A sportsman, lean and lithe, he never drank alcohol, never smoked and looked after himself.

The French have a rather useful expression we should avail of more. *C'est la vie* I think it goes.

Born with a disease called chronic scepticism, I have never been able to take the guff of health promotionists too seriously. If doctors were meant to preach, we should be wearing collars around our necks, not stethoscopes which purport to help us listen. The doctor with all the answers is often the one who has not been listening to the questions.

WORLD CUP HEALTH

June 2010

There is no escape from the dodgy doctrines of food faddists and scaremongers in modern healthcare. The soccer ball of the 2010 World Cup is swerving towards a weary conclusion, and the tournament has gifted its captive male audience a whole new set of boring do's and unproven don'ts. About as useful as an England goalkeeper.

This year's classic soccer scare is the Vuvuzela, once a tin musical instrument, and now a plastic horn that's a handful of decibels louder than a referee's whistle. When these instruments are played together they can perfectly drown out all the inanities of modern sports commentary. Such was the numbing effect of dull football at this tournament, I hadn't even noticed the din until the media drew my attention to it. The newspapers had their attention drawn to vuvuzelas by press releases from hearing aid manufacturers, happy to cash in on a tournament without stumping up cash for official sponsorship.

The initial source of the vuvuzela scare was the AFP news service in Johannesburg who received a press release from a hearing aid company on the 7th of June last.

'Football fans risk permanent damage to hearing' ran the blurb - 'Hearing damage can occur in fifteen minutes'. With assistance from modern newswires and intrepid column fillers, the press release went around the world as quick as you could shout Jimmy Magee Allstars. Local hearing aid merchants in Ireland and elsewhere were then invited to comment by journalists keen to re-nationalise this breaking story. One compared the decibel level of vuvuzuela with a chain saw. Another raised the mortal danger stakes by invoking the sound of an airplane jet engine.

In truth, there is precious little medical evidence that football fans around the world won't hear the doorbell when the final whistle goes in South Africa. On the positive side, perhaps they now have an excuse to ignore domestic calls for a trim of metre long grass in the back garden.

The Irish Times health supplement also got in on a bit of world cup nagging with some frivolous advice on keeping television snacks healthy. In a week when real news wasn't short - threatened hospital closures, dodgy ultrasounds and unaccounted-for funds at the HSE - the newspaper chose to harass world cup viewers about their choice of snack food. "If you do one thing this week . . . keep those world cup snacks healthy" they preached before launching into a sermon about the benefits of raw carrots, yoghurt based dips, hummus and celery. In truth, they were simply parroting banalities from the Safefood Agency whose staff must have escaped the public sector purge. The safe foodies had time to prepare a world cup menu of twenty two dishes to keep you 'match-fit' . The last one was bananas wrapped in bacon which just about says it all. Nuts all of them.

Across the water, things are obviously getting back to normal in Cumbria after a recent shooting spree. One of the region's 'leading GPs' has urged football fans to behave responsibly warning that 'World Cup football, sun and alcohol can be a heady cocktail which can land people in hospital if they are not careful. 'Six years of medical training allowed him issue 'expert advice' to fans on behalf of Cumbria NHS including such pearls as 'dress appropriately for the weather' and 'don't place yourself in danger'.

Over in Hong Kong, perennial non-qualifiers from the goalposts of Asia, things were worse. Their department of health nannies advised that 'even though crispy snacks (such as potato chips and fried food) and alcoholic beverages could add to the world cup festivity, it's important to maintain healthy eating, avoid tobacco or excessive alcohol'. They warned that that insufficient sleep during the tournament 'can lower immunity, make you prone to illnesses and affect work performance'. They went on then to issue a lengthy list of banalities that would do the EU press office proud. Included were gems of modern wisdom that simply confirm the untimely death of Confucius.

Consume snacks only when you are hungry. Do not snack for the sake of snacking.

When you feel like smoking, wash your face, do stretching exercises, try deep breathing and drink water to divert your attention from the urge.

And they go on - if you drink, drink sensibly
and on - drink sugary tea and water

175

and on - stretch and move around while watching the matches

and on - sit properly while watching the soccer match to avoid muscle aches afterwards.

Such petty, incessant and chronic nagging may well explain why the burghers of Hong Hong lost three nil to Turkmenistan in the World Cup qualifiers.

Here at home, we now have something called Healthy Men's Week to look forward to. I'm going to bed.

TOO HOT
IN THE KITCHEN
June 2005

Two years ago, celebrity chef Gordon Ramsey promised to introduce drug-testing for all staff working at his Chelsea restaurant. What prompted such a radical addition to the menu was the death of young protégé who worked as £50,000 a year head chef in his flagship London outlet. The lad had previously helped the former soccer star win a coveted Michelin star in Glasgow.

In May 2003, the junior chef fell 60 feet from a block of apartments of the King's Road in south London. He was just 31. The inquest heard evidence of bizarre behaviour that evening culminating in the chef being on a window ledge smashing windows with a golf club. A very high cocaine level was found in his blood, a dose that could have proved fatal without the fall. Friends and family agreed that such behaviour was very much 'out of character' although it was known by some friends that he took the odd bit of 'Charlie'. The coroner recorded an accidental death verdict and suggested the case might serve as a warning about the unpredictability of cocaine.

Just three months earlier, France was rocked by the suicide of one its most famous chefs. Bernard Loiseau, the 52 year old proprietor of the three Michelin Star *La Côte d'Or* in Burgundy, prepared an exotic €250 dish of truffles and then went home for his usual afternoon siesta. Instead of a nap, he chose to discharge a hunting gun into his head, leaving a traumatic display of colour for those who found his corpse. Loiseau's hotel-restaurant was legendary in France with 32 opulent suites, exquisite dining rooms and stunning gardens. It provided a welcome retreat for the great, the good and the politicians of France who regularly dined there at taxpayer's expense. Loiseau was happily married with three young children and the entire French nation was baffled as to why he had ended it all. Newspapers pored over his faultless personal and professional life. Eventually they tried to apportion blame for the suicide at the doors of restaurant raters, inspectors of haute cuisine establishments and publishers of guidebooks. The strains and stresses of maintaining the perfect score were too much. Only two dozen chefs in France held the 3 Michelin stars and there were rumours that Loiseau may have been about to lose one of his. (In fact his restaurant still has three today). Great significance was given to the fact that the eminent Gault/Milau guidebook had downgraded his establishment from a 19 out of 20 to a mere 17 just days before his death. Across France, and indeed Europe, a debate raged about the rat race of restaurant ratings.

Loiseau's certainly wasn't the first culinary suicide in France. Back in the 17th Century the late arrival of a consignment of fresh fish caused Vatel, personal chef to Louis XIV to top himself with a gutting knife. And in the swinging sixties, Parisian chef Alain Zick shot himself in the head, supposedly because of the loss of a Michelin star.

This year there are signs that chefs are switching down the heat in the kitchen and turning their backs on ever-demanding league tables. A number of chefs have already handed back their stars to Michelin, branding them as poisoned chalices that simply lead to higher costs for everyone. A new book on Loiseau's life and death suggests that there may have been more to his death than guidebooks. He had suffered all his life from bipolar disorder or manic depression. Like many of his 3 star contemporaries, he was an absolute perfectionist. And it has long been rumoured that despite his long-running success, Loiseau was burdened by impossible debt in his 10 million euro establishment. In fact for many in the restaurant game, issues of debt are always bubbling away in the pot. The experience of Irish celebrity chefs bears this out. It's interesting that Ramsay's young chef had borrowed a few thousand pounds from his boss before his death. And in 1966 Alain Zick also faced financial ruin when his Michelin star was reefed away from him. If there is a chef in your life, don't toss him like salad, roll him in flour or drown him with wine. Knead him gently, keep him at a warm steady temperature, and make sure he can pay his bills.

THE ANATOMY OF HANGING
January 2007

There is never any shortage of spoilsports intent on ruining Christmas. The latest fad is seasonal execution of dictators, expertly timed to coincide with slow news days and the grizzly left-over's of turkey. First we had Mr and Mrs Ceauşescu, sub-machine gunned on Christmas day a few years ago. Mr C started to sing a few bars of the *Internationale* whilst Mrs C screamed at the onlookers to go to hell, including the man with a video camera. Last month, the executioners at least had the good grace to wait until the brandy balls were eaten before sending Saddam Hussein down the longest drop in Baghdad.

My own family once had a connection with the execution business. Not as guillotine sharpeners in Paris, but here in Dublin city just 70 years ago. As a young UCD graduate intent on specialising in psychiatry after the civil war, my grandfather took a resident medical officer's position in Mountjoy prison so that he might further study the subtle distinctions between an insane mind and a criminal one. One of the M.O.'s duties at the prison was to attend executions, to ensure they were conducted properly but also to act as a medical witness and certify the actual death itself. Family lore has it that my grandfather hated every single second of his association with state execution. He did not speak of these events, and we assumed that he was involved in quite a few hangings. But recent research suggests that he only had to perform this task once, in June 1937. The prisoner due for hanging was a 43 year old Wexford man called John Hornick. A Protestant farmer, and father of three young children, Hornick was a descendant of the Palatine refugees who arrived in Ireland in 1709. He was convicted of the murder of a neighbour, James Redmond, who lived in a gypsy-type caravan just outside Taghmon, south of Wexford Town on the Rosslare road. The evidence was purely circumstantial. There was nothing to connect Hornick with the death of Redmond. He was sentenced to hang on the basis of some convincing evidence that he travelled to a bank in Dalkey, County Dublin to withdraw cash belonging to the deceased. A huge petition and intense lobbying by well-heeled supporters failed to help John Hornick, and he was hanged first thing in the morning of the 17th of June 1937. Executioners were the UK based uncle and nephew team of Tom and Albert Pierrepoint. Their line of work left a lasting impression both on the corpse and on my grandfather.

In my own medical student days, we were introduced in the very first week of anatomy to the subject of hanging. All students were asked to purchase *Case Studies in Anatomy* by Professor Ernest Lachman, a renowned human anatomist from Oklahoma College of Medicine. I still have the book to this day and remember from coffee room banter that the first section most fellow students went to was the Anatomy of Hanging. It began with a chilling description of what happened Mr L.K., a murderer in America.

"Hands and Feet were tightly secured. The knot was fixed under the chin and in front of the angle of the left jaw. A hood was then placed over the head to spare the onlookers. The trap door opened. Torso and limbs convulsed violently for several minutes. The pulse slowed, It weakened. Then it became faster. Then irregular. Heart action stopped 13 minutes after the trap had been sprung. He was pronounced dead by the prison physician."

The aim of a modern gallows hanging is to induce what is known in the trade as the 'hangman's fracture' - a snapping and dislocation of the second cervical vertebra high up in the neck that is caused by the long drop. Not too long mind you. There is a fine line to be drawn between a clean dislocation that severs the spinal cord and a clumsy execution which completely decapitates the victim. Some basic mathematics and physics training is required for all hangmen. The greater the weight of the victim, the shorter the drop is required. Professor Lachman pointed out that German executioners preferred shorter drops of six feet, which they claimed reduced the number of decapitations. However the corollary of this is that a short drop may result in death by asphyxiation rather than the quicker snapping of the neck. The whole concept of the long drop had its origins amongst Irish doctors in the mid 19ᵗʰ century who felt it was a more humane way to execute prisoners. William Marwood, an English executioner popularised the method in the 1870s and indeed was well practised in its use when he was asked to hang five Irish men at Kilmainham Gaol in 1883. The men had rather unfortunately called themselves 'The Invincibles' as they set off to murder Gladstone's nephew in the Phoenix Park. They were anything but when the Marwood rope appeared.

Marwood's techniques were greatly celebrated. Bureacrats at the UK Home Office helped hangmen all over the world by printing his *Official Table of Drops* in 1892. It was republished twenty years later, minus the errors. I believe it is still used as an executioner's handbook in countries not yet civilised enough to disown the death penalty. Beginning at rope lengths for eight stone bodies and ending with suggested drops for fourteen stone ones - it would probably benefit from another updating given our expanding trouser sizes and the fact that 14 stone is almost slim nowadays.

What I recall from Professor Lachman's lesson is that the location of the knot is paramount. Those of you who witnessed Saddam's last moments may recall that the knot was pulled close to the chin on the left side of the jaw. This ensures that the body's own weight thrusts the head back violently at the end of the fall, severing the spinal cord as the bony vertebral column snaps.

The good professor's musings on judicial swinging finished with a rather stern warning about the consequences of 'unprofessional' judicial hangings conducted by untrained executioners. Complete severance of the head with blood spurting over the witnesses and execution chamber is one outcome. Other 'unforeseen events' he describes as temporary or permanent recovery. He cites reports of executed convicts showing signs of life after the noose is removed, and some even recovering completely.

I have been reading a new collection of John McGahern's short stories on recent evenings. One is a touching story about a man who witnessed the gruesome execution of a 16 year old boy in Mountjoy Prison in 1919. Perhaps the whole gory spectacle of

Saddam's end might persuade a more enlightened generation to campaign against all state-sponsored killing. And if they succeed, Professor Lachman's book might be issued in revised form, without the chapter on hanging.

EVEN MORE MALAPROPISMS
February 2007

I have received a nice letter from a lady doctor who writes that she is sorry she didn't write down all the wonderful expressions overheard in her surgery over the years. She did recall speaking to a local woman who told her that a neighbour had a *malignant casanova* (melanoma) removed from her face. Once she happened upon a student garda who had to fill her in on the details of an accident. She found it hard not to smile when the future officer of the law said he saw a car being driven *erotically*. And an elderly gentleman told her proudly in surgery one morning that his daughter had installed *BBC* windows (pvc) in her new house, as well as a *fertility* room (utility).

A nurse wrote to tell me of a lady patient who described her *high-eating* hernia (hiatus hernia) and the *tagamints* (tagamet) she was prescribed for it. She also sent another one that is far too rude - even for my readers. A Dublin man wrote to tell me that one of the lads working with him in a factory fell off his bicycle on his way to work. The following day another workmate reported that he was ok except for a *hare lip* fracture (hairline) in his back. My ban garda friend wrote to me again with a new collection. There was a gentleman who raved about the benefits of *alcopuncture* (acupuncture). And following the execution of Saddam Hussein, a man told her he had it coming because of how badly the former dictator had treated the *kerbs* (kurds). Once in an electrical shop she overheard a friend asking for a *low life bulb*. A rural doctor told me of a patient who made him quite jealous by saying he suffered from *sleep euphoria syndrome* (sleep apnoea syndrome).

And there's a doctor in the south west of the country who collects funny things people put on their sick notes. He sent me a selection some time back.

Things like

'My son is under the doctor's care and should not take P.E. today. Please *execute* him'. His all time favourites are 'Please excuse Gloria from Jim today. She is *administrating* (menstruating)' and 'Please excuse Roland from gym class for a few days. Yesterday he fell out of a tree and *misplaced* his hip (displaced).'

There was an elderly lady who wanted to tell her GP something in great confidence. Doctor I want to tell you something on the *QE2* she whispered. And a man claimed that a nurse in the public clinic had dressed his leg wound with *gelignite* (jelonet). Another doctor was taken aback one day when an old lady asked him for *low sex* (losec) to heal her peptic ulcer.

A number of people have told me over the years about mispronunciation of hospitals. I told you before about the *sentimental* hospital (central mental) in Dundrum and the *eye and rear* (eye and ear) on Adelaide Road. The Bon Secours in Cork also features. A Tipperary man told me that in a Thurles chemist his mother overheard another customer telling the proprietor that his wife had been taken back into hospital. 'Is she here in the District?' asked the Pharmacist. "Oh no, sir, she is down in Cork with the *Bunch of Hoors*." An American trained doctor told me of a patient whose heart he once treated for *atrial tribulations* (fibrillation). And in Hume Street hospital, now sadly deceased, they once had a case of *cirrhosis of the Scalp* (psoriasis).

And a retired lady GP told me about a man who was always requesting medical certificates to say he was unfit for work. She would usually ask him what diagnosis he wanted her to put on the certificates. On one occasion he replied *fatal injuries*. If he wasn't so concussed he might have got the diagnosis correct - facial injuries was what he meant to say.

SUICIDE BOMBERS
July 2005

I suspect the bulk of today's doctors are a lot less accomplished in traditional clinical skills than their medical predecessors. Most of us have little everyday experience of delivering babies, performing operations, inserting tubes or dealing with everyday emergencies and injuries. The profession has become so super-specialised, that many of the everyday proficiencies patients assume we still possess, have simply vanished without trace.

Take the recent spate of suicide bombings in London. You may remember that the number 30 bus had its roof peeled off on Tavistock Square before spewing mangled wreckage, dead bodies and grotesquely wounded ones out on the street below. As luck had it, the explosion took place right outside the headquarters of the British Medical Association. There were a few dozen doctors inside the building, some attending conferences or meetings and others who work full time in medical publishing, writing and administration.

Within minutes most of them were out at the front of the building, surveying the carnage and doing what little they could to console, whilst the ambulance sirens drew closer. Many have been describing in print exactly what they saw and how helpless they felt without their usual hospital equipment and attendant nurses. One academic doctor described the scene. "There was blood and flesh on the walls of BMA House, up to the second floor. I could taste metal and smell burning flesh. It was 18 months since I had seen a patient and my speciality was geriatric medicine."

Chefs from nearby cafes handed out plastic gloves to the doctors. Security guards gave out blankets to the wounded. Office workers were unscrewing the tops from their desks to make temporary stretchers. They were using their heads. Meanwhile the doctors were busy trying to remember what they would have done in their younger days when faced with a sudden mass of casualties. Some recalled their ABC of resuscitation: Make sure the Airway is clear - tend to the Breathing - assess the Circulation. Once the ambulances arrived they had some equipment to work with - intravenous drips that could be set up to replace lost fluids, bandages and tourniquets to prevent further blood loss, collars and splints to stabilise bones and joints.

Just days after the July 7th bombing, the *British Medical Journal*, whose staff worked heroically at the scene, published an article educating doctors about how to manage patients injured in a suicide blast. Little surprise that much of the research in this area now comes from Israel. We learned that suicide bombs detonated in enclosed spaces such as buses and tube trains cause more deaths but less injuries to bystanders than those set off at open air gatherings. We learned about the three types of injuries that such blasts cause. Firstly body parts that contain air such as the ear, the lungs and the gut are damaged because of shock waves between tissue and air. The second type of injuries are caused by the collision of high powered fragments emitted from the bomb or glass shattered by the blast. And thirdly, bodies are moved forcefully by the blast causing external burns, displacement of joints, broken or amputated limbs. For patients who survive, there is a checklist of things that doctors might be on the lookout for . . . collapsed lungs, smoke inhalation, perforated eardrums, shock and severe fluid loss, damage to internal tummy organs and pockets of air in the circulation (air embolism).

What worked particularly well in the aftermath of the first London bombings was the excellent on-street triage systems that were set up. Emergency personnel were faced with over 700 casualties in just one hour. Those with relatively minor casualties did not flood to emergency departments in ambulances but were in the main treated on the streets or in buildings close to where they first sought help. This meant that hospital casualty units were free to deal with those who had life threatening injuries. Heaven forbid - if we should ever witness more bombs in this country, would we get the same on-street service here?

There are important lessons medics can learn from these bombings on our doorstep. The mere presence of calm doctors, no matter how poorly equipped or qualified they are, can have a very positive effect on any accident scene. And it can motivate others to perform all the extraordinary feats our training makes us forget.

THE MALE COLLECTOR
May 2007

Many men have a secret passion for collecting things. Lots of us do it. Tom Hanks collects antique typewriters. Quentin Tarantino collects board games. Psychiatrist Dr Raj Persaud was dragged kicking from his couch recently to tell television hosts Richard Madeley and Judy Finnigan that he collected spectacles. Then Richard couldn't help himself and blurted out about his penchant for torches. He admitted to secretly stashing more than twenty pen lights and flash-lamps in various locations around Judy's mansion. BBC's *Antiques Roadshow* programme recently featured the family of a dead man who had allowed his children to grow up in relative poverty, so that he could indulge his passion for hugely expensive silverware. The story had a happy ending - with the man's death - and the family were able to start living again having auctioned off his collection The urge to collect and hoard, with the obvious exception of shoes, tends to be very much a male thing.

Can we draw any conclusions about men from the type of things that they hoard? Perhaps men who collect coins have a secret fear of losing money? Do politicians who collect more votes than they need and refuse to share quotas with colleagues harbour a bigger fear of rejection? What about men who collect dickey-bows - have they issues about their station in life? These are all difficult questions to answer.

What is a bit clearer is what causes men to collect in the first place. One simple explanation that appeals to me is that it is simply a remnant of the hunter gatherer instinct in our forefathers. A habit that is two million years in evolution is not easy to kick.

Psychiatrists and psychologists speculate that the phenomenon has anthropological, socio-biological and psychodynamic roots. Which proves two things about them. Firstly they collect big words and secondly, I'm not sure they know what they are talking about. Sigmund Freud had a simpler explanation, probably quite untrue, but one that befitted a man known for major obsessions himself. He suggested that the collecting mentality had nothing to do with sex, but everything to do with pooh. His ideas on adult hoarding (his potty theories) suggested that some children build up a lifelong resentment to having their faecal waste flushed down the lavatory by pesky adults. They take it personally, as a slight on their abilities and a signal from the world that everything they produce is of little value. Freud's theories are interesting, terrific fodder for medical dinner parties, but applicable I think more to the very few than the many.

Years after Freud's theories were discounted, pooh-poohed if you will, his fellow mind professionals still struggle with the concept of men who collect things. They have even collected a whole array of collecting types. The systematic collector, who collects things just as they do, is deemed mentally well. But three other varieties, the addictive collector, the obsessive collector and horror of horrors, the messy collector are all invited to bring chequebooks for long sittings on the couch.

As a medical student I committed one of the seven deadly sins of medicine, spanophilia. Weird, wonderful and rare diagnoses fascinated me. Diseases that were common were much less interesting. This inclination to reading up about rarities made exams difficult to pass, unless the professor examining was himself a spanophiliac, in which case he might pass you as a wonderfully interesting fellow, even if you did place a thermometer in the wrong orifice.

A mental affliction called diogenes syndrome, first described thirty years ago, has long fascinated me. Patients who tick its boxes tend to be neglectful of their own hygiene and of the appearance of their homes. By choice, they tend towards a life of extreme squalour. They withdraw from friends, family and community, and many will hoard what the rest of society considers to be rubbish. The condition is named after the freed slave and philosopher Digoenes, who made the streets of Athens his home, espoused extreme poverty and preached the superiority and simplicity of a dog's life. He believed that the human race could learn more from looking at how dogs conduct themselves and less from constantly looking in the mirror And you know what, I think he may have had a point. Woof. Woof.

UNDERARMS
August 2011

I have just finished reading a most interesting article on armpits, and how the beauty industry have identified their radiance as a new marketing frontier. A captive market is ripe for extra spraying, rolling, shaving, soaping, creaming, toning, firming, lightening and whatever other gimmicks they can think up along the way. One company makes the extraordinary claim that they have 'given women the confidence to go sleeveless'. Armpits have even been rebranded. Henceforth they are to be known, not as pits or oxters, but as underarms. With enough public conditioning and grooming, underarm care will be established as a regularly tolled beauty routine. The daily wash and long-lasting soap bar is to be consigned to history. Underarm care will have its own quasi-science. Anti-perspirants will have motion-sense technology, deodorants that are supposedly activated by movement rather than sweat. One will probably win a gold medal for endurance at next year's olympics. Those daft patronising public surveys are upon us already. 77% of women feel sexier when their underarms look good says one creamery. Oh hang on - that's the same creamery that sells skin-lightening deodorant to women in India. And here's another, from the company that allowed women 'bare their beautiful underarms'. 500 ladies surveyed. Do you find your underarms unattractive? Answer. Yes, yes, my mountain flower, yes, yes, all perfume - oh yes, they all answered as yes, yes, they drew the underarm surveyor in closer for a sniff. He must have phoned Molly Bloom.

We medics have our own term for the armpit - on correspondence between doctors it's referred to as the axilla. Hardly a hotbed of disease activity, but traditionally a good place to stick thermometers if you don't possess veterinary training. Your two axillae are occasional sites for infections and rashes, and doctors checking for certain cancers or arm infections will usually feel them for swollen lymph glands. Armpit fetish or sexual attraction to the oxters, is known to psychiatrists as axillism. It's extremely uncommon, particularly I would say amongst members of the medical profession. Despite what the beauty industry may pay a fortune to tell you, nobody really wants to kiss a chemically enhanced armpit. A soft plain bar of soap is your only man.

A SHOCKING STORY
July 2005

Good health news for the folk of rural Ireland. You may have lost your primary school, your post office, your dance hall, your clergyman, your grocer, your GP and your telephone box to the march of modern Ireland - but those wonderful politicians you elect to corridors of power are going to make sure you don't make a quick exit yourself. They are hell bent on modernising de Valera's dream and installing a defibrillating machine at every crossroads around the country.

For those of you happily in the dark, defibrillators are machines that deliver electric shocks to hearts that have stopped. They are NOT used (as is commonly assumed) on every patient who has a heart attack. They should be used only on those who suffer a cardiac arrest i.e. their heart has stopped beating.

The deep freeze maestro of Tipperary North, Mr Michael Lowry TD told an empty Dáil chamber this Summer that automatic defibrillators should become as commonplace as fire-extinguishers. Considering the size of Michael's house in Holy Cross, I'd be surprised if he hasn't installed half a dozen of them there in strategic locations. Now you may think it odd that a half educated medical quack like myself would argue against life-saving devices when a learned humanitarian of Mr Lowry's pedigree clearly believes otherwise. But there comes a time in every person's life (unless you are elected to Leinster House) that you have to sit down with an abacus, work out a budget and prioritise spending. If the likes of Mr Lowry gets his way and every kitchen aga in the country has a defibrillator hanging with the cooking utensils, then you might be wiser to invest your money in the companies that manufacture defibrillators than actually installing the latest kitchen model yourself.

The average cost of mounting one automatic defibrillator in Ireland and training volunteers to use it is currently in the region of €5,000. At first sight that doesn't seem too bad, but the five grand doesn't cover the cost of keeping volunteer skills up to date for years after installation, servicing for decades to come and upgrading the machine every time a new model comes on the market. But my major problem with installing defibrillators in every townland is quite simply that the vast majority of them will never be used.

The last time I wrote about defibrillators I had some contrary correspondence from fans of amateur heart-shocking who suggested that you cannot put a value on the saving of human life. Doctors and health planners would love to live in that sort of utopia (some already do) but the facts of the matter are that this country would bankrupt itself very quickly if it fell hook, line and sinker for every health fad that hit the airwaves.

A Scottish study which looked at more sensible defibrillator placement in busy airports, railways and bus stations showed that you would have to install 12 defibrillators at a cost of €60,000 in these locations to add just one year to one person's life. Thus if a solitary 60 year old man was successfully defibrillated and lived a healthy life until he died of something else at the age of 80, the cost to the exchequer of adding 20 years to one life would be in the region of €1.2 million. It may seem callous to put healthcare in these terms but these are precisely the terms that need to be discussed if we are to have a defibrillator with a dead battery next to every pothole.

And in case you were wondering, yes they have already treated themselves to automated external defibrillators in Dáil Éireann. For a workplace that sits less than half the year, opens for full business on occasional Tuesdays, Wednesdays and Thursdays, and has more empty seats than a camogie final, you get a sense where their priorities lie.

Postscript: *This little country did file for bankruptcy itself about two years after this piece was written. It did come as a shock to some, but I think it would be unfair to blame it all on superfluous defibrillators.*

CHECK-UP FOR BIFFO
March 2009

It's the 17th of March. Lá Fhéile Phádraig. Ireland's exemplary statesman, Brian Cowen, is in the oval office presenting fellow Offaly man Barack Obama with a bowl of medicinal clover. Oops. Biffo Cowen recites from the wrong autocue and welcomes President Obama into his own home. Back in Dublin, a Garda enquiry continues into who painted a picture of our Taoiseach in his underpants and left it in the National Library. His ministers have punched the over seventies by threatening to take away their medical cards. They also deny a life saving vaccine to a generation of schoolgirls. And then they implore us not to talk-down the country. You couldn't make it up. The funny thing is, if he ruled America, Mr Cowen would be forced to publicly strip down to his underpants once a year.

Summer is the traditional season for the annual physical examination of the U.S. President. In August 2006 George W. Bush submitted himself to nine doctors for a four hour check-up at the National Naval Medical Centre in Maryland. A four page medical summary was released to the press stating that the president was 'fit for duty and will likely remain fit for duty for the remainder of his term.' Hardly the stuff of headlines so the media chose to pick up on the weight gain of 4lbs since his previous medical and the fact that a tiny pre-cancerous lesion had to be frozen off his left forearm. President Bush fed the journalists more tittle-tattle by owning up to cake gluttony at his sixtieth birthday party and promised to wear a hat and sunscreen whenever out in the midday glare. His cholesterol measurements were made public, as was his pulse, his rising level of body fat, his declining vision, his vastly-improved stomach reflux, a fondness for cigars, treadmill test results, daily exercise regime, abstinence from alcohol, and his solitary medication - a daily multivitamin to fuel America's war on terror.

Bill Clinton's medical history as President was more interesting. Whilst in office he had five exercise tolerance tests which tested the strain on the heart under pressure 'to predict' future coronary disease. On his final examination in 2001, this test was left out as his doctors said it was unwarranted. Clinton began taking medication for a slightly raised cholesterol and went on a fad diet. As we know he ended up having an emergency quadruple bypass operation in September 2004 when 90% blockages were discovered in the arteries that fed oxygen to his heart. So much for preventive medicine.

There is no onus on American politicians to disclose personal medical records to the public. Only the results of the annual presidential overhaul are released, albeit in an edited format. Bill (and indeed his wife Hillary) never released their medical files to the press, fuelling wild and idle speculation about personal, marital and psychiatric details they might wish to keep secret. To our knowledge, Mr Obama has yet to reveal the colour of his Y-fronts to the White House physicians, but during his long electoral trek to the oval office, he did release a letter from his Chicago family doctor about the state of his health over a ten year period. It revealed a spectacularly low blood pressure for a man well into his fifth decade, at just 90/60. In some countries, particularly those where doctors don't derive enough income from sick people, they'd be rushing in to treat that.

I remember being told in medical school that the treatment of hypotension, low blood pressure, was taking off in what was then East Germany.

Obama's last cardiograph was fine, as was his urine. A blood test for prostate cancer (more common in men of African American heritage) was ok too. His fondness for alternating cigarettes with nicorette gum was recorded, but as all smokers know, a penchant for fags can be every bit as hard as ditching your personality.

This modern fascination with presidential health has its roots back in 1944 when citizens elected Franklin D. Roosevelt to his fourth term of office. Roosevelt's health had been declining since the early part of the second world war but the public had been kept in the dark, and he died in office in 1945. The nation grieved like never before and questions were asked about the fitness of future candidates and holders of high office. The interest was genuine, as Roosevelt was pretty much loved by most if not all. Free speech prospered when essayist H.L. Mencken declared in his own personal tribute that Roosevelt 'had every quality that morons esteem in their heroes.'

Which brings me neatly back to Mr Cowen. Do we, his loyal subjects, have a right to his personal medical records? Should the state pay for him to have an annual check-up and release the results? Does his right to medical privacy supersede the public's right to know if he's physically up to the job? Two years before his unelected accession to Bertie's throne, I wrote a piece in the medical press gently probing his health and speculating on whether it might stand-up to the rigour of the most important office in the land. The article ended up in the national press and dare I say, did not find much favour in his Fianna Fáil party. We should be grown-up enough to have a debate on this and with such a gloomy future ahead of us, it's a matter of no small importance. I'd be more than happy to examine our emperor in his underpants. Nothing we haven't seen before.

INTOLERANCE
May 2007

I had occasion to visit a cancer patient in hospital recently. He wasn't in his bed on the oncology ward. Instead I found him standing in the rain outside the front door of the hospital, with a raincoat over his pyjamas. He had his cigarettes with him for company. Beside him blared a loudspeaker straight out of big brother house. Every few seconds it bellowed out a message about the institution being 'HEALTH PROMOTING HOSPITAL' with 'NO-SMOKING POLICIES'.

As we chatted about the unfairness of life and the inevitability of death for us all, an ultra-diligent security man turned up. "It's illegal to smoke here" (meaning outside) he said and ushered both of us further out into the campus. "There's a shed around the corner - you can have your fag there". Soon we were in a freezing shack, not unlike the school bicycle shed where my first furtive drag of tobacco smoke took place over 30 years ago. The wind howled through the trellis fence - we were open to the elements on all four sides. My clinical eye roved and within minutes I had spotted a young man with advanced AIDS, a lady with severe burns and a hunched little old man who couldn't have been a day under 90. All were in their pyjamas and looked thoroughly miserable. So much for a health promoting hospital, I muttered. My friend wondered if the same zero-tolerance attitude to smokers might be better be applied to superbugs. It was also the same health promoting hospital that once hired debt collectors to hound a very sick patient of mine. She owed a couple of pounds and because she was unable to work with a serious heart condition, she didn't have the resources to pay the bill. The bad debtors list wasn't the only register she was on at the hospital. She was also on their waiting list for open heart surgery. If memory serves me correctly she was warned by letter that her debt could become a serious source of embarrassment as the person coming to her door to collect the money could possibly be a neighbour and be known to her. I still get angry today thinking about it. And all from a health promoting hospital.

There is a growing intolerance, coldness and impersonal feeling about our healthcare system. It was present in isolated pockets when I trained, but has become all pervasive after the move into warehouse medicine. The small local hospitals where staff and patients knew and tolerated each other have gone. Now we have institutions where the staff hardly even know each other, let alone their charges. Little surprise that in such environments, caring ceases and common courtesies to fellow human beings go out the door into the rain. There is an unspoken but understood dogma behind the doctrine of health promotion that patients are to blame for most, if not all of their ailments. I once read a piece of propaganda from an eminent heart specialist, one of the moral doctrine wing of the profession, alleging that virtually all stroke patients he dealt with were personally to blame for their own condition. Regrettably such arrogance is a growing feature of modern medicine.

I was fortunate enough to study for a short time at Trinity College under a very ardent and well-informed critic of health fascism. Professor Petr Skrabanek passed away 13 years ago this month but his legacy lives on in the minds of students he tutored. Petr correctly predicted that the doctrine of lifestylism would readily fill the vacuum left by religion. He said that the middle classes in particular would eagerly embrace healthism as a path to surrogate salvation, erroneously believing that 'the righteous would be saved and the wicked shall die'. Skrabanek foresaw a day when the medical profession would abandon the sick and dying in favour of a new role - expert counsellors to the healthy and arbiters of 'normality' in society. He suggested that politicians would eagerly join in, employing the same facile rhetoric of health promoters to buy votes at zero cost. The late professor would have afforded a wry smile at our recent election when political leaders tried to outdo each other with promises to find a cure for diseases they couldn't even pronounce. Fianna Fáil and Fine Gael promised free annual check-ups for everyone, conveniently forgetting that the health service they preside over cannot cope with the diseases already identified. One can only imagine how many more hundreds of thousands would be churned into the hospital service if the population was screened for everything. You would do well to watch carefully for signs that your doctors and politicians are worshipping at the church of health promotion. It's a slippery slope from well-intentioned advice to a society high on its own intolerance. Iranian television recently showed footage of captured British navy hostages they had arrested in disputed waters. Patricia Hewitt, the UK's health secretary was incandescent with rage. What she found deplorable, was not that her citizens were being held against their will, but that the only female hostage was shown smoking on television. 'This sends completely the wrong message to our young people' she whined.

See what I mean.

SAINTS AND MIRACLES
November 2006

There are some things I simply don't believe in. Fairies at the bottom of the garden, health-enhancing yoghurts and medical miracles, to name but three. This longstanding scepticism about miraculous cures is unlikely to fast-track me to sainthood when I return to the earthworms, but I can live with that. The history of saintliness is an interesting one. Some recent study on this matter tells me that it used to be a more democratic process than it is today. In the early Christian churches, canonisation and martyrdom tended to be 'of the people' - the cult of sainthood was everywhere but it was local. Sometimes local bishops stepped in with a bit of regulation or fund-raising, but by and large, canonisation took place without too much bureaucratic input from the hierarchy.

This all changed in the last millennium when popes began to take an interest in the cloudy business of what constitutes a saint. Four hundred years ago, Pope Urban VIII put things on a formal footing by forbidding the public worship of any person not yet beatified or canonised by Rome. Urban was a wily character, often described as the most astute politician ever to fill soft papal slippers. Born into Florentine nobility, his papacy meant boom times for the building industry. As well as developers, he also patronised the arts, renovating a whopping summer residence from himself at Castel Gandolfo. He was also a great man for the issuing of bulls and notices of excommunication. By greatly enriching his own family's wealth in the process, he took the art of papal nepotism to the dizzy heights of the Fianna Fáil tent. Urban's great weakness however, was a distinct lack of ecumenism. By setting himself a mission of eliminating Protestantism from Europe, he dealt the papacy a weak hand and a series of less than successful wars left his office a much more dejected place than when he went in.

The late Pope John Paul II is the newest name to crop up in Vatican saint-making circles. Little surprise perhaps, as he relished the whole business of saints and was easily the most prolific saint-maker in Vatican history. Such is the indecent haste to beatify him, the miracle investigators, also known as the Vatican congregation for the causes of saints, are already on substantial overtime. They have thirty four members, twenty six staff, and a further retinue of a hundred theologians, relators and consultors. Official Vatican rules suggest that five years have to pass before a beatification process can begin. But at the late pope's funeral, rowdies in the crowd began chanting 'Santo Subito!' loosely translated as 'We want sainthood, and we want it now'. To everyone's surprise Pope Benedict XVI, a known stickler for the rules, did not wave a yellow card at them. Instead he announced a waiver of the waiting period

195

because of 'exceptional circumstances'. A life of virtue and heroism is taken for granted when dealing with candidates for sainthood. The difficult bit is the proof that from beyond the grave, they have been personally responsible for two 'medically inexplicable miracles' in response to prayers of the faithful. One miracle is enough for beatification, a second is needed to go marching in with the other saints. And it didn't take long for the JP II mysterious miracle claims to crop up. The Pope's former secretary, Cardinal Dziwisz, now archbishop of Krakow, predicted that there would be no problem finding miracles to advance his cause, the problem would be to select one miracle from the many.

Late last year, the Vatican was alerted to the case of a French nun who was confined to bed with severe parkinson's disease. After praying for his intercession, she was up and about again working on her hospital ward. Now the archbishop of Salerno is promoting a second medical miracle from his own diocese. Monsignor Gerardo Pierro claims that a young man with lung cancer has been completely cured of his condition. The story runs that his wife had prayed to the late pope, who then conveniently appeared to her in a dream reassuring here that her husband would return to full health.

Of course the congregation of the causes of saints has its own team of consulting doctors to look into both cases. But just who are these medics and might they allow their religious persuasion influence their clinical judgment? Could it be that those who are appointed to conduct miracle validation work might just be scions of the very church that appointed them? Consider this. A recent American poll of more than 1,000 church-going doctors (of all religious persuasions) found that three out of every four doctors believed in miracles. Furthermore, more than half of the medics surveyed said they had witnessed cures of their patients that they would regard as miraculous. Would it be too much to ask that doctors who don't believe in miracles might also be appointed to such important jobs. And before sainthoods are conferred, could they not publish their results in scientific or medical journals and share important clinical details with believers, cynics and sceptics alike? Just a thought. With the miracle that is Ryanair, I could be over at St Peter's in a jiffy.

LETHAL INJECTION
June 2009

Two sacred cows are mooing in the fields today and you criticise either at your peril. One is climate change which is, we are told by our green schoolmasters, very much our own fault and no longer a subject for scientific debate. The second untouchable, cherished by our fawning media, is a certain Mr B.H. Obama. Possessed of a tidy and easy pronounceable name on election posters, and a wise scholarly manner. This summer he left his paddock to preach in the land of Islam and smooched his hosts as effectively as a late night Barry White track. By the time Mr O got home to Washington, he had the whole world and their media corps eating from his plate. Now don't get me wrong. I like Barack very much. He reads to his children every night and pens thought-provoking books. I have two of them on the shelf beside me. What worries me about Mr B.H. Obama is that he is in favour of putting his own citizens to death. I know this because many of his erudite speeches are available on YouTube, including the one where he first declared his hand on the death penalty. Using an old Irish expression, he said that US citizens whose crimes were 'beyond the Pale' could expect death sentences under his leadership.

Barack is happy for his army to travel the world chasing extremists who murder American citizens in cold blood, yet appears untroubled that his own country casually sponsors the killing of their own extremist citizens, especially black ones, at home. There have been 31 executions already this year. In the past twelve months, Americans have syringed to death men by the name of Bradley, Murray, Moore, Gardner, Morris, Riley and Kelly. Relatives anyone?

If you watch Barack Obama's speech in support of the death penalty, you may get the impression that his heart is not really in this punishment. Don't forget, he was in vote-attracting mode at the time, and politicians rarely rock boats when they are outnumbered above deck. Currently over 60% of Americans want to retain the death penalty. Their main crime is that they hold themselves up to the rest of the world as a beacon of tolerance, civility and godliness, whilst at home in the dark recesses of their own backyard, they continue a dirty practice that degrades us all.

In a numbers game, the United States is very much little league when it comes to politicians knocking off their own voters. China leads the world in this cruelty. Amnesty International reckons that 2,000 Chinese prisoners were executed last year. Death sentence statistics are a state secret so the figure could be much higher. Some are guilty of nothing more than being born Chinese. Serious questions continue to be raised about the fairness of its trials, torture during interrogation and political interference in the judicial process. When Irish politicians trot off on their next Beijing trade jaunt to the Great Hall of the People, they might keep an eye out for MEUs on the streets outside. MEUs are the mobile execution units, death buses that now carry out most of the death sentences conferred on naughty citizens of the people's republic. There are almost 70 crimes in China that could land you on the back seat of these buses - ranging from violence and murder, to the lesser offences of tax evasion, corruption, bag snatching or involvement in prostitution. These MEUs were launched in 1997. Chinese politicians were quick to heap praise on the execution buses hailing them as 'discrete', 'civilised' and 'convenient' - making them sound like more like sanitary towels than killing wagons. They are certainly less messy than the traditional manner of official Chinese execution which roughly translated as 'Open your mouth wide please as I'm just going to shoot you in the back of your skull and the bullet needs somewhere to exit.'

The whole project of Chinese death on wheels was driven by economic concerns. It was cheaper to have visiting executioners on the road than building and staffing death chambers in every prison. There are now 40 death buses motoring around this vast country. To spare the blushes and anxieties of fellow motorists, the MEUs are unmarked. If any delegates on our next trade mission are reading this, they might keep an eye out for a bus with a staff of four that has no windows in its rear third. Condemned prisoners are strapped to a stretcher in their detention centre and get their final glimpse of sunlight as they are wheeled out like day-trippers to the visiting bus. Electronic arms grab the stretcher from the ground and lift the customer heavenwards into the rear chamber. The door closes and the small team of paramedics switch on the camera equipment that records their dirty work.

Details about what exactly happens once inside these buses are unclear as nobody outside China ever sees the tapes. In the 'civilised' world of death by injection, Obama's USA for example, a triple therapy of drugs is used - sodium pentothal knocks the brain off to sleep, pancuronium bromide paralyses the lungs and potassium chloride delivers a lethal rhythm to the heart. The kindly politicians of Ohio changed the law just this month to allow the warden pinch you in between your first and second injections. This change followed two botched executions where the second drug was given before the first one had worked. Press reports suggest that new law worked very well on June 3rd last when the late Daniel Wilson became the first US prisoner to receive such a pinch. This execution took place just as preacher Obama was wooing Islam.

There are suggestions that executions in China have been conducted with single high doses of Sodium Pentobarbital, the favoured euthanasia method of vets worldwide. I have never witnessed a human execution. But I have observed many times the gentle euthanasia of much loved pets with a single high dose of liquid barbiturate. I can testify to the serenity and dignity of the passing it induces. It is the circumstance and the intention that are so different in China. Our civilised world will eventually outlaw human execution. It may take time in China, but if America follows where Europe has led, there is hope that this degrading practice might end. Now that President Obama has called time on human torture and closed some of his least admired prison facilities, we should remind him that the American death penalty ill serves a nation that many admire from afar. By all means let's have the Kearney grandson over for a shindig and a pint of plain in Moneygall. No better place than the fringes of the Pale for him to announce that the land of the free won't be executing any more Irishmen. Or anyone else for that matter.

BOWEL SCARES

January 2005

Spoilsports at the American Cancer Society at least had the sense to wait until after Christmas before scaring the feathers off us about bowel cancer. The latest wheeze from these anti-neoplastic do-gooders is that those of us who enjoy a decent quantity of meat on our dinner tables are increasing the risk of tumours in the back passage by as much as 40%. To drive their message home and ensure nobody sleeps tonight, they list out the offending fare: bacon, sausages, hamburgers, cheeseburgers, meatloaf, casseroles, minced beef, steaks, roast beef, stew, meat sandwiches, pot pie, liver from all sources, pork chops, roast pork, hot dogs, ham, sausage bologna, salami and deli-meat slices.

It's an interesting list, because the society that represents the country's 14,000 bowel specialists, the American Gastroenterological Association state clearly on their website that 'the exact causes of colorectal cancer are unknown.' So if one medical community knows so little about the cause of disease, why is another so quick to issue warnings that achieve little but confusion, fear and risk-factor fatigue amongst patients.

We doctors are slow to own up to the fact that ascertaining the cause of many diseases is simply beyond us at the present time. As a cover-up, we all too readily resort to a flexible science called statistics to show that at least we are one step above ignorance. I read of one such thoroughly useless study last week in a medical journal. It announced that multiple sclerosis patients are more likely to be born in May and less likely to be born in November. My immediate reaction was that it mightn't be long before we hear that patients who develop tumours in their bottoms are more likely to have been married on a Wednesday.

Much of what passes as earth-shattering medical research these days is absolute piffle. There are now in excess of 300 risk factors for heart disease should you care to listen. If you live in Scotland, don't take a daily siesta, and hate mackerel, you should book your coronary care bed now. The medical community's record on bowel cancer risks has never stood up to scrutiny. When I was passing through lecture halls, we were told that the risk factors were a family history of the disease, a history of inflammatory bowel disease and a low fibre diet. The first two risk factors still ring true, but the fibre theory, beloved of breakfast cereal merchants, was completely turned on its head five years ago when it was conclusively proved that fibre was about as protective against bowel cancer as Speedo togs against a tsunami. But risk-factor doctors never sleep. Fibre may have let them down, but they went about identifying new baddies like fried food, working night shifts, being aged over 50, holding in a big waist, less than 30 minutes exercise a day, high fat dairy products and a family tree that includes ashkenazi Jews from eastern Europe. Now they are chasing our dear butcher out of town as if he had smoked in front of the baby. Eat, drink and sleep well tonight. For tomorrow the alarmists will still be ringing bells

MORE PATIENT BLOOPERS
January 2007

January is upon us and you are probably all in need of happy pills. Alas, all I have to prescribe today is a new collection of medical malapropisms, bloopers which have mainly been sent to me by doctor colleagues in answer to a recent request. A public health medic in the North West sent me a lovely story from twenty years ago when a 'very proper' country lady in her 30s related to the doctor that she once suffered from *honeymoon cirrhosis*. (honeymoon cystitis is a well recognised bladder condition - once prevalent in new Irish brides, less so now). And a gentleman patient, perhaps a student of Roman history told his baffled doctor that he once had a painful excision of *multiple legions* from his skin (lesions). A GP in Galway told me about the elderly lady who came into him having recovered from a major operation. She announced that the hospital had given her at least ten *blood confusions* (transfusions). A lady doctor in Dublin was told by a man that he had *gremlins* inserted into his ears when he was a child (grommets). A female patient told her that she had recently undergone a *skin autopsy* (biopsy) whilst an elderly male patient with back pain bragged about how he had two *slipped dicks*. We assume he meant discs.

And an elderly lady surprised her family doctor one day when she presented with a nasty rash that she said was *fleabitis* (phlebitis). It turned out that she was correct in one way, she had actually been bitten by insects. A junior doctor texted me the other day to tell me about a family who rushed their son to hospital with a severe headache. When questioned in detail, it transpired they were particularly worried as there was a family history of *brain haemorrhoids* (brain haemorrhage). And a specialist in the south east told me of a recent referral letter, written by a doctor, which claimed the patient had *involuntary health insurance* (VHI).

I had letter about a soldier who described his painful wrist as a case of *corporal tunnel syndrome* (carpal tunnel syndrome). An elderly patient with dizzy spells kept referring to his *sinkable episodes* (syncope). A gentleman kept turning up at the cardiology outpatients not unreasonably referring to himself as being a *heart failer*. He had Heart Failure. And a man with polyps in his bowel announced that he was going in for a *clonostomy* (colonoscopy). A lady in her sixties who attended for breast check was feeling the pressure when she said it was three years since her last *manogram*. (mammogram). And a retired casualty consultant wrote a lovely letter to me telling of a now deceased elderly female relative who, as he put it, was a proper malaprop. She was once heard referring in true Hilda Ogden style to the *sycamores of Lebanon* (cedars) and on another occasion remarked that a certain lady's bosom was 'covered with *dynamite*' (diamante) !

An anaesthetist up north told me about a patient who ended up in ICU having abused prescription hypnotics. When he had sufficiently recovered, the patient owned up to taking the odd *marzipan* (temazepam). Another family doctor was chatting to a gentleman whose niece took part in the special olympics. When asked about the nature of her disability he replied that she was subject to *olympic fits* and was now on *anti-olympic medication*. (epilepsy/epileptic). On a similar tack a GP in Mayo told me that he discovered a wonder drug that may change the face of Connemara society. He received a letter from a consultant stating that his patient was going be to started on an *anti-conversant* (anti-convulsant). A colleague sent me an e mail to say he was once confronted by a very healthy lady in his surgery demanding prophylactic treatment for *rabies*. She said that she was alright, but that her sister had the condition, and that all the household had be treated. When she explained that he beloved sister 'was destroyed with the itch' it dawned on the doctor that she had meant to say scabies.

And I heard a nice one recently about a customer who asked a counter-assistant in the chemist for some *euthanasia drops* for her daughter. Fortunately, the pharmacist overheard and realised that she had in fact meant echinacea drops. Last but not least, an old classmate of mine sent a me a list of malapropisms from his dugout in the midlands. One dear lady wrote to him requesting an appointment to have her *marina coyle* inserted (mirena coil - an intra-uterine contraceptive device). Another requested a social welfare cert with *fibromyallergy* on the diagnosis page (fibromyalgia). And a poor elderly lady suffered a fall on her wrist and told him the hospital diagnosed tenderness in her *atomic snuff box* (There is a little hollow area between your thumb and wrist doctors know as the anatomical snuff box it gets tender when you crack your scaphoid bone). And a poor lady who reported that the hospital consultant believed her palpitations only started on *excretion*. I hope she meant exertion.

ASPERGER DOCTOR
April 2010

A gentleman wrote to me the other day asking why it was, that his doctors no longer look at him. He is not particularly ugly and I am assured he doesn't smell like a brown bin you forget to put out in August. Nor is he what doctors rudely term a heart-sink, the sort of patient who makes doctors want to give up medicine and become cloistered sisters in an enclosed nunnery. My correspondent's problem is that all the doctors in the fancy practice he frequents, prefer to stare at their computer screens. They don't eyeball him in conversation and seem to have forgotten to examine him. Now this isn't an idle complaint. It may not top the chart of unprofessional offences kept by the medical council, but it's a perception that has a whiff of truth to it. In the days before computers and practice nurses, there were similar grumbles about

GPs who spent consultations buried in books, notes, prescription pads or secretaries.

In defence of this charge, many doctors now keep your medical records on a computer hard drive or USB stick rather than on the old fashioned brown envelope kardex system. If they seem more anxious to look at their screen than your warts, it might be that they are scanning your medical history for clues as to the origins of your complaint. If however, you notice that they are on PaddyPower.com placing a 20 euro bet on surgeon Neligan to become the next CEO of the HSE, while you are describing the intimate workings of your ano-rectal valve, then you do have grounds to carp.

By rights a standard consultation should begin with a handshake, followed by an acknowledgement that you are still alive and have settled your last bill. This should be followed by a brief how's your father, mother or thyroid gland - delete as appropriate - according to the GP's mood and time management skills. Once your gory details have been dragged up on screen, it's only fair to expect that the doctor should engage you with a modicum of eye contact until the presenting complaint has been dealt with. In my own bygone practice days, I had a routine of neither writing any notes nor averting my gaze until the consultation was over. It didn't make my diagnoses any better. Nor would it help me in court if a senior counsel, wise ten years after an event, wanted to raise pertinent questions about the veracity of my record-keeping. But it did help to keep a flow of chat and personal engagement going. To my untutored mind, that was at the heart of the doctor-patient relationship.

I read a very good book recently. It was called 'Look Me in the Eye' and though it dealt with a certain amount of modern medicine, it had nothing to do with doctors peering at patients through Microsoft windows. The author was John Elder Robinson, a fascinating yet ordinary American who services classic cars and once built guitars for the rock group Kiss. John had a difficult childhood. He related better to grown-ups than he did to his peers. By the age of five he was affected by a 'crushing loneliness'. When another boy said 'Look at my Tonka Truck', John was likely to say 'I want some cookies' or 'I rode a horse at the fair'. When he was nine, he began to understand some social skills that hadn't come to him naturally. When John learned to reply 'That's a neat truck - can I hold it', his world changed and he started to become accepted by other kids. John had symptoms we might now place in the asperger pigeon hole, though it was never picked up in his childhood. His avoidance of eye contact, a classical aspergian trait, made him less likely to pick up on the facial expressions and nuances of others. He read prodigiously and became expert on anything and everything. When John was forty, a friend with some psychology expertise gave him a book on asperger's syndrome and told him that he might be a poster boy for the condition. We are told by revisionist medical historians that Sir Isaac Newton, Hans Christian Anderson, Albert Einstein and our own Eamon de Valera all had the condition. Well maybe, just maybe, your computer geek doctor has it too. Some reckon the highest incidence is found in countries where access to medical school is subjected to genetic and academic control. Your plea to look me in the eye doctor may be slightly more complicated than you think. Show him your Tonka Truck and see what he says.

INDIAN HEAD MASSAGE
June 2005

Like many alternative quackeries, Indian head massage and reflexology are shrouded in clouds of myth, half-truth and exaggeration. Last week I nearly choked on my toast when I read that both 'therapies' had been introduced to a public psychiatric hospital in the south east. The *Irish Medical Times* reported that since 2004, two nurses at St Otteran's hospital have been offering regular sessions to patients.

This is an extraordinary development in a health service supposedly based on current research and devoted to rational science. Allow me begin with some thoughts on reflexology. It's based on a particularly daft notion that each and every organ and part of the human body is miraculously represented on your hands and feet. Despite hundreds of years of careful anatomical study followed by extraordinary recent advances in human body imaging, not a single solitary shred of evidence has ever backed up the primary absurd assertion of the reflexologist. There is clear proof that many parts of the human body are well mapped out in the brain, but the idea that you can assess or even influence a person's health by taking their socks off is bizarre. Your toe bone is connected to your foot bone, and your foot bone is connected to your ankle bone, but the song is about as far as it goes.

Reflexologists train each other to believe that by pressing on specific areas of the hands or feet, these fumblings have therapeutic effects on other parts of the body. Like many vacuous therapies, the jargon of reflexology is tarted up in emperor's clothes. Clients will hear mumbo-jumbo about energy flows, pressure zones, nutrient diversion, toxin elimination and that favoured flatulent cry of the fanatical quack - the 'immune system boost'.

It's to the shame of the medical world that some of the greatest quackeries have been introduced from our own ranks. Reflexology, or zone therapy, was introduced into the United States in 1913 by Dr William Fitzgerald, a young ear, nose and throat specialist. It was his latter day disciples who began the process of exaggerating its benefits claiming that it could 'cure the worst illnesses safely and permanently' and could reverse the ageing process. Practitioners of unscientific therapies pose greatest danger when they venture into the area of diagnosis. Many reflexologists still claim to diagnose abnormalities all over the body simply by feeling the hands and feet. Sadly patients join them in this delusion. Family doctors are used to being asked by confused patients for particular organs to be 'checked out medically' because they have been told of hidden malfunctions by their foot ticklers.

As for Indian head massage, until recently I pleaded ignorance of this area of human endeavour. Some recent swotting tells me that it was first introduced to these islands by a Mr Maeda, an Indian gentleman who was taken aback when all he received on a visit to a London barber was a haircut. Back home he was used to getting a traditional head massage as part of his short back and sides so he set up a training school to introduce the practice to the West. Indian mums were renowned and revered for putting aside time to massage the growing heads of their offspring. Traditional Indian massage involves more than pressuring and caressing the scalp - there is poking at the face, tugging of the ears and stretching of the earlobes too. Practitioners also have madcap motions about the entire human body being mapped out like an atlas on earlobes, as well as hands and feet. Anyone who has had a vigorous shampoo or scalp treatment administered knows there is much to be recommended in a head massage. The more correct term for this is champissage - the source from which our word shampoo derives.

Every quack to his own, but when massages are dressed up and cloaked in delusions of grandeur they deserve to lose custom entirely. Practitioners may well believe it to be a 'subtle chakra-balancing procedure that delivers a powerful energy to rid your system of the energetic debris of everyday life'. But the truth is that human massage is neither a science, a healing art nor an essential treatment to be administered by health staff to the mentally ill. It is simple pleasurable one-to-one contact with another human being. Scorn not its simplicity. But there's no need to adorn it either.

MAGNETIC ATTRACTION
December 2005

Pardon the pun, but I have never been able to see the attraction of using magnets, bangles or copper bracelets to cure anything. For decades Irish pharmacies have been stuffed to the rafters with clinically useless jewellery, despite overwhelming evidence that they are without a solitary clinical merit. Golfers seem to be particularly susceptible to wasting money on them. Not the fittest athletes in the world, they regularly suffer from ligament strains, tendonitis syndromes of muscle overuse, and plain wear and tear of joints as the years advance. Without golfers, the sale of magnet therapies (and hideous jumpers for that matter) would have died out years ago. Nobody shouts about what the magnet and allied copper bracelet market is worth in Ireland today. But I have discerned from reliable non-sticky contacts that about five million euro is spent annually on these dubious remedies. The market peaked a few years ago when copper bracelets were all the rage, but punters have wised up to disappointing success rates and their pulling power appears to be on the wane.

Magnets are nothing new. Charlatans - medically qualified and otherwise - have extolled their potential ever since the more rational scientific discoveries of Isaac Newton and Benjamin Franklin. A champion of their cause was the Viennese physician Dr Franz Mesmer who in 1775 was summoned before a medical commission in Bavaria to show how his 'animal magnetism' cures could be duplicated by science. It was Mesmer's belief that all disease was the result of inadequate supplies of magnetic fluid. The medical establishment at the time was reported to have been jealous of his rising popularity amongst patients and the high fees he was able to command. He failed to convince his colleagues, and the commission concluded that magnetic theories about ill health belonged firmly on the fiction shelf. They considered, probably correctly, that reports of his previous successes were more attributable to showmanship than any clinical skill. His legacy to mankind is not his treatment. From Dr Mesmer comes the verb *mesmerise*. Something he singularly failed to do to his peers.

Magnets have been well studied in the intervening centuries. According to *Quackwatch*, which is dedicated to fighting health fraud, there is no scientific basis to conclude that small, static magnets can relieve pain or influence the course of any disease. They conclude that many of products on pharmacy shelves produce no significant magnetic field either beneath or at the skin's surface.

There is limited evidence that electromagnets - combining magnetism and electricity - may speed up healing in bone fractures. And psychiatrists, including one or two in Ireland, are currently showing interest in a new brain technique known as transcranial magnetic stimulation which claims moderate success in treating serious mood disorders, obsessive conditions and even some forms of parkinson's disease. Other researchers are studying the effects of magnetic pulses on disabled stroke patients.

These potential successes bear absolutely no relation to

household or shop magnets, magnetic patches and other adornments that are hawked as panaceas for everyday aches and pains. They have been shown time and again, to be no more effective than non-magnetic placebos. If you are still convinced that magnets work, I might make a suggestion. Instead of handing over good money to health hucksters, stick the offending body part between the magnets of your kitchen press or wardrobe. The treatment looks a lot less ridiculous in the privacy of your own home and costs nothing.

TASERS
August 2009

In the mid 1970s, a Dublin TD called Noel Lemass put down a parliamentary question for the minister for justice asking if the import of new-fangled Taser electric dart guns would be prohibited. The minister was sympathetic, saying that he didn't see any likelihood or circumstances in which a licence or certificate for such weapons could be granted. Thirty years later, with Michael 'Lugs' McDowell at the helm in the justice ministry, the Taser gun arrived quietly in Ireland. Oireachtas records clearly show that there was no debate and no consultation.

It happened in the wake of some botched siege operations involving the Gardaí, when it was decided that their non-lethal arsenal of pepper spray and bag shot should be beefed up. Sometime after their introduction, McDowell's ministerial successor, Brian Lenihan, told the Dáil that Garda authorities carried out extensive research and consultation with relevant professional bodies, including other law enforcement agencies and medical professionals, before the introduction of taser to Ireland. This 'extensive research and consultation' was news to me. I suspect it was news to most other doctors in the country too.

Tasers, named after the Thomas A. Swift Electric Rifle of an old science fiction novel, were born in the USA in the early 1970s. They act as a sort of stun gun, shooting needle tipped darts from a distance of 20 feet. Each dart contains two tiny electrodes that conduct an electric shock of 50,000 volts through a wire that stays in contact with the gun. The electrodes have to be needle-tipped to penetrate clothing but there are also barbed like fish hooks to prevent recipients from ripping the wire out. The effect is extraordinary. The victim buckles as if hit by a painful bolt of lightning. They have uncontrollable muscle spasms and hit the deck in seconds.

Amnesty International reports almost 250 deaths which they attribute to Taser use. Tasers can induce dangerous cardiac arrhythmias resulting in sudden death. They can impair breathing and have been implicated in spinal fractures due to the heavy and uncontrolled falls they cause. Pre-existing medical conditions and consumption of alcohol, medication or drugs exacerbate the risk of fatalities. If hit in the head, a full epileptic convulsion can result. In March of this year the *Canadian Medical Association Journal* reported on the case of a police officer shot accidentally by a colleague during a chase. He was found unresponsive, incontinent, foaming at the mouth with eyes rolled upward. His body jerked violently for one minute and once awake he was confused and combative. He complained of chest discomfort and a severe headache. For weeks after the incident he had dizziness, back pain, persistent headaches and chest tightness. Seven months later he had symptoms consistent with anxiety and depression.

In the UK, police officers tasered a man 'acting strangely'. Subsequently it was revealed that he was simply a diabetic whose blood sugar had been going low. In Florida, police tasered a wheelchair bound woman ten times. She died and her killing was adjudged to be homicide. In Canada, there were four taser deaths in a two month period in late 2007. One victim was a Polish migrant who spoke no English and died two minutes after being tasered five times for alleged non-compliance and being agitated at Vancouver International Airport. UK police forces have been trialling Taser use for five years now. They have been deployed in over 5,000 incidents and fired in about one third of these. In August of this year, the Home Office trumpeted interesting statistics about their rising use. You are five times more likely to be tasered in Newcastle than you are in London. When asked why this was the case, the Chief Constable for Northumbria, the Newcastle area, said that more of his police were trained to use them. Which is the point really. The more of these things you buy, and the more officers you train to use them, the more indiscriminate their use and the higher potential harm will follow. UK Prime Minister Gordon Brown has just sanctioned the purchase of six thousand new tasers for the UK at a cost of eight million pounds.

There is increasing deployment of these weapons by non-firearms officers worldwide. Studies from the city of Houston in Texas reveal that Tasers have been used hundreds of times when no offence has been committed. In many Western European countries they have been deployed against political protest, such as anti-globalisation gatherings and marches. The weapons can also be used for 'contact tasing' where instead of firing, the gun is simply held to the body of a victim and is used to deliver painful electric shocks to improve 'pain compliance'. The United Nations committee on torture has rightly expressed its concerns about the onward march of Taser into modern society.

As happened with superfluous and under-utilised defibrillators, Tasers are now being marketed towards an American public who now fear life and death in equal measure. A nifty line of pink or leopard print Tasers are being promoted for women. The Taser marketing punchline is 'Who says safety can't be stylish?'

In this neck of the woods, Tasers are unlikely to be appearing in handbags any time soon. But do we really want to see US style stun-gun policing on the main streets of Wicklow, Waterville or Westport? Don't expect to be consulted. For 'operational reasons' we don't know exactly how many Taser guns the Gardaí have at their disposal. What we are told is that their use is strictly limited to the Emergency Response Unit. The last Garda firing range was quietly closed down some years ago because of problems with ricochets. Could the same health and safety legislation not be used to protect the rest of us from Tasers?

ANTIBIOTICS & PROBIOTICS
September 2009

The dreaded return from summer holidays rarely leads doctors to win Nobel medicine prizes. But a sojourn away from his cluttered desk eighty years ago proved a famous exception. Fleming was a forty year old Scottish microbiologist (bug expert) who atoned for unspecified sins against patients by toiling in the laboratory at St Mary's Hospital in London. He would grow all manner of bacteria on small petri dishes and observe how various chemicals or laboratory conditions might affect their growth. Up to his breakthrough with penicillin, Fleming's only renown was for some work he had conducted on the antiseptic quality of human tears. His own, probably. But when he returned from the beach in the August of 1928, he found that one dish which required washing contained a mould (or fungus) that was happily devouring the bacteria colonies it had landed on. These days, hygiene auditors and infection control staff would probably have his lab shut down for unkempt worktops discovered during risk profiling. They might also have put a closure order on the laboratory one floor below Flemings. It was from here, the laboratory of mycologist C.J. LaTouche, that spores from a rare penicillium mould had escaped to infest Fleming's dish.

It was 17 years later, in 1945, when Alexander Fleming received his Nobel prize. His fortune and skill in finding penicillin, was tempered by the fact that he did not really recognise its value. It was during World War II, thanks to the foresight of two Oxford scientists Howard Florey and Ernst Chain, that Fleming's work was rediscovered in dusty research papers and reached a potential unrecognised by the Scot in 1928.

Fleming, Florey and Chain, the three champions of penicillin, travelled to Stockholm for their joint Nobel prize ceremony in December 1945. They were praised for the fact that they had quickly made their work available to the warring populace and had not sought to make personal fortunes. Professor Theorell of the Nobel Institute of Medicine recited a Grimm-type Fairy Tale about a poor student who heard a wailing voice under a tree begging for freedom. On digging he discovered a corked bottle with a little frog in it. The student pulled the cork, and out came a mighty spirit, who thanked the student and gave him a two-sided plaster. With one side he could heal all sores, with the other he could turn iron into silver. The student used both, and became the most famous and richest physician in the world. Professor Theorell turned to his three prize-winners and praised them for using only the healing side of their plaster.

The word antibiotic was not invented by Fleming, Florey or Chain. It was coined by Selman Waksman, a soil scientist who migrated from Ukraine to the United States in 1910 and subsequently went on to discover 15 antibiotics. One was streptomycin which revolutionised the treatment of tuberculosis. Waksman became a Nobel laureate himself in 1952. We hear very little about antibiotics these days. Patients and their physicians rather take them for granted. Over prescription remains rampant, and will continue for as long as lawyers attach parasitic tendrils to healthcare and doctors retain five or ten minute consultations.

A word we hear rather too much of these days is probiotic. Now this is a very different fishy kettle altogether and one which is, in my humble opinion, light years away from Nobel ceremonies. I don't consume probiotics, nor am I impressed by the advertising blather that accompanies them. The money generated by probiotics is way out of all proportion to any scientifically verified value.

They are a marketer's dream. Target she who buys groceries. Pluck at her insecurities - her monthly bloating, her lazy bowels, the behaviour of her hair and the future health of her babies. Dress it up with the language of NATO - boosting defences, meeting challenges, all of us huddled together in the war on bad bacteria. Use some cod latin titles for 'ingredients'. Great fun making up your own - How about Goodybacillus Longus Crappus for those stuck for hours in a digestive transit lounge? Or Naughtibus Journipuss to ease long faces on challenging road trips with children? Finally, invoke a few meaningless scientific endorsements, hire a microscope for making your advertisement, and watch the cash roll in. Britain now spends almost 200 million euro a year on probiotic drinks. That sort of money could fund a cervical cancer vaccine for a whole female generation in Ireland.

We are not even sure where the name probiotic comes from.

It appears to have been coined in the early 1950s as a kind of opposite to antibiotics - something that actively favours the growth of bacteria. Mysteriously, in recent years, the definition has been smudged and stretched to a 'food supplement that beneficially affects the host animal by improving its intestinal microbial balance'. Even more inexplicable is the fact that in farming circles, probiotics are touted as products that actively promote weight gain.

Now I wonder why those adverts aren't shown on prime time television.

DIAGNOSING CHILDREN
June 2011

A debate that we have never really had here, is underway in Britain. They are reconsidering the whole concept of childhood autism. There is concern that the diagnostic goalposts have been set so wide as to hinder the care of those children who are most affected, and display the classical signs. A recent RTE *Prime Time* documentary on carers showed clearly how children with the most severe disabilities are suffering most because of the paucity of community resources.

One father of a severely affected child, a man who helped found the UK's National Autistic Society in 1962, recently wrote to the *Guardian* newspaper suggesting that the whole concept of an autistic spectrum may be having a detrimental effect on children who display classic autism - severe lack of speech, bizarre mannerisms and social unresponsiveness. He went on to suggest that the focus of support groups and health authorities has become too much centred on those at the 'higher functioning' side of the spectrum i.e. those with a diagnosis of asperger syndrome, and that patients who are more severely affected are suffering most from the lack of specialised schools and adult residential units. It does appear here that too much of our own debate (and resource allocation) centres on the role of special needs assistants at school, for what in many cases are mildly affected children. Not enough resources are spent on one-stop diagnosis facilities, early intervention services and ongoing facilities and joined up healthcare for the most severely affected children.

The whole arena of diagnosing children from an ever younger age with vague psychiatric diseases, of ever broadening parameter, needs to be opened up for debate and challenge. As does the classification of their educational strengths and weaknesses into state-endorsed abilities or disabilities. Even the language employed in this field has Orwellian undertones. In the classic novel 1984, Big Brother banned all antonyms and synonyms in favour of the singular adjectives, good, ungood and plusgood. There are some of you reading this who were perhaps a bit clumsy or absent-minded in your schooldays. Today you might attract a modern catch-all diagnosis of dyspraxia. I have heard children who are not particularly gifted at mathematics described as having dyscalculia. Children who fail to keep the beat in music classes have dysmusica. Those who struggle with writing have dysgraphia. And it goes on. And it will continue to go on, until we see the light beyond the pigeonholes, and afford most of our tender loving care to those who need tender loving care the most. All the rest of us will survive.

MEMBER OF A HEALTH BOARD
March 2006

Seven years ago, in a moment of mid-career madness, I put my name forward for election. The health services of Dublin and its satellite counties were being offered a multi-million makeover by government and fifty five swanky leather seats complete with personal microphones were up for grabs on the Eastern Regional Health Authority. Nine seats were warmed exclusively for doctors - with a free laptop computer, a choice of still or sparkling Tipperary water at every meeting, and a guarantee of national and international junkets for a full five year term. I filled in the nomination papers, signed the vote-begging letters and waited for

215

the ballots to roll in. From absolutely nowhere, your weekly scribe topped the poll. One medical newspaper christened me the 'most popular doctor in Dublin' so I dutifully sent the clipping to my mother and waited for the work of reorganising the health services to begin.

Now to begin with, I did think there was something a bit unfair about the make-up of this new authority. For a start there were four and a half doctors for every nurse. This was a complete reversal of life as I knew it and if replicated during my younger days, I might never have got a slow dance at the hospital disco. Worse still, there were four county councillors for every doctor. Now as a medic, I was rather green about political matters and knew very little about the form of what we were politely brought up to call public representatives. I set about researching their role in Irish society and was told that the wise one to consult on such matters was the late satirist, Flann O'Brien. Mr Collopy, a grouchy character in one of his books, *The Hard Life*, had a particular take on them. 'A gang of ignorant, pot-bellied, sacrilegious, money-scooping robbers, very likely runners from the bogs, hop-off-my-thumbs from God-forsaken places like Carlow or Leitrim.'

My time as a member of the authority and a local health board was not happy. Indeed I found the habits of some councillors, city and county, rather hard to stomach. At one early meeting I tucked in beside one such creature and found that he spent the entire two hours of a meeting on acute health matters, collating his expense claims. Indeed he was only half way through when the gong went. There were compensations. I enjoyed getting out and about the countryside on hospital and clinic visits. One day we'd be down in the jockey's hospital in the Curragh, next we'd be out in windswept Portrane surveying a cemetery full of forgotten and nameless patients at St Ita's. But certain things troubled me. Particularly the number of board members who would drive many miles to a particular location, sign the visitors book, and disappear into thin air long before anyone noticed they had arrived. Or those who would arrive after the visit or meeting, seconds in advance of the most wonderful imported finger food buffets you have ever seen. I say imported, because the food served up was often very different to that dished out to patients. At the time I had a weekly column in a medical newspaper and used to comment frequently on the 'spontaneous combustion' of elected councillors. At one stage I was tempted to ask the public health department of the health board to investigate these strange evaporations. But I was always reassured when the self-same councillors would turn up hale and hearty for the beginning or end of the next day trip. My literary musings on the habits of fellow health board members got back to them and I was hauled up, on more than one occasion, in front of the serious procedures & protocol sub-committee for a dressing down. If corporal punishment was allowed, I'd have had six of the best, and not on the hands. What particularly stuck in their collective craw were comments I had made about health boards paying conference expenses for meetings that had nothing whatsoever to do with health. All manner of strange summer schools and winter solstice colleges would invite us to small seaside towns scattered far and wide in four provinces to wine, dine and play 18 holes of golf at the expense of the taxpayer. Seeing as expenses for these trips were already being paid by the county council that had co-opted the member on to the health board in the first place, I could never quite figure out why the health board was offering to pay them too. One county councillor proposed that the board's communications department should scour the nation's newspapers every day for adverse comments by yours truly and have posted them out to all the members for their perusal in advance of each meeting. I was making an impact, but not perhaps the one I imagined.

My clinical records of this interesting life period have yet to be collated and bound, but if some kindly publisher would like to take a chance on '*Secret Diary of a Health Board Member*' and brown envelopes a six figure advance in this direction, it might hop off my thumbs into the printing press. The good news for patients is that all county councillors (and scribbling doctors) were taken off all health boards with the arrival of the Health Service Executive. The bad news is that they are campaigning vigorously to be taken back.

MORE ON HEALTH BOARDS
April 2007

I wrote in the previous chapter about some of my experiences on an Irish health board. But I held some back for today - I didn't tell you about the motorbikes for instance. Within hours of being elected, topping the poll if you don't mind, the couriers were revving up outside my bungalow - at all hours of day and night. I had gone from being a humble GP, a simple backwater ear-syringer, cert-provider and soother of sore throats to one of the most important greasy cogs in the machinations of Irish healthcare. From dawn to dusk, evil knievels in garish helmets would whizz up to my front door dropping off all manner of public interest documents. The sort of thing that would rock the state to its foundations if found out. At 4pm I might get a delivery stating that the day trip for all 55 authority members to Ballysore Health Centre (all 200 square feet of it 20 miles away) the following day was going ahead. Then at 7pm another helmet would arrive telling me that refreshments would not now be served beforehand in Johnny's Bar but had been moved to the nearby five star golf resort hotel and that members who wished to play eighteen holes after the public health nurse had demonstrated her varicose vein bandaging techniques should bring their sand wedges with them. This sort of nonsense continued day in day out. With four or five day-trips organised for almost every week, and more meetings of boards, committees, sub-committees than there were boxes on the expenses forms, it was boom time for fizzy water bottlers, hoteliers, restaurateurs, contract caterers and preferred providers of health board courier services. When I asked about the cost of sending speed bikes on a almost daily basis to 55 members in the East of the country alone, the service ceased overnight. At least they ceased coming to my house. I suspect it continued for the 30 something county councillors who would park their rear ends moon up in a pig shed if a couriered note mentioned lobster thermidor and health board in the same sentence. My GP colleagues were most interested in the courier service for health board glitterati. Because for decades they had asked health boards (to no avail) if they might provide a similar service for urgent blood and urine tests from real patients that needed to go to real laboratories.

Next on the agenda were the free computers for all health board members. And not just top of the range laptops and desktops from preferred health board IT providers. As well as the screens, keyboards and mice there were free printers, modems, telephone cables, home installations, surf time, refundable phone calls and as many hours of free computer training as you liked. Not only that, printers have to be fed so there were free envelopes, business cards and enough personalised stationary to write to every man, woman and giant panda in China. This made matters even worse. Because now the health board was inside your house and 24 hours a day we were treated to hot e mailed news on important matters of state business. What actually happened was that those e mails that did not relate to where you could get free refreshments the following day, were copied press releases from publicity hungry ministers and junior ministers at the department of health.

Vast hoards of money were spent on high-tech corporate headquarters for three separate boards and one overall authority. They all lasted a mere four years. There were major IT developments that allowed corporate communicators to e mail county councillors up-to-the-minute news about virus populations in Chinese fowl, whilst frontline doctors up and down the country would receive illegible photocopies of faxes, by snail mail, three weeks after the news was current. I grew to loathe with a passion the meetings of these boards during my short years 'in office'. Now I would like to state here and now my admiration for the people who have staffed these boards, authorities, executives and whatever they are called by the time you read this. They resemble in many ways patients on long stay psychiatric wards - there are far too many of them and some exhibit distinct signs of institutionalisation. How senior staff sat through so many meetings without being committed themselves I will never know. Are all Irish civil servants immunised with a top secret vaccine against elected representatives and their antics?

Meetings always finished with far less attendees than they began with. Some gougers had it down to a very fine art. They would park the car outside, sign the arrival form and before you could ask whether they wanted a still or fizzy water, they were long back in the townland that elected them. It's not that their contributions were missed, the warblings of politicians that did stay were often party-centred, parochial and only relevant to the press release that the said member would be issuing after the meeting. Health board photographers were omnipresent. Idle groups of members were always happy to be snapped carrying some weighty report they hadn't read, or posing beside some new sign or other that needed to be officially unveiled. The results of these photo-ops would be fed to lazy elements of the local press. Every so often group snaps of men and women wearing gold chains would be slotted into a health board's own fanzine.

I have very clear recollections of early board meetings. On my right sits a county councillor who transcribes expense claims from his diary to the official claim form. On my left is a TD, sorting through an array of gold-embossed invitations to openings, closings, launchings, briefings and assorted photo-callings. Every so often there are winks, tics or nudges and groups of members depart for the men's lavatories. Important transactions of state, like which member of which party would chair the finance committee and claim the appropriate annual stipend would take place, as members wiggled their woggles over the urinals. Prize jobs would be bartered with enemy parties, proposers and seconders arranged, and before flies were hauled up to full mast, the procedures and protocol committee would have a new chairman to decide on the resort for the next foreign trip.

Early meetings were often rudely interrupted by the mobile phones of members. Rather than agree that members should switch them off completely prior to each meeting, it was decided (by protocol sub-committee) that the health board should fully fund any member who wished to upgrade their phone to one with a silent or vibrating mode. Some poor administrative sod, who probably should have been liaising with patients about their hip replacement operations, was given the task of writing a letter to each and every member to see of they might like to avail of this facility. I cannot remember whether this letter arrived by courier. It probably did.

I used to wonder what might happen if the tax-paying public really knew what went on at health board meetings. Not that they would ever find out mind you. Difficult matters were always discussed at private committee session. Board meetings were for rubber stamping and mouthing off. Journalists were thin on the ground - public meetings were usually held when ordinary human beings would be safe at home with their families. After a few short months, I got the distinct impression that to be a successful member of the political classes, it helps to care more about the ego of self than the id of your family.

Then it was all over. There was a brief thank you letter from the same minister who was positively orgasmic about launching us just four years before. It was time for a new logo to adorn grotty health centres on the east of the country. The new logos which the ERHA, east coast, south western and northern area health boards had just paid for were scrapped by ministerial dictate. Members were dispensed with overnight, their sudden demise sweetened by a cosy deal on back-dated expenses. As for staff and patients, it was time for belts to be tightened. Cut-backs were on the way in the form of a staff embargo. Finance minister McCreevy called for prudence in health spending. Exiting members didn't let him down. They awarded themselves a top notch dinner and champagne reception at the five star Four Seasons hotel. A light airy lobby, graciously decorated interiors and an atmosphere of traditional comfort and ease as the hotel brochure goes. Guests of the Nation indeed.

MINISTERS, MOSQUITOES AND MALARIA
July 2006

If our embattled health minister, Miss Harney, hasn't enough on her plate these days, she can add midges, mites and mosquitoes. When a local councillor in the town of Drogheda got bitten this summer and had to rouse a doctor in the middle of the night, Fine Gael's garden bug policy division sprung into action and sent shockwaves through the insect establishment. Mr Gay Mitchell, TD, member of the European parliament and party spokesman on entomology and all things creepy crawly, convulsed our national parliament by throwing down a Dáil question to the health minister. He demanded that she come to the chamber and make an official statement on mosquitoes. More specifically, he asked her to report back to him personally on the level of mosquito bites in Ireland. He also asked if she was satisfied that adequate measures were being taken here to prevent mosquitoes breeding and to prevent them becoming a public health nuisance.

Doubtless the minister didn't have the facts to hand but had to rouse that section of the Health Service Executive which deals with parliamentary questions on the nocturnal feeding habits of all creatures with six legs. When the answer was given in Dáil questions on the fifteenth of June, it was brisk and biting. No, the minister does not record the number of mosquito bites in Ireland. Furthermore the minister for health and children has no function in relation to the matter of the sex life of the Irish mosquito. She advised that persons bitten by mosquitoes should follow normal procedures and visit their local general practitioner if any health problems arise from the aforementioned bite. Deputy Mitchell's response to the minister's slight is not recorded. Perhaps he took the matter up with higher powers in Brussels or set about making plans to bring the flea olympics to Ireland.

Across the water in the queendom of her majesty, rather more serious mosquito matters were discussed this summer. The eminent London School of Hygiene and Tropical Medicine is worried about the rise in malaria cases amongst holidaymakers returning to Britain from high risk countries. They discovered that a growing number of patients are ignoring conventional medicine and taking advice from barmy alternative medicine clinics who offer malaria prevention 'remedies' that don't work. Together with 'Sense about Science', a charitable trust that campaigns for rational science, they surveyed ten homeopathic establishments using an undercover researcher. Each and every one recommended products that contained nothing useful but water. Not one recommended consulting a trained medical doctor as they should have done. The BBC then sent an undercover reporter from its *Newsnight* programme to a number of stores to ask what malaria protection measures she could take on a trip to Malawi in sub-saharan Africa. Instead of being directed back to her GP or travel health clinic, she too was advised to take nonsense homeopathic products. In one well known homeopathic chemist on Oxford Street, she was told by an adviser that the homeopathic compounds would 'make it so your energy doesn't have a malaria shaped hole in it so the malarial mosquitoes won't come along and fill it in'. She was further advised to purchase garlic, oil of citronella and vitamins. At another homeopathic institution in Covent Garden, the reporter was told that she only needed homeopathic compounds to protect her and that she didn't need anything else. Even in a so-called mainstream chemist on The Strand, she was offered a homeopathic consultation 'to ask about malaria' for £58 sterling.

Now let's be serious for a minute. You won't pick up malaria in Ireland from home-grown mosquitoes, even on Kildare Street. Like horseflies and wasps, their nibbles rarely cause more than an itch, though occasionally skin infections and allergic reactions might require medical attention. What is worrying is the reported rise in the number of imported malaria cases here. According to figures from our health protection surveillance centre, the number of cases took a fair jump last year from an annual average of twenty something to forty four with one recorded death. We are now just over half way through this year and the number of cases has reached last year's all time high already. Looking through the figures, it's clear that holidaymakers, business people, missionaries and armed forces personnel who visit countries with an endemic malaria problem need to take precautions. But the groups most at risk are Africans who return to live and work in Ireland having visited their families back home, and new visitors to Ireland from sub-Saharan Africa. I think the health care needs of these people are far more deserving of Dáil questions than home-grown mosquitoes.

SCHIZOPHRENIA
June 2007

Political correctness, or as they say in Naples, *politicamente corretto*, is a drug I don't prescribe. But I do make exceptions. For many years now, support groups dealing with mind diseases have challenged the media to write with more tact and consideration for the real people whose lives are blighted by mental illness. When Dublin's Central Lunatic Asylum was built in Dundrum in 1850, it was the first 'criminal lunatic asylum' in these islands, pre-dating the more famous Broadmoor by a decade. Dundrum was the brainchild of Lord Chancellor Sugden, head of the Irish judiciary, who said that 'the advantage of bringing together all the criminal lunatics is obvious. . .their security could be easily provided for, and strangers could be prohibited from visiting out of curiosity'. Things were more black and white in those days. Keep a few people in, and keep others out.

Psychiatric classification began during the late thirteenth century reign of Edward I. It became necessary to distinguish between various categories of insane people so that their property rights could be ascertained. The idiot patient (taken from the Greek *idiotes* for a private person) held a very different meaning from the lunatic patient (derived from the Latin *luna* for moon). Descriptive words such as defectives, imbeciles and simpletons were used interchangeably over subsequent centuries but lunatic lasted in the phrasebooks of psychiatrists well into the 20th century. I remember well the word lunatic or the shortened version, looney, being frequently used term of mild abuse in the school yard. Perhaps it still is. In recent times, Dundrum changed its name to the Central Mental Hospital, but the nomenclature employed in and around mental illness continues to cause difficulties.

Last month the *Irish Times* ran a story with the headline 'schizophrenic jailed for life'. It concerned a Belfast man who was found guilty of the manslaughter of his mother. I paused to think when I read it, because I cannot ever recall seeing headlines like 'epileptic jailed for life', 'diabetic gets parole', or if you may permit a note of sarcasm, 'man with haemorrhoids gets bail'. People with ongoing mental illness carry heavy enough burdens as it is, and we need to be more sensitive when it comes to reporting the problems and troubles they encounter. Mental health charities frequently write to journalists and editors requesting fair play in the media. A common misdemeanour is to use the term schizophrenic when describing somebody who is 'of two minds'. In fact nothing could be further from the truth. Schizophrenia, known in my grandfather's psychiatry days as dementia praecox, is a condition characterised in its florid state by hallucinations, unusual beliefs and a diminishment of emotional expression. Very few patients with schizophrenia are violent. In fact some of the most interesting, engaging and talented folk you could meet in your lifetime have been labelled with this condition.

I fear we are losing the battle against insensitive reporting, Recently the *Irish Sun* newspaper led with a story about a young man who hurdled over the crush barriers on St Peter's Square as the Pope approached. 'Nut Lunges At Pontiff - You're My Pope Idol' was what the great journalistic minds at News International came up with. And the *Irish Mirror* wasn't much better with its 'Crazed Pilgrim'. How we describe and report mental illness may be a small matter. But it feeds into a bigger one - of the shame, embarrassment and stigma that still surrounds these ordinary everyday matters.

IONA
April 2009

A few weeks ago, the Dublin 'think-tank' known as the Iona Institute, issued a press release. They claimed that if you practice religion, you are likely to be happier. This earnest body of pollsters, pundits and patrons campaign for 'a strong vigorous civil society' with a rather hefty dollop of religion at its core. They draw on 'Catholic thinking' and sponsor research 'from social scientists, lawyers and psychiatrists' to further their aims. I think the Iona Institute is well named. They always strike me as thoroughly isolated, rather cold and far away from real people. The fountain of their newfound wisdom, is a paper by a person who is also a patron of the aforementioned institute. To my knowledge the paper has yet to be published in any peer-reviewed medical or psychiatric journal, but here is a quick summary: Religious people have less sex, consume less drink, take less drugs, endure longer marriages and suffer less madness with a lot less bother from their offspring.

The Institute issued a press release which mentioned a call from senior hierarchy members for mental health practitioners to be more open to the positive contribution that religion can make to wellbeing. Echoes I thought of Dr René Louis Villermé, the ex-army surgeon turned public health expert, who when asked in the 1820 how the health of les misérables could be improved, suggested that impoverished flea-ridden Parisians packed like maggots in their filthy tenements should undergo moral regeneration and religious indoctrination. If the Iona Institute have their utopia, psychiatrists in this thoroughly modern recession might hand out indulgences, decades of the rosary and the best of Roman incense with their prescriptions.

I assume in these informed and more tolerant times that this rose-tinted view of religious practice on mental health now applies to all faiths. Such a position has not always been shared by luminaries of the church. Pope Urban II wasn't too impressed by the lower rates of alcohol and drug abuse amongst his religious contemporaries when he launched his own personal brand of butchery known as the anti-Islamic crusades. Nor was Pope Pius IX too bothered about the effects of bigoted and hateful sentiment on the mental wellbeing of family-centred Jews when he described them as 'dogs that bark in the street'. And Pope Leo III did little for family tolerance and ecumenism when he declared all Anglican ordinations as 'null and void'. In fairness, I won't mention Pope Stephen VI who exhumed the body of a predecessor Pope to make his corpse stand public trial.

If I had a moral agenda, which was not so enamoured with the effect of religion on society, I might cherry-pick those pieces of research that best suit my moral agenda. I could quote from *Fools and Mad* - a *History of the Insane in Ireland* written by the late Dr Joe Robins of the Department of Health. Dr Robins suggested that religious fervour in the 19th century was responsible for some of the 'more extreme instances of abnormal mental behaviour'. He describes an account by one overseas observer of Irish psychiatry who said in 1891 that 'Religion always has a powerful effect on the insane and its effect is most commonly not for good. There was much worry about the harm caused by religious excitement and doctors were often concerned that asylum chaplains might be having a disturbing influences on patients. His book also mentions the disproportionate number of clergymen and other religious that took refuge as patients in the same asylums. Most institutions of the day had chaplains, but notable exceptions were Clonmel, Armagh and Belfast. The governors of the latter asylum were particularly adamant, suggesting that a situation where three or four chaplains each conducted a Sunday service under the same roof was 'calculated to cause no small excitement, even among the sane'.

Or I could pluck more recent cherries - published research papers from less God-fearing frontiers of Canada and the UK. They suggest that psychiatric patients have higher levels of religious beliefs and attitudes than do non-psychiatric comparison groups. One study compared psychotic or depressive inpatients, some of whom had self-harmed, with a cohort who were attending orthopaedic outpatients with broken bones. They found more Godliness amongst the mentally ill, and suggested that those who were more severely ill had the greater intensity of religious belief. Organised religions, no matter what colour flags they wave, are fine by me. I am just wary of them dressing up their dogma in science and feeding it to the masses as a public relations crusade.

HOW DOCTORS THINK
May 2007

Imagine you are out to dinner and order a medium rare steak with béarnaise sauce, sautéed potatoes and fresh runner beans. Twenty minutes later you receive a blackened red snapper marinated in lemon, with boiled spuds and a side order of mashed turnips. Furious at the incompetence, you storm out of the restaurant and call your solicitor. Legal proceedings are instituted, forthwith, as all the best attorneys say. Bit over the top? Most people would agree it is. But if it the error was made in another walk of life, medicine for instance, you'd be thought slightly mad if you didn't sue. I met an English lady some years ago, who told me in no uncertain terms that doctors simply shouldn't make any mistakes and that those who do, should be struck off the register immediately. When I pointed out that there would be none of us left in practice, she wasn't impressed. 'Let that be a lesson to them' was the reply. The lady was not for turning. Or listening. I chose not to argue my case any further.

The truth is that we do make mistakes and lots of them too. Research based on post mortems shows that between ten and fifteen per cent of our diagnoses are incorrect. The same sort of 15% figure was backed up by a further study where actors were used to simulate real diseases. According to Jerome Groopman, a Harvard Professor who has penned a new book called *How Doctors Think*, most medical errors are not a consequence of ignorance, but rather a result of faulty thinking. Faulty thinking that is often inherited at medical schools. The book is aimed primarily at the patient, that's where publishers' returns are greatest, but in truth the group with which the professor's message will resonate most is the medical profession itself. Groopman challenges doctors to bury their arrogance and learn from mistakes. For a profession with a long tradition of burying its errors, and a political system that demonises troops rather than generals, such a policy in Ireland could be rather painful.

So what do we do wrong? *How Doctors Think* examines the common sources of medical error. We tend to stereotype patients. We assume drug addicts will get drug addict diseases and that the ailments of priests and nuns will all be clerical in nature. When Reverend Mother gets intimate warts and Buzz Murphy expresses religious delusions, doctors get confused.

We are also too quick to 'frame' our patients, slotting them neatly into little boxes from which it is difficult to escape. Medics are also guilty of what Groopman calls 'anchoring', which is latching on to ideas and diagnoses early in the consultation, long before the clinical ship reaches port. Apparently we also interrupt our patients once every eighteen seconds. Another sin that regularly visits our profession is what the good professor calls search satisfaction. Namely that when we find one thing wrong, we have a tendency to sit on our backsides and applaud our own genius. The time could be spent more fruitfully contemplating a second, or indeed a third diagnosis. Groopman invites patients to get more involved in their doctor's decisions and suggests three polite interruptions they might use.

What else could it be, doctor?

Is there anything that doesn't fit?

Is it possible I have more than one problem?

Simple questions that will spur a good physician into reflection, and a bad, or tired one, into standing up and opening the door.

If you are not being listened to - shop around. Groopman says doctors are the very first to kick up and leave when their own medical care falls short of expectation. Second opinions should not be the preserve of hypochondriacs The umpteen examples of real life medical errors described by Professor Groopman cast the medical profession in a naked light we are unused to. But his sheer honesty and admission to a host of mistakes himself wins over the reader.

In our defence, the wider world can also be guilty of stereotyping doctors. We often hear the old adage - Doctors Differ, Patients Die. And in the next breath the same person will tell you all doctors are alike. If you can wade through some veritable turds of jargon - attribution errors, availability thinking and diagnosis momentum, Groopman talks an awful lot of sense for an American. I particularly enjoyed how he contrasted the way doctors work, with the work practices of other professions. We tend to be all whizz, jizz thank you Miss, next please. Whilst lawyers and economists tend to devote painstaking attention to fine detail, they do careful research and pore over the facts of each case. Doctors are trained, or at least believe they are trained, to think on their feet whilst walking and talking. Perhaps it is the workload that has converted the art of medicine to a never-ending laundry list. Modern medics tend not to be good philosophers. Professor Groopman has provided us with plenty of fodder for debate. This is a discourse that patients need to join in on. For eighteen seconds at least.

FORZA ITALIA
April 2010

For more years than you could shake a thermometer at, medical regulators have decreed it a mortal sin to bad-mouth the skills of a fellow doctor who is licensed in the same jurisdiction. Plumbers, palm-readers, pawnbrokers and percussionists - they can say what they like about each other, but physicians have such mutual regard for fellow club members, they behave like a breed apart.

As for denigrating colleagues in foreign climes, well that's a different story. Doctors have a long and honourable tradition of asserting national superiority and disparaging the worth of dastardly foreigners. In BC times, when Greek medicine spread across Mediterranean waters, the first reaction of Romans was to say that society was far better off without clinicians. 'Beware of doctors' was the battle cry of notable writer Cato who favoured his own home brew to the potions of interfering Greeks, who he said simply hasten inevitable death. The great Pliny, another noteworthy scribe of the day, insisted that medicine was a 'luxury' import that macho Romans had no need of. To Romans, healthcare provision was an affair kept within the family. Herbs, charms, magic spells and cabbage soup were dispensed by elders. The Greek usurpers were regarded as barbarians.

Now when I was training, around 1980 AD, there were not dissimilar attitudes here towards Italian doctors. A certain cosa nostra of the Irish profession took quite a dim view of their graduates, deeming them far too numerous for the public good. At the time there was huge unemployment in medical ranks in Italy. They had trained far too many students in the healing arts and there was talk of Italian doctors driving taxis in the evenings to make ends meet. A small number found their way to Ireland, but only supernumerary (unpaid) hospital work was available. I met one or two on my travels and found them to have extremely pleasant bedside manners. However the smug view was that Italian medical schools, had allowed too many not so clever boys and girls into the dissecting rooms.

Some months ago I was speaking to a man who told me a story about his ageing Irish-Italian mother who took very ill in Dublin, where she had been living for donkeys years. She had diabetes and a few other complications, and the family's reaction was to whisk her straight back to Italy for treatment. When I pressed for the reason, I was told in no uncertain terms that the family wouldn't let a dog be treated in an Irish hospital.

Fascinated by this turn of events, I unearthed some scribbled research that I conducted on the Italian health service during a Tuscan holiday a decade ago. I'll bring you my observations today.

There are some very subtle differences between their system and ours. For a start, the Italians actually have a system, a single one, there is no Irish-style apartheid between public and private. In the late 1970s Italy moved from a mandatory health insurance model to the SSN, its own version of Britain's NHS. The Servizio Sanitario Nazionale pays the bills, ranking healthcare as worth over 9% of its GDP per year. Everyone, with the possible exceptions of Senor Berlusconi and Pope Benedict XVI who both recently bone suffered fractures, occupies the same rung of the ladder. Family doctors act as the gatekeepers to the rest of the health service. In return for this honour, they must work at least five days week and not keep more than 1,500 adult patients on their books. Children stay out of their clutches, registering instead with specialist paediatricians who themselves are strictly limited to 1,000 patients each. It's interesting that Ireland has never once considered a quota system for its doctors. Perhaps it's too foreign a concept, of more benefit to patients than clinical bank accounts.

There's a mix of mainly public and a few private facilities, but all feed from the same trough by contracting themselves to the local office of the SSN. They pay nurses about twenty grand a year, and family doctors get double that - about the same salary as nurses get in Ireland. Top job in Italy by the way is pilot - treble the salary of a nurse, double that of an academic. The ministry for health takes an active role in monitoring and planning health services, quite distinct from here where they issue pamphlets about cancer-fighting vegetables, pretend to ward off imaginary disasters and respond to the parochial scribbles of TDs.

The family, treated like a super bug in the Irish system and relegated to nuisance by ONE VISITOR ONLY signs, still has a proud contribution to make in Italian healthcare. In many of their hospitals, families are expected to share duties. especially when it comes to the personal hygiene, clothing and feeding of their loved ones. Some observers say that this has more to do with cutting nurse quotas, however the practice long pre-dates trade unionism, and perhaps more fairly reflects the respect and duty Italians still retain for senior, junior and afflicted family members.

Life expectancy in Italy is a phenomenal eighty two for ladies. Men's graves are dug just two years before that, well ahead of European averages. Italy has long ranked number two in healthcare league tables at the World Health Organisation. Just this month it was rated Number 1 by an article in The Lancet for its care of mothers in pregnancy. In Italy, just 4 mamas die in every million childbirths, two less than Irish mammies. In Britain the number is 8, in France it's higher again at 10 whilst in the United States an astonishing 17 mothers die in every million confinements.

So what do the Italians think of their good fortune and high performing health system? Well true to form, they can be a contrary lot. Survey after survey confirms them as the grumblers of Europe, the most dissatisfied patients of them all. Must be the heat.

THALIDOMIDE
March 2010

The other evening I dug out my extensive library of books dealing with the history of Irish medicine. I wanted to see how the thalidomide scandal of the early 1960s was remembered. It wasn't. I trawled through volume after volume, yet the story of how dozens of children were horribly maimed by indiscriminate use of a 'safe and effective medicine' didn't even merit a footnote. Doctors aren't the only breed who can bury their mistakes. Historians do it too. There was one notable exception. The autobiography of Dublin doctor and one time health minister, Dr John O'Connell, devotes an entire chapter to thalidomide, and the indelible stain it left on medicine. His book, published in 1989, begins with a chilling description of how the tranquilliser was promoted as a panacea and dispensed without the need for a prescription. He depicts the public confusion that arose when serious side effects were uncovered, caused by the fact that the drug had a dozen different names around the world. He details the deaths of newborn babies and the dreadful deformities in those children that lived - missing arms, missing legs, fingers growing directly from shoulders, missing ears, blindness and so on. He goes into painful detail about a repulsive 'points system' that was used to score these children for their compensation claims years later.

Dr O'Connell states categorically that he was able to purchase the drug in an Irish chemist three years after it was supposedly withdrawn. He says that the Department of Health was 'criminally negligent' for failing to have the drug taken from shelves and for failing to alert the public to the dangers. He describes the cold attitude of health minister Erskine Childers in the 1970s when he refused the young TD's request to go to Germany to see the manufacturers on behalf of Irish thalidomiders. In the event, Dr O'Connell went to Germany himself. He was shown documents there that reinforced his belief that 'our Department of Health had been more sinning than sinned against'. In fact he went further, stating that the department did a cover-up job on realising its own criminal negligence. It leaves me wondering how Dr O'Connell was received when, in the latter part of his career, he ascended to the top office in Hawkins House. Did he ever ask to see the files on thalidomide that all governments since the 1960s refused to allow us see?

The number of babies affected by thalidomide deformities was relatively small, but what happened to them and to their families taught doctors, regulators and medical industries a very valuable lesson in the importance of clinical trials and the dire potential consequences of medication use in pregnancy. I have a copy of the British Encyclopaedia of Medical Practice Pharmacopeia from 1962 - the year thalidomide was supposedly withdrawn. This is the drug reference book all doctors in this country would have used at the time. There are 1,800 products listed, and distaval, a trade name for thalidomide, gets a whole half page which I can summarise here:

Relatively long acting sedative and hypnotic. Absence of excitation and narcotic effect. Effective in stress situations. Safe and effective in the old and young. Especially useful in excitability, lack of concentration, nervous conditioned pain, psychosomatic disorders, premenstrual and menopausal syndromes, spastic colitis, valuable hypnotic for sleeplessness. Dosage 25 milligrams three times a day for sedation. Lower doses for children yet higher doses for hyperkinetic (overactive) children. Dosage 50 milligrams for hypnosis at home. 200 milligrams for hypnosis in Hospitals. Side Effects uncommon. Occasional mild dizziness, nausea or rash. rarely peripheral neuritis (nerve inflammation in limbs) in long term use which disappears on withdrawal. Mild constipation which is easily controlled. Even when taken in gross overdose there have been no reports of organic damage or other serious problems.

It is chilling to read the entry today. As many as 20,000 children worldwide had to live or die with its consequences. The number of Irish thalidomide survivors is now very small indeed, just over thirty are still alive. They are an extraordinary group of people who have proved what can be achieved in the face of lifelong crippling adversity. Thalidomide patients have been treated grudgingly and with meanness of spirit by the state since their tragedy first surfaced in the winter of 1961. The written records of many oireachtas debates bear ample witness to this fact. I have knowledge from my own practice days of the extraordinary sacrifices many parents of thalidomide children made to provide security and a future for their sons and daughters. The settlement they finally accepted in the mid 1970s proved to be wholly inadequate and did not take into account that so many of these brave children would survive into middle age.

Recently, governments in other jurisdictions have been living up to their responsibilities. A fulsome apology was given earlier this year in the UK. In Northern Ireland a sum of just over £1 million has been set aside for the welfare of their eighteen survivors. Thalidomide survivors in Ireland still wait. To date they have been successfully fobbed off by government. Like so many health casualties in this state, they must go public and allow the glare of television lights into their homes to bear witness to their daily plight. And as I write, our great men of state in government have just pledged four million euro. But not for thalidomide survivors. That's four million euro going to an ocean race for millionaires. Coming to Galway in 2012.

THE NOBEL PRIZE FOR MEDICINE

October 2005

Another year passes, and once again your scribe has been overlooked for the Nobel prize in medicine. This year those pesky Swedes have awarded 10 million kronor to an Australian bug doctor called Barry Marshall. His accomplishment is straight out of *'I'm so desperate to be a celebrity, get me out of here.'* To prove that bacteria cause ulcers, Barry swallowed a beaker full of another man's stomach contents. Doubtless half of the award has already been spent on outback barbies, bling for Sheila and party packs of Fosters. Now don't get me wrong. It's not that I begrudge this year's choice. In fact two Australians were jointly awarded the prize. The other was a pathologist called Dr Robin Warren who discovered tiny curvy bacteria in the stomachs of patients back in 1981. When he met young Barry Marshall, a plan was hatched for the latter to drink a mug full of another man's bugs. It didn't give Barry an ulcer, but he did suffer from what we medical experts term an acute gastritis. For readers, this means a sore tummy, plenty of vomiting and bad breath that former colleagues described as 'putrid'. Barry enlisted a third specialist to put a peg on his nose and ram a camera scope down his gullet. What they found has been described as the last great discovery of modern medicine. Get rid of the bugs and you get rid of the ulcer. Within 24 hours of commencing antibiotic treatment, Barry's symptoms had disappeared.

The stomach-churning work of Barry Marshall and Robin Warren consigned millions of pages of clinical research, dodgy thinking and professional dogma to the dustbin. In fact it took nearly a decade before the medical establishment believed them. I was a semi-professional snooker player attending a Dublin medical school whilst this research was going on. This was a bleak time to be a student. Barry Desmond took away our medical cards and Charles Haughey closed half the city's hospitals. As if this wasn't bad enough, the medical authorities were warning us that AIDS was a high risk if you were a homosexual, a heroin user or a Haitian.

At the time, peptic ulcer diseases were three a penny in our training hospitals. Hardly a night went by without admissions for a *bleedin' ulster.* If a less well off patient arrived in with a burst ulcer, we were told it was because he had a poor diet, was drinking to excess and was horror of horrors, smoking cigarettes. If a professional man like a politician or barrister arrived in waving all manner of VHI plans, we were told that his ulcer was directly caused by stress - caused of course by an abominable workload, ruthless ambition and headstrong personality.

In awarding this year's prize to Australia's finest medics, the Nobel assembly paid glowing tribute to their pioneering work. "Peptic ulcer disease is no longer a chronic frequently disabling condition, but a disease that can be cured by short regimen of antibiotics and acid-secretion inhibitors" read the citation. As is usual in medical circles, nobody hung around to answer questions about how so many doctors had it so wrong for so long. Why were some patients told that their condition was a result of a life-long struggle against dominant parents? Why were others told that they had returned to an infantile state of wishing to be fed? Why were some ulcers blamed on 'striving, dominant and obsessional' mothers and 'steady, unassertive and passive' fathers? Why was Dublin's ulcer problem put down to a rise in Chinese take-aways and Indian curry houses? Answers to those and other questions were left blowing in the wind.

What distinguishes real medicine from the quackery of alternative health is that the former usually has the guts to learn from mistakes. It builds on solid scientific foundations, dumps on its past and moves on. The lesson from this year's Nobel medicine winners is that we should perhaps admit ignorance more often than we are trained to. It's more scientific than making it up as we go along.

STEROLS
February 2006

This new fad of supermarkets pretending to be pharmacies is relentless. There are now two aisles full of lifesaving lard at my local grocery store, stuff that I wouldn't touch with a barge pole. All this cod science about healthy heart spreads for your toast and dairy peptides to keep blood pressure down. Not to mention fortified milk to keep you alive as long as Moses and unintelligible babble about healthy bowels on yoghurt. They have even moved the campaign out onto the streets. Bus stops and billboards now challenge commuters to lower their risk of heart attacks by forking out cash on over-priced tubs of oily water, mumbo jumbo yoghurt and sugary milks masquerading as medicine. Any doctor worth her pinch of salt will tell you that this new-fangled empire of nutraceuticals has virtually no clothes in its wardrobe.

Hippocrates, the so-called founder of modern medicine, is gleefully quoted by promoters of comestibles for his famous one-liner '*Let food be your medicine*'. You are less likely to read on your tub of margarine that he was also the doctor who first accused patients of lying. Did he not say:

"*Keep watch on the faults of patients, which often make them lie about the taking of things prescribed. For through not taking disagreeable drinks, purgative or other, they sometimes die. What they have done never results in a confession, but the blame is thrown upon the physician.*"

And there is another less well known quotation from Hippocrates designed to keep men healthy, wealthy and wise. '*In winter men should have sexual intercourse more frequently . . . and for older men more than for the younger.*' This kind of puts Hippocrates in context. He was full of well meaning advice. Were he to offer it today, he might be locked up.

I take exception to challenges thrown out like confetti by the food industry to increase sales of profitable lines. If they really believe in their own hype, why don't they conduct their research at their own expense as reputable healthcare companies do. If they want a sample of the population to drop a jean size in three weeks, let them provide free bowls of sugary carbohydrates on the doorstep each morning. If they want us to join some well paid celebrity or other in a challenge to reduce levels of bad cholesterol, let them conduct properly randomised trials. All they need is a couple of thousand volunteers, half of whom are given a placebo and half the real thing, and reputable independent scientists to supervise the study.

Sterols are a problem too. I'm not disputing the fact that some of these 'sterol' based products can lower cholesterol. But what you may not have realised is that 'sterols' are from the steroid family, and are only a 'chole' short of being cholesterols. They have a very similar chemical structure. What is being offered to the punter is a tub, pot or bottle of oily water which has had bits of plants (often the wood pulp of Christmas pine trees) added to them under industrial conditions. Plant sterols then compete with cholesterol for absorption, the theory being that this causes less cholesterol to be taken in.

Contrary to popular opinion, cholesterol is not all bad. It's essential for the absorption of certain vitamins in a balanced diet, especially vitamins A and E. This is one of the reasons you need good eyesight to read the miniscule print on the packaging of these products advising young children, and women who are breastfeeding or pregnant not to consume these products. It also helps explain why patients with seriously high levels of cholesterol and are on medication for their condition, are also advised (in equally small print) to consult with their doctors before parting with their money on products that are up to ten times dearer than own brand 'ordinary' products.

It's a free country. By all means spend your earnings on expensive challenges. But somewhere, deep in a bottomless bunker of my heart, I suspect the lives of those who hard sell supermarket remedies will end up more enriched than your own.

FLOGGING FLAKES
June 2007

The silly season began in earnest this month with a dawn skirmish between the Irish consumer's association and purveyors of breakfast carbohydrates. The former conducted a survey which showed that morning cereals marketed at children contained massive amounts of sugar and weren't in the least bit 'healthy'. Their work mirrored an almost identical survey conducted by UK counterparts three years ago. Flake Floggers were indignant and their public relations battalions countered quickly. They issued their own press release rejecting the findings as not being based on real life portion sizes (whatever they are) and then quickly changed the subject to blather on about the large numbers of Irish children who are deficient in iron, folic acid and calcium. From a distance, this battle of the breakfast bowl is fascinating. On one side we have the obesity hype brigade forecasting that all the nation's children are going to fill graves that were purchased for their parents. And on the other side we have the save your soul with breakfast troops and mercenaries, whose sole mission is to convince you that everything your life lacks can be sold to you in a giant carton. All you have to do is dunk the stuff in milk and bob's your aunt in a red Baywatch bikini.

I veer towards a neutral view of all this nonsense and defer to the wisdom and maturity of parents. Especially those who can read, think and make choices for themselves. Yes, there are parents who feed sugar lumps lightly coated with cereal to their children for breakfast, lunch and supper. But there are others who leave watery porridge steeping overnight under a tea towel and watch with grim pleasure as their children gag on a bowl of gruel each morning. For the record, our own early day cupboard is stocked with best before five years ago muesli, last year's corn flakes and ample stocks of glow in the dark ready brek that are regularly replenished. For what it's worth, I prefer the traditional breakfast of a lightly salted egg, two slices of wholemeal bread and a fat pair of sausages. To be eaten no earlier than two hours after rising.

I've never really bought into this 'most important meal of the day' patter peddled by sugar cereal merchants. Ham sandwich makers might say the same about lunch if their profits were as high as those of the breakfast industry. Regular meal times are important if you have to carry an insulin supply with you, but for thousands of years, our ancestors ate when they were hungry and when they could. It's only in recent times that we have turned into a race of three meal a day grazers.

A trawl through the archives of the world's biggest breakfast brand, Kellogg's, is fascinating, Their corn flakes were launched in this part of the globe in the early 1920s and the company's job was to persuade a nation hooked on bacon, egg and porridge to try a brand new morning food. They used the oldest technique in the book. Armies of door knockers, mainly casual labourers and boy scouts, traversed the country giving away millions of free samples. Within a decade, they had their prey and so it remains to this day. Ireland and the UK have the highest per-capita cereal consumption in the world. The company is a little less forthcoming about the discovery of the first corn flake. There were two brothers - Mr Will Kellogg sold brooms whilst Dr John Kellogg, eight years the elder, worked as a medic at a religious sanatorium in Battle Creek, Michigan. Working together at the health farm laboratory, they produced the first flaked cereal. For reasons which have never been explained on cereal packets, even those carrying the *Horrible History* series, Dr John Kellogg has been written out of breakfast history. It's William who gets the credits. He seems to have swept the good doctor under the carpet. Why so? Well Dr John Harvey Kellogg was a bit of a fruitcake, a nut amongst berries. Like many of today's health faddists, he enjoyed telling his patients that their diseases were all their own fault, a consequence of moral failure, physical failure, or both. As befits a man who thought he knew everything, Dr Kellogg held strong racist opinions - though in his day and the country of his birth, this didn't mark him out as being particularly unusual. Despite a medical training, Dr Kellogg was no man of science. Rhetoric became his business and he quickly developed a fad for all seasons. His passions, in no particular order, were enemas, the bible, sexual hygiene and cures for masturbation. He once produced a 600 page book which documented 39 suspicious signs that a person was indulging in solitary vice. Clearly a man with time on his hands. You can still buy this title, *Man, the Masterpiece, or Plain Truths Plainly Told about Boyhood, Youth and Manhood* at a hefty price from antiquarian booksellers. A cheaper option might be to watch Sir Anthony Hopkins playing John Harvey Kellogg in the wonderful 1994 film *The Road to Wellness*. Perhaps our favourite cereal maker might give the DVD away free with our Frosties?

NURSING HOMES
May 2007

"Purpose Built Nursing Home. Built in 1996 and extended in 2001. Registered with Health Board and VHI. Premium 24 Hour Nursing Care in a safe, secure and dignified environment. Services include 24 hour GP cover, Occupational Therapy, Chiropody, Physiotherapy, Hairdressing and all Spiritual Needs."

Sounds good? Somewhere you'd be happy to park your slippers as your independence ebbs away? Actually it's Leas Cross Nursing Home - and I'm quoting from a profile sent to me three and a half years ago. We published the profile in the 2004 edition of the Irish Medical Directory. Much has been written about nursing home care in Ireland since the RTE *Prime Time* documentary revealed the truth behind what was one of the most profitable private care facilities in the country.

Leas Cross was not the first scandal involving care of our elders. You might remember back in the mid 1990s, there was uproar at a retirement village in County Wicklow. A particularly nasty dispute arose between the so-called 'care company' and elderly residents. At one stage the relationship was so strained that villagers had their water and electricity supplies cut off by management - an all time low in respect for the elderly in this country. One Sunday, sometime after all the media coverage had died down, I decided to pay a visit to the retirement village. My initial impression was that it was a particularly dark and dismal place, built as most of these retirement villages are, right in the middle of nowhere. When I stopped the engine, an elderly man appeared. He began to run towards my car wielding a walking stick like a truncheon. He was extremely angry. 'Get out' were his first words and the language deteriorated after that. I mumbled something about being a doctor who was keen to see conditions at the village but he was having none of it. I got the distinct impression he thought I was sent there to harass residents. Driving home, I ran through a laundry list of possible diagnoses - acute paranoia, early dementia, migrant psychosis? When my heart rate had settled back to normal rhythm, I concluded that he was simply one elderly resident living out his last years in an atmosphere of fear, siege and resentment.

In recent years we have seen successive ministers for health and finance pay lip service to the care for older people who have lost independence. Much attention has focussed on money. In Ireland of 2007, we put a value on the care of our grannies, granddads, granduncles and grandaunts at about €700 a week. Informed commentators argue that this needs to increase to €1100 immediately to meet minimum care standards, and probably needs to double if we are to provide some degree of privacy, decent medical care and comfort to society's veterans.

Money is important. But of equal importance is exactly where we dump elderly citizens and I use the word dump advisedly. Mushrooming up in fields all around the country, cross-pollinated by politicians, doctors and heavily fertilised by tax incentives to their business friends, are so-called 'green field care centres' catering for numbers far greater than in traditional nursing homes. You can see these places all over the place - up airy mountains and down beside new motorways. Close to heaven, miles from civilisation. Is this really where we want to site Granny's armchair? Away from community, shops, neighbours, relatives, young people, animals, church and memories. A one-stop feeding and sleeping station where 'all spiritual, medical and recreational needs catered for'.

I'm afraid it's simply not good enough.

Over in the Netherlands, the lowlanders on their bicycles have seen the light when it comes to residential care of the elderly. Nursing homes 'without walls' are all the rage. Built in towns, designed by civic planners with attitude, Dutch citizens can now live out their golden years in 'on-street' residential homes - complete with wings of self-contained apartments, their own kitchens, bathrooms, bedrooms, chapels, supermarkets, courtyards, café bars and beer gardens. They shop with staff, prepare their own meals and dry their own dishes. Locals, family members and children are encouraged to visit. Some are deliberately built adjacent to schools. Teenagers are recruited to visit residents in the evenings. All staff, and there are plenty of them, receive specialist training. And each home has a permanent doctor on site.

The model home is called Daelhoeven - a haven for 120 older folks in the town of Soest outside Utrecht. Back home I read that planners in Sligo have refused permission for owners of a nightclub to turn their disco premises into a nursing home. Objections raised include the proximity of an existing public house, potential traffic hazards and the adverse effect a nursing home would have on the residential amenity of the adjoining property.

Back up the mountains it seems for poor old Katie Daly.

A MODERN SURGEON GENERAL
June 2009

Can you trust anyone to give independent and truthful advice on healthcare matters in Ireland? A straightforward question, but one that is not answered easily. We have hundreds of stand-alone health bodies - from government departments to royal colleges, medical schools to councils, boards to trade unions, insurers, executives, professional organisations and voluntary groups. Each and every one has its own agenda and their primary interests tend to be personal to their members. Patient organisations, and we have many of them too, are deliberately kept lean and many by the state, almost to the point of starvation. Family doctors tend to come out tops in patient surveys of trustworthiness and independence, probably because they practice and preach fairly autonomously. It also helps that most patients can change family doctor as easily as they can change socks. Yet, despite all the billions we have poured into our public health service, we have no real independent voice of authority to speak on everyday health matters.

For many years I have advocated that we look at the American office of surgeon-general. It's far from perfect, but for 140 years, he or she has been charged with providing current medical advice on a range of issues to the great unwashed. To date there have been twenty five wearers of the gown, including eight locums. Up to the early 1950s the surgeon general led an independent public health service, but in more recent years the office has been reined in. It has been embroiled in many public controversies, principally on issues where there is a policy conflict with the serving president or the one true church of America.

Professor Joycelyn Elders, an eminent paediatrician, was appointed surgeon general by Bill Clinton in 1993. She hailed from his home state of Arkansas, and had studied her way from nurse's aide to army physiotherapist to a medical qualification in 1960. As Clinton's first surgeon general, she was only the second woman to hold the position, and the very first African American. Her Dad was a sharecropper, who picked weeds from the base of cotton plants. As a child she remembered him carrying her younger brother on a mule to see a doctor late one night. A few hours later the boy returned with his father - prostrate on the same animal. Her brother had a large red tube sticking out of his abdomen. The diagnosis had been a ruptured appendix - his treatment was a simple tube to drain out the poison. Black children were not admitted to hospitals in those days. They weren't even opened up. A staunch supporter of universal healthcare, Elders campaigned against teen pregnancy - advocating better sex education and more widely available contraception for young people. She was also interested in studies that showed how legalising certain drugs could reduce crime.

But in certain hind quarters of her fearful and hamstrung country, Dr Elders became a marked woman. Within 18 months of taking office, she had lost it. Clinton sacked her, supposedly because she advocated teaching about masturbation at school. What actually happened was that she was speaking at an AIDS conference organised by the United Nations. She was asked if masturbation could be promoted as a means to prevent young people from engaging in more risky sexual behaviour and she replied 'perhaps it should'. Apparently she has not spoken a word to the great Arkansas adulterer since.

Dr Richard Carmona served as George W Bush's surgeon general from 2002 until 2006. Raised on Harlem streets in a Puerto Rican family, Carmona worked his way up from paramedic to nurse to qualified surgeon. He detested the strictures placed upon his office by central government, once claiming to a congressional committee that he had to mention George W. at least three times in every page of his speeches. By the time his term had expired, the Bush administration had forbidden him from speaking about stem cell research, sex education, emergency contraception, prisoner health, mental health and climate change. His passion was passive smoking - he blamed it for everything, and the Bush administration felt he was being a bit extreme about Daddy's corporate buddies who grew tobacco on their allotments. Carmona was regularly prevented from attending conferences and his dreadful experience spurred previous office-holders to say that the post had succumbed to extreme partisanship and a certain maliciousness on the part of government.

Of late, the office has been reduced to schoolmasterly whining and finger-wagging about the dangers posed by fat children or teenage drinking. Surgeon generals, like medics anywhere, have their follies, foibles and hobby horses. One went public with his concerns about the dangers of walking with knitting needles. But through the years there have been some very fine advocates. Under JFK, Dr Luther Terry first got Americans interested in the dangers of cigarette smoking. Harry Truman appointed Dr Leonard Scheele who had to steer the country through the dreadful Cutter Incident, when a laboratory produced 120,000 doses of contaminated polio vaccine that maimed and killed many children. Jimmy Carter's surgeon general Dr Julius Richmond is fondly remembered for his neighbourhood health centre plan which brought accessible healthcare to disenfranchised Americans during fiscal cutbacks.

Public representatives of various hues have made calls over the years for an Irish model of a modern Surgeon General. Gay Mitchell MEP, to his credit, is a fan, when he's not planning a Dublin Olympics or fretting about flea-bites. In these times of supposed austerity, it's interesting to note that the annual salary for a US Surgeon General is currently just over $150,000 which converts to a rather neat €110,000 at home. By my reckoning, that's about one quarter of the current take-home pay for the chief executive of our HSE and two and a half times less than the current salary of our minister for health. Peanuts indeed. But I can think of many medical monkeys who would like to fit the bill, and they might do a very fine job too.

ALONE AGAIN WITH GILBERT
April 2010

I think they call it reminiscence therapy. A recent *Arts Lives* television documentary on Gilbert O'Sullivan certainly had me reeling in the years. Transported back to a time when you could write a song about throwing yourself from a tower (Alone Again, Naturally) without incurring the wrath of professional suicide preventers. A forgotten era when you could croon about a lovely child you once baby sat for (Claire), without having to apply for a police clearance certificate.

Every child of the 1970s had more than a passing interest in Gilbert. He wasn't just an Irish pin-up, Gilbert was an international superstar. And unlike today's karaoke goons, he had those twin delights of a real hairy chest and phenomenal song-writing talent. Gilbert O'Sullivan didn't wait for someone to discover him or embarrass himself on talent shows. He picked up a pen and confidently wrote to the best pop guru in the UK, appointing him as his manager. Whenever he appeared on *Top of the Pops* with that gravity-defying hairdo and garish tank tops, we happily educated any passing adults to the fact that Gilbert was one of us. Born, bred and buttered in Waterford city, his family moved to Swindon for work in the 1950s. His father died young, and his mother, who 'ruled with a rod of iron' and wasted nothing, brought up a young family of six on her own. She provided well for her brood. Gilbert the teenager was installed in the garden shed with a second hand under-pitched piano where he taught himself that distinctive style of left hand chopping coupled with right hand melody.

In 1972 Gilbert O'Sullivan was the biggest selling solo artist in the world. And then he vanished. Had we bothered to read papers we might have learned about his legal battle with the pop industry. How he went to the high court for the rights to his music and won the case, giving him a pot of seven million sterling that would otherwise have gone to industry bag men. Needless to say, the string-pullers of the entertainment world didn't invite Gilbert to many gigs after that.

The day after *Arts Lives* aired, Joe Duffy's *Liveline* was fielding calls from across the country with wildly differing accounts of Gilbert's demeanour. There were those who thought he was a right 'pain in the bum' petulant, moody, grumpy, like a big child looking for recognition. But there were others, like me, who were in awe of the man, his intelligence, his passion for hard work, musical genius and doggedness in adversity. A documentary does not make a man, but it can sketch some valuable insights. There was something of the Leopold Bloom about this programme, a pen picture of an under-celebrated mid-life man displaying trophies and vulnerabilities in equal measures. A portrait of a very ordinary chap, a shy husband and a dad, burdened by extraordinary talent, fleeting fame and the everyday limitations and human contradictions that beset one and all.

The minutiae of his everyday life were particularly interesting. His passion for tea cosies and real china tea cups. His hatred of hotel rooms and rented accommodation. His aversion to stage make-up, barber shops and mirrors. His compulsion to clean things, especially taps - not only in his own house, but on visits to the apartment of his daughters. 'Just a quirk' he said, 'a freaky little thing I do.' His predilection for straightening rugs that have gone crooked. ' I am very obsessive-compulsive' said Gilbert at one stage, 'I don't suffer from it. I have it.' He went on to describe his horror at bins have not been emptied. 'Work that one out - very Freudian' he volunteered. There was an element of suspicion which perhaps verged on paranoia at times. He used brother Kevin (his personal assistant) to 'deal with enemies' of whom there were 'plenty' and would often write e mails but use Kevin's name to sign them.

A degree of envy of other artists is also apparent. Those who manage to sell huge volumes of records without the pain of touring come in for sharp rebuke, as if their success is somehow undeserved. Sensitive to criticism, he can dish it out himself. He happily described a strange compulsion to tell fat people that they are fat. Gilbert also had rather old-fashioned ideas on the roles of men and women in marriage. Not to mention a strange take on couples who are married and do not have children. Everything has its place in Gilbert's world and nothing much is thrown out by this self-confessed hoarder. One has the impression of an artist whose reluctance to cede control, even of minor matters, can cause him daily grief. There is an impression of a much-loved man who is slighted easily. He possesses that keen Irish sense of having being overlooked. He admits to anger, but not to bitterness, for that might affect his song-writing. A perfectionist, the documentary followed his dark moods after one forgettable concert where the sound was not right and contrasted this with the transitory elation that follows successful gigs.

Gilbert comes across as a warm, humorous and well-read man, a *Guardian* reader who is not terribly happy about all aspects of the workplace he has chosen for himself. What he has is a thirty year marriage to a delightful Norwegian wife, two grown-up children and two fabulous houses, in Jersey and Nashville. He also has a catalogue of some of the best tunes in pop history. Perhaps even enough money to rescue a Greek bank.

But is he happy? He envies his band members who can hide behind their instruments.

'The ultimate success for me would be to be Number One and for nobody to know it's me.'

Someday there will be a best-selling biography of Gilbert O'Sullivan. The hoarder has enough material to fill many volumes. In the meantime, you can buy his current or old work direct from the artist (I have struggled to find his discs in record stores) and listen to the extraordinary lyrics of a major song-writing talent who feels forgotten in time. And is probably right about that.

GUT HEALTH
June 2010

The ever-changing nomenclature of healthcare must utterly bamboozle patients, as it's a real puzzle to me. No longer are you advised to contact your doctor. The new term to appear from the vapours is health care professional, abbreviated to HCP to confuse grey matter further. This vague and thoroughly useless label might refer to a caring experienced nurse or a studious pharmacist with a keen eye for detail. But equally it could apply to a quack with a three month correspondence course from a college in Wigan or one of these new breed of 'nutritionists' who seem to have a single day's tuition in biology and twenty seven days training on pyramid sales techniques.

Another respected, if fallible discipline of medicine, is also on its way down. The term psychiatry, and the psychiatrists who guard our cerebral neurones, are being quietly phased out of existence as a vague coalition of 'mental health professionals' come into vogue. I assume the professional tag is used in case somebody mixes them up with mental health amateurs. Nobody really knows why these ambiguous changes are happening, least of all the civil servants who are chief architects and perpetrators. There has been no debate. No consultation. The pen-pushing lexicographers of health, who wouldn't know an orthopaedic patient from an embalmed Egyptian mummy, decree that we must change for the sake of change. Challenge is not invited.

Another new-fangled whimsy phrase to catch my glare of late is this nebulous term of 'gut health'. It is a mangle of the very American 'gut' and the popular idea of longevity that governments aspire to for their subjects. I believe it is thoroughly meaningless. Recently a free magazine came my way that focused in its entirety on 'best tips for gut health'.

Opening gambit was 'We need to think about our insides', followed by farcical and quite ludicrous windy comments about how you might 'make your gut happy'. Television and sporting personalities expounded on nutty scientific theories concerning apricot 'super foods', nocturnal self-repair mechanisms that kick in with eight hours sleep and an unchallenged 'fact' that 'our bodies don't absorb nutrients very well'.

The publication was liberally sprinkled with promotions for honey (contains unique plant phenols that support gut health), nutrients (protects health and maintains internal balance) and good bacteria (encourage regularity, natural colon cleansing and stimulation of poor elimination). Interwoven with these scatterbrained distractions were advertisements for reputable cancer clinics and patient support organisations that do good work. There were interviews on unrelated matters with medical doctors and the whole magazine lent a cosy feel of sure it must be alright if some professors are in it. In my day, the only gut health in medicine was gastroenterology - a clinical field that focused on real diseases of the stomach and bowel. It was revolutionised was I was passing through medical school with the introduction of scoping tests that used bendy cameras. Symptoms that warranted checking out were tummy pain, unexplained weight loss, bleeding from either end and a substantive change in a previously regular toilet habit. In the absence of real disease, the gut was quite capable of looking after its own health and happiness, without the intervention of supplements, minerals, plant food or tubs of bugs priced higher per millilitre than the finest champagne.

Quite by accident I tuned into the comedy channel the other evening. Dara Ó Briain, Bray's finest funny-man, was on strutting his stuff. His stand-up routine, in front of a huge audience in middle England, was about how gullible people are, in the face of health fears. He was particularly interested in how populations were being scared s**tless by bacteria wars - those imaginary battles between good and bad. And he pondered the great disaster that might befall mankind should a bottle of dettol be poured into a bottle of yakult. Before finding a real job, Ó Briain had educated himself in the physics department of University College Dublin. He wondered out loud why quackery was allowed to flourish so easily in healthcare, when it would be laughed out of the room in his own discipline. He speculated on how the worlds of physics and astronomy might react if somebody claimed there was no sky above us, and that we are surrounded by a giant blue furry carpet that has been hand-painted by heavenly bodies. The tolerance shown to pseudoscience in medicine is quite extraordinary in this country.

For generations, our national broadcaster and television licence collector has prayed with extraordinary deference at the oratory of alternative healthcare. Quacks of all hues are welcomed to prime time television and encouraged to spew out whatever balderdash comes first to minds. For the most part they are unchallenged and unedited. Recently, to their credit, Prime Time made an interesting programme on the lure of unproven stem cell clinics in Holland. For some reason they have yet to devote investigative talent to the dodgy health content, spurious use of language and dressed up sham science that is peddled during advertising breaks from Donnybrook. Yes, once could complain to the advertising standards authority. But as with so many of our gummy regulators, they are all ears and lip service, and have precious few teeth with which to bite those who purvey false promises.

It's interesting that those in charge of our nation's finances now make chastened noise about listening to dissenting voices in the future. If we are to believe the grapevine of our business pages - contrarians, sceptics and assorted bluebeards may now be corralled into the fold of approved economist sheep and encouraged to kick against the sticks of financial mandarins. But in the health world, we continue to rely on our Dara Ó Briains to poke fun where ridicule is more appropriate. It's a source of disappointment and shame that so few of our leading doctors, or should that be health care professionals, bother their barneys to challenge media spun guff masquerading as scientific fact. It's also a great pity that so many journalists lose control of the discerning part of their brain when faced with the health advances of public relations firms. Our silence makes all of us complicit in the decline of science. And leaves me with a rather bad gut feeling.

DARTS IN THE OLYMPICS
January 2006

With London's Olympics just six years away, and Ireland tendering to provide pre-competition training facilities, we could do worse than join the campaign of the professional darts corporation. These brave men with well-upholstered bellies and war cry of *wun-undred-and-haiti* want their sport included in the Olympic games. I reckon Dublin's pubs could offer an excellent smoke-free environment to the planet's finest exponents of hand-eye coordination.

The battle to elevate darts to the status of a true sport has been underway for some time. It has the political support of Bob Russell, an MP of the Liberal Democrats. Now this is a political party whose hierarchy have been busy of late chasing their own leader out of the pub. More significant perhaps is the official backing of Nuts magazine, which along with world champions Phil 'the Power' Taylor and Andy 'the Viking' Fordham is seeking signatures for a petition to persuade Beijing to accept big boys in 2008.

In a well spent youth, that covered all the lounging bases, I played a mean game of darts, once achieving an elusive nine dart finish - the darts equivalent to Snooker's 147 break. Alas it was in my bedroom, un-witnessed and unheralded, and no, it wasn't a dream. I once had the steady hands of a surgeon. Darts was a big sport for those Saturday night men of the late 1970s who never quite fitted into the skinny white slacks and John Travolta winkle-pickers. The game has had its ups and downs, its heroes and its villains, but it's still a big pastime north of London's equator. I am reliably informed that it's the second most watched attraction on sky television. After the weather ladies.

Yet darts remains unrecognised and unloved by the blazers and ties of sports councils and games federations. What stands between it and its Olympic holy grail is simple middle-class snobbery and a degree of health fascism for good measure. Just the other day the very idea was pooh-poohed by the former director of coaching for British athletics. Tom McNab said that an Olympic sport had to involve a minimum level of physical activity and that darts therefore could not be considered. What he then said better explained his considered position. "Look at the bellies on these guys" he wrote in the *Guardian*, "some of them are more like places than people." So there you have it. That Olympian special dream might be somehow tarnished by seeing rounded or wobbly people compete for real medals.

Of course darts detractors cannot explain why grown men with rifles and other weapons of war are welcomed to the Olympian fields with open arms. There are no fewer than seventeen shooting events in the modern Olympics. That's fifty one medals for bullets but not a prize in sight for the beautiful flight of the dart. Archery is in. They even allow curling, that strange winter pastime where teams of four 'athletes' slide a 40lb stone on an ice rink and help it roll into target circles by fidgeting with sweeping brushes. The International Olympic Committee recognise synchronised dancing in swimming costumes as a sport. They also recognise bridge, chess and boules as sports. But there is an uneasy discrimination against larger-than-life men who play their favourite sports in pubs.

Andy 'the Viking' Fordham is a hirsute British publican and a recent world champion at darts. At one time he had a track and field athletic career and went under the nickname of 'the whippet.' Andy now weighs in at 25 stone. Once he went to his doctor for a check-up. Tests on cholesterol, heart and liver were all normal.

His doctor said "Andy you drink too much, you eat too much, and you smoke too much."

Andy replied that he never smoked in his life.

"Well you are still overweight and you still drink too much" was the reply.

As Fordham said himself "If I went with a sore arm I'd get exactly the same".

OBAMA'S MEDICAL
March 2010

The hottest story in healthcare this month is the medical status of Barack Obama. A few weeks ago he flew to Bethesda in Maryland with his personal physician Dr Jeff Kuhlman, to submit to his very first physical examination as commander-in-chief. Check-up location was the National Naval Medical Centre and whilst Dr Kuhlman (himself a navy captain) led the investigations, reading between the lines, he was probably assisted by various specialists who have dedicated their lives to hearts, bowels, waterworks, eyes and joints. Within hours of a battery of tests being completed, the west wing press office released a 3 page memorandum detailing Mr President's current state of health. It's standard procedure now for all US presidents to make most of their healthcare findings public. I use the word 'most' advisedly, because the release by his doctor of a publicly accessible 'executive health summary' has to be authorised by the boss, and one assumes the most powerful politician in the world has the authority to bury personal details that he does not wish to disclose to his fellow citizens.

Much commentary has focused on Obama's use of nicotine gum, but close study of the report reveals that this is not the only medication being used by the president. I was particularly interested in the entry for treatment of 'jet lag/time zone management' which mentioned that he was on a 'direct physician prescribed program' that allowed occasional medication use. This may refer to some sort of melatonin therapy, but more likely I feel to suggest that Obama takes minor tranquillisers, perhaps short acting benzodiazepines, during his frequent trips abroad. Nothing remiss with this practice per se, it's just interesting to note the way his doctor phrased it in his report.

Obama also uses anti-inflammatories to remedy persisting aches from old basketball injuries. Another medication mentioned is 'malaria chemoprophylaxis', pills that are taken whenever the President flies to swampy parts of the globe. Looking through his travel schedule since taking office, there haven't been too many locations where mosquitoes were the main terror threat. During his first year in office, he spent just twenty odd days abroad, but managed to visit Canada, England, France (twice), Germany (twice), the Czech Republic, Turkey, Iraq, Mexico (twice), Trinidad, Saudi Arabia, Egypt, Russia, Italy, the Vatican, Ghana, Denmark (twice), Japan, Singapore, China, South Korea and Norway.

Perhaps the best chance this country has of getting him to sip a pint of plain is for the midland general hospital - Tullamore branch to tender for his next medical, scheduled for August 2011. Local TDs, especially those on Obama-like salaries, might need to divert some walking around money into fancy equipment. I was fascinated to read that Obama had his entire large bowel screened for cancer using a new high-tech process called CT colonography. This test is slowly being introduced here and looks set to compete with and compliment the traditional colonoscopy, where a flexible tube is inserted deep into areas you don't want to read about over Sunday brunch. Instead, the colon is filled with warm carbon dioxide emissions through a small tube inserted into the rectum. A radiologist will know just how much inflation is required for the best snapshots to be taken, thereby reducing the 'burst gut' risk to one in two thousand. This 15 minute test was used to screen Obama's large intestine. For those interested in where all the air goes, let's just say that a very small amount is absorbed and the rest follows gravity rather than Boyle's law. Though Barack's test was clear, Mrs O would have been well within her rights to banish him from the oval bedroom on his return from Bethesda. Or at least to arrange to have the windows opened.

Most of Obama's medical test and vital sign data is bog-standard for a thin man in middle years who still has his own teeth, hair and faculties. Much ado about little was made of his lipid levels. At one stage in recent medical history, what we considered a normal cholesterol level was coming down faster than bank shares. I think we are now realizing that cholesterol has a rather useful brain and nerve function in human beings, and that we may have been too aggressive in passing death sentences on it, particularly in well people. If you have a family pre-disposition to early coronary disease, a genetic disorder of cholesterol regulation or have had a documented heart attack, then of course your cholesterol could be a factor worth worrying about. But a significant number of doctors still subscribe to that old medical philosophy made famous by the

Beatles. Let it be.

In addition to making remarks about the president's efforts at smoking cessation (lapses are frequently admitted), Dr Kuhlman does suggest moderation in the president's alcohol intake. Now there is absolutely no evidence that Mr Obama does not follow this advice, but were you or I to go for a medical, we might expect a little blood sample to be sent for LFTs (liver function tests), one of which gives a subtle indication of whether you finish a bottle of fermented grapes in one sitting, or put the cork back on for tomorrow. That result, if the test was done (and one would expect it was), is omitted.

So that's it. All over until August of next year when the President turns 50. Sobering to think that by the end of his first term in the White House, Barack Obama will have outlived both his father and his mother. 'Fit for Duty' says Dr Kulhman - and despite the fags, the gum, the sleepers, the drink, the malaria tablets, the myopia, the astigmatism, the presbyopia, the cholesterol, the weak left hip, the crackly left knee and that ominous family history, who are we to argue? Good Day Mr President.

THE PRESIDENT'S PHYSICIAN
September 2005

Doctoring is like any walk of life. There are good jobs, and there are bum steers. Looking after the health of the most important man in the world might sound like one of the better ones. But appearances may deceive. One of the first appointments made by an American President is his personal physician, the man (or woman as was Bill Clinton's choice) who takes over if an assassin's bullet hits target, a pretzel lodges in the Presidential gullet or stabilizers fail on the White House bicycle. I said man, but of course there was one woman who took this job. Dr Connie Mariano, a Filipino American was appointed director of the White House medical unit in 1994, by Bill Clinton.

A previous medic to occupy the White House surgery was Daniel Ruge and sad to report, he passed away on the last day of this summer. Back in 1981, at an age when most doctors are dreaming of tying flies or making bogeys, 63 year old Doc Ruge took a phone call from the oval office. Ronald Reagan wanted him as his presidential physician. Like many male bastion appointments, Ruge was offered the job because of family connections. His medical partner was step-father to Nancy Reagan and he recommended to the first lady that Ruge would be a good man for the job. It just so happened also that Nancy's step-brother had also once worked for Dr Ruge, so the references were glowing. Dr Ruge's speciality was neurosurgery, his special expertise was on the spinal cord end of things, rather than on the brain.

This farmer's son from Nebraska was initially reluctant to accept Reagan's invitation. He told Ronnie that what he really needed was a bright young doctor, somebody who wants to make a name for himself. The President hit the ceiling "That's exactly what we don't want" he screamed. Ruge accepted the honour being offered to him and carted his medical bag up to Washington. Four years later, unlike his political master, Ruge turned down the chance to have a second term at the White House. For a decent, active and well-educated man, the job turned out to be a drudge. For somebody taken in to Presidential confidence, he also showed admirable honesty. He once described his position as vastly overrated, boring, and not in the least bit medically challenging. He spent his days preparing for emergencies that never happened and issued regular bulletins about the rude health his solitary patient was in. Most of his evenings were spent in his White House office dressed up in a tuxedo doing crossword puzzles. He was always looking for other things to occupy his time. The White House directory at the time also listed him as chief usher and curator of White House artifacts.

Ronald Reagan's medical history wasn't too exciting when Ruge took over. I have been reading up on Reagan's early days and imagining how the President's medical notes might have read:

Difficult birth. Healthy childhood. Alcoholic father who smoked 60 a day. Died of heart attack at 60. Mother survived 1918 flu pandemic. Ronnie is 6 foot 1 inch, weighs 190 lbs. Severely myopic all his life (never saw a butterfly until he got contact lenses). Pneumonia 1945, Fractured femur 1949 (fell off horse. Gave up smoking when brother got cancer of larynx. Minimal alcohol intake. Moderate hearing loss (perhaps due to gunshots in Western movies).

Urinary tract infections and stones successfully treated in 1966. Degeneration of tempero-mandibular joint in his jaw 1977. Severe hay fever - gets regular shot. On anti-inflammatory medication for arthritis of his thumb. Occasionally forgetful (toasted the people of Bolivia when in Brazil).

Ruge's skills were called upon early in the Reagan presidency when his patient was shot in the chest by John Hinckley. Ruge decided that the critically wounded President should be treated in the nearest hospital by whatever surgical team was on duty and decided not to call in experts from afar. This quick thinking has been credited with assisting Reagan's good recovery as timing is absolutely crucial when managing internal injuries. Reagan also underwent surgery for an enlarged prostate, and had two operations related to bowel cancer during his term of office. Alzheimer's was not officially mentioned until 1994. And as we know, Reagan slipped away peacefully last year. Pneumonia isn't known as the old man's best friend for nothing.

America makes very meticulous preparations for the health care of its leader. Last year, when George W. Bush was visiting these shores, I had a call from the US Embassy looking for the most up-to-date edition of the *Irish Medical Directory*. They were taking no chances if their man fell ill on these shores. In the wake of the recent flooding catastrophe at New Orleans, it seems they don't plan quite so meticulously for the health of their poorer citizens.

COTTON WOOL CHRISTMAS
December 2006

The paganisation of our cousins across the Irish sea is gathering pace. I read that British Airways has entangled itself in a 'health & safety' mess by trying to ban staff from wearing little brooches with crucifixes on them. The Church of England was so incensed they threatened to sell shares, and send their pilgrims on Ryanair. BA's chief pilot, Willie Walsh. was quickly ordered to put on reverse thrust. Now Rupert Murdoch's satellite broadcast service, Sky Corporation, has changed the name of their annual 'Christmas party' to 'Winter party' in case it gives offence to non-Christians. And the politically correct puritans of the Scottish parliament have asked elected members to send 'neutral alternative' messages to *Christmas Greetings* on their annual cards. Such slogans are now 'potentially offensive'. The Red Cross in the UK has banned staff in their charity shops from adorning their windows with decorations, in case minority groups feel excluded. And not to be outdone, the Royal Mail has decided that this year's Christmas stamps should not have a Christian theme.

Here at home, the party poopers have a slightly different tack. As I write, our GAA brethren across the country are being asked to swallow some very unwelcome advice this Christmas. County board members and club alikadoos up and down the empty terraces of Ireland have been circulated with a manual that was launched at their recent coaching and medical conference in Croke Park. Amongst other things, it advises a complete ban on alcohol in all clubhouses and avoidance of pubs for post-match celebrations. Interestingly, the conference was sponsored by Kelloggs, a company founded by Dr John Harvey Kellogg, a medical doctor who was big into alcohol abstinence and other odd fads which I have written about in other chapters of this book.

Some years ago, health insurers BUPA instituted a 'code of conduct' for staff engaged in putting up Christmas trees in their offices, clinics and nursing homes. The *BUPA Care Services Health & Safety Manual* insisted that a 'risk assessment' must be performed by staff before the erection or removal of any Christmas tree or decoration. If a larger than usual tree was to be put up, they advised that a separate 'manual handling risk assessment' must be carried out and appropriate eye protection and protective gloves must be worn. If it was a tall tree, then staff must carry out a further 'working at height risk assessment and refer to the company's 'policy on heights' for guidance.

This is the sort of nonsense that results from letting nay-saying medics and ludicrous lawyers run our lives. They have also now started to intrude on the sacrosanct world of office parties. A UK legal firm recently found itself with the time to conduct a survey of 5,000 employers and came up with the earth-shattering news that 90% of managing directors have had complaints about employee behaviour at Christmas parties. Warnings have been fired out to firms up and down these islands about the hidden dangers of 'office romances'. One solicitor, shuddering no doubt at the news that one in four affairs begins on top of a photocopying machine, was quoted as saying that instead of an outright ban on love (only because it was unlikely to work), all companies should now institute 'love contracts' with their staff. This would ensure that all relationships would be 'officially declared' to the employer and the small print would include stiff penalties if work performance was to suffer as a result.

Plato the philosopher was there before me. He warned of the dangers of allowing society be dominated by medical vultures and legal eagles. He went so far as to say that it was shameful for any person to need a lawyer at all - proof to everyone, he said, that you cannot manage your own affairs. And as for doctors - he said that their practices should be strictly limited to the treatment of battle wounds and seasonal afflictions. Hear, Hear and Joyeux Noël.

RECESSIONARY MEDICINE
April 2009

With the Gruffalo still in charge at the Taoiseach's department, and Shrek retained as recession expert at the department of finance, these are scary bedtimes for the nation's children. Budget A, the one that had granny and granddad shouting obscenities at government TDs in a Dublin church should have been enough to topple the whole regime. But Gruffalo and Shrek, with their terrible tusks, and terrible claws, and terrible teeth in their terrible jaws, survived in a fit of hair-combing and personal grooming, to present us with Budget B, the one that tried to shut the whole country down.

Yes, things are looking bleak. But we are island folk, and we have the survival instinct of an adaptable people. This week I thought we could look at how you might survive this painful era of Gruffalo government and save a few bob on your health bills. For southern citizens, the financial advantages of a day-trip to

Newry and its hinterland have been well documented. When you get through the worst car queues in the world, your budgetary and travel headaches can easily be sorted out by purchasing a packet of supermarket brand paracetamol for about 25 pence. The same pills in the independent south of the country would set you back at least six times that amount. Securing an address in Northern Ireland is an even more drastic measure, but it is more widely practised than is let on, and can confer very great health benefits. You could try a holiday home address or even a relative's dwelling. A residency in the six orange fields, means that regardless of your resources, you can not only register with a local GP, but can obtain free NHS treatment with minimal prescription charges until the day your hearse is called. In recessionary times, family doctors in the north see an increase in 'dual citizenship' and today are recognising many more southern accents in their surgeries. If things get any worse, their undertakers are more than competitive and would I'm sure be only too delighted to bury you north of the border too.

Shopping around for cheaper private health insurance can also pay dividends. I had supper recently with a friend, who for the first time ever had gone looking for quotations, as one would with car or home insurance. The results were staggering, but what I found most surprising was that when he rang his original health insurer with a much better quote from somebody else, a new policy emerged and they agreed to match the quote exactly. There are also a growing number of younger couples who could, but don't pay private health insurance. Instead they put a sum of money each year into an account for health emergencies and plan only to take up private health insurance when they reach about fifty five. Other parents I know cover themselves, but don't include children on their policy. They argue that there is virtually no distinction between private and public paediatric care in this country. Once you get under the wing of a paediatrician who can be paid for consultation services rendered, there is more than one kernel of sense in this.

Can you shop around general practitioners for best prices?
Of course you can.
'I've only got 40 euro on me, would the doctor see me for that?'

Of course he would.

Fees shot up during the latter years of the Celtic Tiger - particularly when the euro was introduced. When I started practice in 1992, my beginner's fee was struck at thirteen punts, the average consultation fee was about fifteen. Eight years later when we all got millennium candles for our surgery windows it was twenty punts. Another eight years on and fees hovered between fifty and sixty euro. Even allowing for the change of currency, there was some remarkable medical inflation during this period, not all of it justifiable. You should get the lowest prices in those areas where money is tightest. It was after all the more salubrious suburbs that were first to demand €60 plus. It would be an interesting exercise if all healthcare professionals, such as doctors, dentists and various therapists, had to put their basic consultation prices up outside their premises just as petrol retailers do. There mightn't be much competition, but there is some. The chain gangs are getting ready to pounce on Irish general practice (some are here already), and central branding of groups of doctors' surgeries will follow. But if you expect real price competition to result, you could be a long time looking at the waiting room goldfish. My expectation is that in twenty years time, most surgeries in Ireland will be run by insurance companies with the doctors paid a set salary. The prices will still climb, it will be shareholders rather than doctors who profit.

I am always amazed at how few families keep all their healthcare receipts in a box in order to re-claim tax. Less than one in five patients ask for a receipt on a surgery visit. This should increase as the recession bites. Simple things like thinking ahead can save you money. If you are attending with a dose, why not ask for your driving test form to be signed at the same time or request a prescription renewal that mightn't be due for another month or two. If you pay for a full visit and then have to go back for a quickie, you should not in my mind have to pay the full fee again. A reduced or waived fee is more appropriate. 'Thank you so much doctor. You are wonderful. Now do I owe you anything for that?' is a disarming tactic often used by the shrewdest of patients. Few quacks are mean enough to resist. There is a perception out there that practices with lots of support staff have higher costs and therefore charge higher fees. But the corollary might be that the doctor who practices very much on his own is too mean to pay staff, so you mightn't necessarily get a lower bill.

Many years ago, when I had to subsidise casualty officer wages with some GP locum work, I discovered the extraordinary uses to which people try and put their medical cards. One day I was filling in a very long repeat prescription for a lady in her seventies as she called out her tablets from her shopping list. My ears pricked up when she mentioned a well known contraceptive pill. Marvelling at her chutzpah, I thought it prudent to ask how long she had been taking the product. "Oh it's not for me doctor" she replied "that one is for my grand-niece. She doesn't qualify for the card !"

SWINE FLU
July 2009

There's an old joke that pokes a gentle dig at the discredited art of weather forecasting. It goes something like this. 'Tomorrow will be Muggy. This will be followed by Toogy, Weggy, Thurgy and Frigy.'
Influenza prediction isn't much different.

My clever hospital colleagues know a lot about very little whilst ordinary family doctors like myself know very little about a lot. Although undergraduate microbiology was an exam I passed without either cheating or repeating, I claim minimal expertise on the matter of influenza's named after animals, be they bird, swine, or kangaroo. I do know enough however to see that the experts in this field aren't half as expert as they would like us to believe. And that could be an under-estimate.

The *British Medical Journal* recently carried editorial on swine flu. It began with an extraordinary statement claiming that 'the world needs to know how many people are likely to die from the new flu virus'. Says who? Ireland needs to know if signor Trapattoni will get a squad of has-beens and never will-be's to South Africa. We also need to know if our charming low-visibility Taoiseach, half-man half-cowen, will last another bleak winter. But that's the beauty of the unknown. Predictions on emerging medical illnesses have all the scientific rigour of an 'okey-dokey what do you think lads' soccer panel on the television. The gist of the *British Medical Journal* piece was that 'We have to forecast if we are going to plan'. It mentioned nothing about wildly inaccurate predictions of the past or indeed the human cost of these mass panics.

Perhaps we'd all be served better if the words 'professional prediction' were removed from the medical vocabulary and replaced with two smaller ones, like 'wild guess'. The UK's Chief Medical Officer, Sir Liam Donaldson is a great man for the guessing game. Four years ago when all the talk was of birdy flu, the good doctor told a gasping media that a human death toll of 750,000 was 'not impossible'. This time around, he has revised his estimates downwards cheerful predicting that 65,000 people across the channel 'might' die from piggy flu, although then again it could be as low as 11,000. They should really give Dr Liam his own newspaper column, on the racing pages.

To get some sense of proportion, let's charter a flight back to Mexico where this current bout of swine flu fever began. It's now reckoned that the H1N1 influenza strain was already circulating many months before you heard about it from Brian and Sharon on the RTE News. The first reaction on the other side of Mexico's border was of true grit and heroism. Mexico sneezed, America caught a panic. There were calls for border closures, flights in and out of Mexico to be halted, quarantining of gauchos and so on. Until it was pointed out that the flu strain was already in America and that these measures would be a waste of time. Surprise, surprise, there was no subsequent talk of banning flights in and out of the United States.

Poor Mexico, a basket case economy before all of this, virtually shut down. Export bans kicked in. All public gatherings and festivals were banned. Schools closed. Tourism was devastated. Wildly inaccurate data, sweeping predictions and public panic were the order of the day. Later, it emerged that estimates of swine flu deaths had been greatly exaggerated. In a medical first, the death toll began to decline on a daily basis. But the damage was done. The international monetary fund and world bank were asked to make house calls, and they are still negotiating fees out in the cactus garden.

So how many people died in Mexico with swine flu? Well as I write today the death toll has not even reached one hundred and fifty. Worldwide, the swine flu death toll is under a thousand. Compare this with the common-or-garden winter flu that sweeps the world once a year kills 500,000, and doesn't merit a mention in the death columns.

There is a cumulative dangerous effect to hordes of professional scaremongers making wild predictions that are unsubstantiated and usually left unchallenged. The public will not only lose trust, they will lose interest too. UK politicians have already admitted on camera that they would rather over-react and be wrong than under-react and be caught out. I find it rather embarrassing to see doctors embroiled in the hysteria that now accompanies each emerging disease.

Having watched how many governments and their state-sponsored doctors have managed a number of successive scares now, I have come down with a serious dose of not being very impressed. Each time you see a public health doctor on television, whether he is advising you on budgie flu, toxic rashers or the perils of drink, you should remember that above all he is a civil servant. He is a state employee. He is a person whose family relies upon his day job. Whatever he says at a press conference may not be quite the same line he tells medical mates in the pub.

'I don't know' are three words which medical students know well but which doctors have a tendency to forget during the course of a self-important career. It takes a very special kind of 'expert' to possess the wit to use them. I could be wrong about the nature of this swine flu. Like the great outbreak of 1918, there may be a 25 million deaths sting in the tail. Just when we thought the worst was over. But I suspect not. When they write the medical history of the early twenty first century, they will mention hype, overkill and misplaced panic. They may suggest that words like epidemic and pandemic were so over-used, as to become meaningless. And most worrying of all they will conclude that the people were injected with so many vials of misplaced fear, that they stopped listening altogether.

CROOKSLING
November 2011

Noel Browne's opus *Against the Tide* is often held up as the classic testament of twentieth century medical and political in Ireland. But another important work received much less acclaim in its day and I'm not even sure if it is still in print. It's the autobiography of another former health minister, John O'Connell, called *Doctor John - Crusading Doctor and Politician*. First published in 1989, a few years before the author fulfilled his minister for health ambitions, his sharp observations about the medical services in his impoverished early years deserve an airing, particularly as the same two-tier service exists today. When Dr John's older sister Kathleen developed tuberculosis, Mrs O'Connell was told to seek out a famous TB specialist who subsequently admitted her daughter to the Richmond hospital. However, the specialist was under a misapprehension that the family had money. When he found this not to be the case, Kathleen was transferred 'in the dead of night' to the South Dublin Union where nursing care was rudimentary and shame was a predominant emotion underlying all admissions. Dr John's family were not even given the courtesy of being informed of the move. Kathleen was later transferred to Crooksling sanatorium in the foothills above Tallaght and Dr O'Connell described in great detail his family's visit to see her each Sunday. The beds in windowless huts. Pretty patients with flushed cheeks. Progressive loss of weight. Weekly updates on ward arrivals and ward deaths. Incessant rosaries and demands for new novenas. The ominous onset of night sweats. The 'agony for ice' that couldn't be got. And the inevitable death of so many girls in their first flush of youth.

Crooksling, renamed as St Brigid's home, has in recent decades operated as a facility for ladies with dementia.

A farm once worked side by side with the facility and animals, including wild deer, still wander the ample grounds at Brittas. The home has been a great stalwart of pet therapy and dogs pay frequent visits to the eighty or so lady patients still resident. The HSE announced last month that it will close in spring of next year. It will be seventy seven years old and whilst recent reports from

HIQA have been very positive about the staff, the buildings have not kept pace with modern standards. The place is still described as 'draughty' which was all very well in times of TB sanatoria but is not ideal for care of older people. Crooksling certainly had its successes and figures from the 1940s show that about two hundred patients were discharged as 'medically fit' each year, fifty took their own discharge and a dozen would be 'expelled' for unspecified behaviour,

During the war years, national purse strings were held very tightly. Health debates and committee work in Dáil Éireann focused very much on the cost of patient keep rather than on the quality of their care. It's interesting to note that the average cost to the state of keeping a patient in a sanatorium, including Crooksling, was about two pounds and ten shillings, whilst the equivalent cost of keeping a patient in a mental asylum was just over one pound. Seventy years on and our state still obsesses about the 'burden' of maintaining patients in long-term care. Today, the cost of public nursing home care greatly outstrips private nursing home care and slowly, but surely, the number of public beds for older person care is being quietly halved by the State. When that happens, it will be halved again. Hung, drawn and quartered I believe is the medical term.

Postscript: *Crooksling was granted a temporary reprieve from closure in early 2012 and will stay open for at least three more years.*

REAL MEN IGNORE YOGURT
January 2005

Ernest Hemingway wrote about the four things all men must do in their lifetime to prove their manliness. They must plant a tree, father a son, fight a bull and write a novel. The bull market in Dublin is rather depressed these days. Had Hemingway chosen to live amidst the dust of Terenure instead of his beloved Pamplona - I suspect he might have added doing the weekly supermarket shop to his list of masculine chores. I've noticed a steady rise in men manoeuvring trolleys around Dunnes Stores in recent times. The old hunter gatherer instincts are beginning to reassert themselves. Real men are developing new expertise in the strange ways nappies are packaged and priced. Less slavish to brands and better judges of value, we form orderly queues around the four pack value kitchen rolls for €1.50 whilst the ladies stick their nails into the €6 two-pack pussy-cat ultra-soft super-absorbent treble-layered pastel-toned towelettes that would vanish after a single dog-pee.

Men are also less impressionable at the dairy counter - home of intensive care yogurts, defibrillating dessert mousses and health claims cloudier than milk. I'm not sure exactly when popular yogurts first arrived in Ireland - somewhere between the adverts for blue band margarine and boyzone's first appearance on the *Late Late Show*. My first memories of late 20th century yogurts were of cheap and cheerful little pots with silver lids, promising no more than a couple of mandarin segments, or a sugary strawberry if you were lucky. Nowadays yogurts are making so many health claims you'd expect them to be driving ambulances. It's all probiotic this, lactobacillus that and immuno-boost whatever you're having yourself. This is the age of functional foods - everyday groceries that claim to improve health and wellbeing without ever being asked for an ounce of proof. In truth, it's one of the most dysfunctional marketplaces in the world. Writing in the *British Medical Journal* last year, Dr Martijn Katan, a professor of nutrition in Holland stated that some 'functional foods' are no more than quackery. Shoppers can't be expected to assess the veracity of health claims, yet governments, slaves to food industry lobbying, have been notoriously slow to step into the breach. Some countries such as Canada and Australia have begun to regulate but our stooges in the European parliament have been debating these issues for twenty years now, with nothing to show but handsome expense claims. Two years ago the European commission finally published a proposal for regulation, but even optimists believe it may take another twenty years for regulators to grow teeth.

Last year, a rather large nail was driven through the heart of the probiotic industry when one of its oldest claims, namely that lactobacillus can prevent antibiotic-induced thrush, was rubbished by a scientific trial in Australia. So forget about your gut mucus barrier, don't fret about your faecal transit time, ignore your digestive immune response and pay little heed to the balance of your intestinal flora. The male bowel has more important things to worry about. Black stools, bloody diarrhoea, prolonged constipation, tummy pains and weight loss are words your doctors will be glad to hear about. Life support yogurts? No thanks.

MORE RESEARCH NEEDED
June 2009

Many moons ago, I began this dazzling literary career by filling a blank page every month between must-have accessories and alluring scents. I was writing for Dun Laoghaire's finest periodical, *Image* magazine. They needed a health columnist and my style seemed to fit the bill. I reckon the D and R letters before my name swung the gig, but I was a little taken aback that there was no interview, no training, not even a health and safety demonstration before the fee offer was put on the table. For three long years, in the era before electronic mail, I drove out to Crofton Road late at night to put monthly copy in the *Image* letterbox. In return, the editor would pop all the magazine's 'health post' in a large padded envelope and have it regularly delivered to my house. You wouldn't believe the medical baloney that public relations companies send to women's magazines for transcribing. I was always grateful to the power-dressing ladies at *Image* that they had the good sense to leave their resident quack to his own devices. They trusted me to bin any twaddle masquerading as health news and allowed me compose regular medical tripe of my very own.

Health columns the world over peddle absurdities to their readers. Recipes for longevity, half-truths about dietary advances and downright lies about exercise and healthy living pervade this entire sector of popular health reportage. Medical journals are not immune to the disease, but the more reputable ones have rules that lend them a modicum of respectability. First off, the author of any published scientific paper has to declare his or her interests.

If a scientist submits a paper extolling the live-saving benefits of a probiotic yoghurt or makes claims for the sporting benefits of an energy drink, the very first line of the research will make clear whether money from the purveyors of these products have been put at the writer's disposal. No such rules apply in most of the popular media, hence the old adage about not believing what you read, can be particularly apt when it comes to health news.

Secondly, doctors receive a certain amount of training in how to decipher medical fact from health fiction. Before settling down to read a scientific paper they will scan the piece for some clues as to its provenance. Who is writing it? Why are they writing it? Who is paying for the writing of it? What journal is it published in? Who owns this journal? When these questions have been satisfactorily answered, doctors will proceed to dissect the research, examining the way it has been conducted, and collating merits with defects. They are encouraged to respond in the next edition of the journal, pointing out omissions, bias or obvious mistakes. In this orderly way, medical science moves on. There have been many frauds perpetrated in the world of medical reportage. Its strength is that so many of them are found out.

Not so on newsagent shelves. Our current dose of health news nonsense concerns curry. Now I've nothing against it - mine is mild with added fruit if you are doing the cooking. But in this month's big fat lazy media, curry is a 'new super-food' which could help you lose weight, avoid cancer and prevent dementia. One paper says to eat it once a week, another twice a week and a third says you should eat it two or three times a week.

The meaningless phrase 'scientists claim' begins each piece. In fact the scientists involved made no such claims. They were American psychiatrists who had published very preliminary research on animals. They simply said much more work is needed. The curry claims focused on turmeric, a plant of the ginger family, which is boiled up, dried out and ground into a spice. In India it's a kind of poor man's saffron. It has been loved the world over for its vibrant colour. Or at least it was, until the world saw the communal toilet scene in *Slumdog Millionaire*.

Claims have been made for turmeric's medicinal value for generations - it has been suggested as a panacea for cancer, liver disease, arthritis, life-threatening infections and anything else you care to name. The fly in the turmeric ointment is the salient fact that in countries where it is most popular, life expectancy tends to be twenty years lower. Now there are very few health websites worth a toss for scientific advice, but one gem worth saving in your favourites folder if you are prone to health neuroses is Medline Plus at the US National Library of Medicine. Here's what they say about turmeric, and its important ingredient, curcumin.

Blood clot prevention - cannot be recommended, more research needed. Cancer - remains unclear if it has a role. Dementia/ cognitive function - currently not enough evidence to suggest the use of curcumin to improve cognitive performance. HIV - no reliable human studies.

And you can ditto all the above for claims that curry cures arthritis, high cholesterol, irritable bowel and any other condition you care to mention. Whilst I am there, here's what Medline Plus say about probiotics. "There is limited evidence supporting some uses of probiotics. Much more scientific knowledge is needed about them, including about their safety and appropriate use. Effects found from one species or strain of probiotics do not necessarily hold true for others, or even for different preparations of the same species or strain." They also suggest that you seek advice from your doctor before starting on probiotic products. Funny, that's not what it says on the television adverts or on the supermarket packaging.

Try this library yourself with whatever new-fangled poison is being peddled as a panacea for modern life. Fish oils, antioxidants, echinacea, garlic, tea tree oil, vitamin supplements. You will get almost identical results - Not enough evidence. More research is needed. Unless you write a health column.

PROFESSORS
May 2010

The doomsday brigade of the medical press predict a dire summer of discontent for our health service. Inside sources predict shortages of nine hundred junior medics from this July. There are fears that rule changes on jobs for apprentice doctors, coupled with the economic depression. may be used as cover to permanently close casualty units up and down the country. It would be a criminal deed to mention the names on the executioner's list in polite company, but it's not difficult to imagine who will get the chop. Small hospitals of the 'county' variety without the saving grace of the word 'regional' in their title will be amongst the most vulnerable. Hospitals that have not had dedicated casualty or emergency consultants appointed during Bertie's boom years can worry too. And if your local almshouse has been filling vacancies with temporary overseas consultants for the last decade, then you might be advised to secure a car and plenty of petrol for the emergency use of sick relatives.

You will not be told that your services are being cut, chopped, removed or even centralised. Instead you will have your family's care needs 'rationalised'. You may be informed that your current batch of doctors and nurses have become deskilled as they do not have that 'critical mass' of patients to keep them up to speed. Promises will be made about the latest equipment being available at your new 'centre of excellence' (including automatic letter opening machines). You will receive reassurance about the expertise of your new clinicians, the amount of research they do and the number of journal clubs they participate in. And as you penetrate bendy potholed lanes darkened by overhanging trees that haven't been pruned since the famine, and queue at motorway junctions that give spaghetti a bad name, rest assured that your longer journey of healing, in agonizing pain or mortal peril, is 'patient safety driven'.

Your politicians, your bureaucrats, and yes it pains me to say, your doctors too, have decreed that ordinary punters have been spoiled for choice for too long. What they prescribe now is a countrywide dose of far away medicine in a non-smoking warehouse that doubles as a part-time incubator for MRSA. Don't worry. You won't be the only stranger. Even the staff have never heard of one another.

You might think that the medical profession had a hotly contested debate about centralisation of your health services. Not so. Your family doctor and your local hospital consultant had zero input into these decisions. Much of the impetus for these changes emanated from the academic side of the profession and the well-resourced teaching hospitals they inhabit. We hear much from our learned professors about how they can spot problems quicker when they have large volumes to deal with. They regale us with tales of better outcomes - claiming that stroke victims, cancer sufferers, traffic casualties and heart surgery patients all do much better when they travel greater distances to bigger waiting rooms. Our academics have been quick to recommend closure of small hospitals, outpatients and casualty departments. All in the best interest of patients.

But they have been extraordinarily quiet on the rationalization of their own establishments. We now have an extraordinary seven medical schools on this small island, all receiving state funds. That's five too many by international standards. There are three in Dublin and one each in Cork, Galway, Belfast and Limerick. Every now and then, when feeling a bit peripheral, the parish of Waterford clamours for one too. If big is best for patients, why then is big not best for their doctors too? Professors will tell you about the wonderful and rational things they find on a fact-finding missions to New Zealand, but may just fail to mention that the identically populated country has just two medical schools and trains future doctors with a tiny fraction of the number of professors we have here.

Your leading professors are also fairly quiet on the topic of what goes on in private hospitals and whether they too have a 'critical mass' in each discipline to keep their skills up. In fact one wonders how so many of today's professors can do private practice at all. Thirty years ago, a professorship meant that you did not have private rooms but devoted all ancillary time to your students, your research and your family. Today the professor who does not engage in private arrangements with patients is the exception.

Jealousy, rivalry and twin desires for self-propagation and pontification have long been features of medical colleges in Ireland. In the 19th century, such schools were six a penny in Dublin - many hospitals had their own training establishment, usually driven by the reputation of its senior clinician or tutor. Two hundred years ago, Dr John Kirby set one up on Peter Street, and awarded his own certificates to students who wished to train in military and naval medicine. He was wildly popular as a lecturer and in order to train students in the art of removing bullets, he would prop human corpses up against the wall of his anatomy room and discharge his pistol into them. When corpses were in short supply, live animals were sheepishly led into his dissection room. Jealous of his popularity, and fee income, other doctors refused to accept the bona fides of his medical certificates. One charge levelled against the continued running of his school was that his hospital had only one bed! Kirby's school closed in 1832, the same year parliament passed an anatomy act to end the practice of body snatching. But by then Kirby had kissed and made up with his rivals. The real reason his school closed is that his colleagues conspired to award him a professorship of medicine. Nothing much changes, does it?

BLACK LUNG
May 2011

Tony Bennett left his in San Francisco. Hank Williams tried to melt one that was extremely cold. And Billie Ray Cyrus said that if you relate bad news to his achy-breaky one, it might just kill him off completely. No bad thing perhaps for those who have had to listen to him on long car journeys.

For what is merely a pump and actually has a very minimal physiological role in romantic matters, the human heart has had more than its fair share of popular songs written about it. The same cannot be said for its neglected, but equally important chest cavity partners, the lungs. Songs about lungs are a real rarity in popular culture. The British band Radiohead did record a rather abstract tune called *My Iron Lung*, but perhaps the best known ode to the human bellows is *Black Lung*, a bluegrass number composed and performed by American songwriter Hazel Dickens who died last just month.

Hazel was the eighth child of a West Virginian family that were steeped in the mining industry. The coal business and its deleterious effects on workers was never far from her mind and featured in many of her protest songs.

Black lung, black lung, Oh your hand's icy cold
As you reach for my life and you torture my soul
Cold as that water hole, down in that dark cave
Where I spent my life's blood digging my own grave

The medical term for Black Lung is coal worker's pneumoconiosis. In its severe form there is a progressive deterioration in lung function and shortened life expectancy. As with cigarette smoking, chronic cough and shortness of breath are early signs of disease and it can progress to heart strain and subsequent failure of the aforementioned achy-breaky organ. There was some confusion as to the real age of Hazel Dickens at the time of her death. She exercised the old lady's prerogative of a certain vagueness about the exact date of her birth. It is thought that she was about seventy five. She died from the complications of another lung disease. It was pneumonia that took her down.

THE GREAT NORTH RUN
October 2005

You may not know a lot about the Great North Run. And if you check out the website devoted to this thirteen mile jogging event, you won't find many details about what happened during the race last month. Forty thousand professional and amateur runners set off on a pleasant Sunday to complete this annual 'fun-run' between Newcastle upon Tyne and South Shields. Four of them came home in coffins.

Described as the world's biggest half-marathon, the event glorifies good health, clean living and human longevity. It's happily sponsored by BUPA the health insurers, bottlers of fizzy water and assorted corporate purveyors of health and fitness. The event is long established on the UK's sporting map. It has proved so successful that there is now even a mini version sponsored by a supermarket chain. Entrants can be as young as two years of age. Those who complete the course, alive that is, receive a goody bag, a t-shirt with a number on it, a certificate, a medal and a bottle of mineral water.

Previous winners of the Great North Run women's event include Sonia O'Sullivan, Liz McColgan and Paula Radcliffe. The men's trophy has been lifted by legendary Kenyan athlete Benson Masya and Ireland's John Treacy. No laurels however for 28 year old Reuben Wilson of Leeds, 34 year old Kieran Patching of Kent, 43 year old David Mahaffey of York or this year's oldest fatality, 52 year old Philip Lewis of Durham. Like Pheidippides, the Greek messenger credited with inventing the marathon, they paid a heavy price for jogging. With their lives. Two and a half thousand workers are employed at the Great North Run every year. The organisers say they provide extensive medical services. There are 'medical facilities' every half mile among the route. There are five water stations, three mobile shower units, sixteen ambulances all equipped with defibrillators, two paramedic motorbikes and two field hospitals at the finish line. All very well, except that the four deceased runners didn't reach the finish line. So what went wrong?

Well the excuses came in thick and fast. Mike McLeod, the winner of the first race in 1981 and the man who fired the starting pistol this year, said that 'some people do push themselves too far'. He said he had 'heard of people who had a skinful the night before and then turn up in the morning and run like hell.' A theory perhaps. But it doesn't exactly tie up the loose ends. The late Mr Lewis for example was a deputy head teacher who played regular football, was an accomplished skier and had run every Great North Run since 1982.

Dave Bedford, another former athlete, is the race director. He said that when you have a large number of people in one place there is always a risk of someone having a problem. Sure. But four deaths in a fun-run - that's sounds like more than an acceptable risk. He then suggested that if you do have a problem, an event such as the Great North Run or the London Marathon is the safest place to have your problem because of the high-class medical facilities on hand. Little consolation there then.

Next up on the excuse podium was sports minister Richard Caborn MP who managed to complete the run alive. 'It might be good for UK Athletics or Sport England to look at the dos and don'ts advice for runners' he waffled. Translated into reality speak this means "I am really saying nothing of any substance but just want to deflect the problem onto someone else's desk." Mr Caborn is not a top politician and half marathon man for nothing. 'I don't want this to distract from what was a big family event which is brilliantly organised' he added. Finally, when all about him were scratching their heads in the aftermath of the greatest catastrophe ever to afflict 'fun-runs', Mr Caborn turned on the weather gods. 'It was very warm' he said.

Indeed it was warm. Pleasantly so at a maximum of 68 degrees. Others blamed the humidity. At 70% it was higher than average for Tyneside, but hardly Singapore's Changi prison. The organisers kept up a marathon stream of top notch excuses. 'Our medical services were busy but kept up with demand' they said. 'All competitors are sent a booklet asking them to seek medical advice from registered doctors.'

So is that it? Blame their doctors now, registered ones. Perhaps their crystal balls need to be sent back to the manufacturers for recalibration. These aren't the first fatalities of the Great North Run. This year's bad run brings the cumulative number of deaths to twelve. According to the event's website doctors estimate that more than 11 and a half million breaths were taken in the Great North Run this year. They are less forthcoming with the statistic that four of them were terminal ones.

VIDEO SHOP SLIMMING
August 2005

Film rentals must be on the wane. Our local video shop is now masquerading as a pharmacy. The other evening I was browsing through their collection of the most forgettable movies in history, when high up on the back shelf, near the fast-tan lotions, I spotted bottles of anti-obesity pills. For the price of two new cinema releases, you could have a three day trial of a product 'that is very similar to products that are now being prescribed by doctors to the

277

most obese 19,000 people in the country'. I found that particular claim interesting, as I had no idea there was any product being prescribed by doctors to the most obese 19,000 people in Ireland. As a slightly porky doctor, I think I might have known. I made further enquiries from the lad in the shop but he simply referred me to the leaflet which I had already picked up. The document was so fascinating I still have it in my pocket. Amongst the many claims it makes is that the counter staff at the outlet where I got the leaflet were all highly trained in thermogenics. That had never struck me before. I thought most of the staff were language students who were paid by the hour to watch re-runs of the Simpsons during the day and catch out account defaulters in the evenings. It never dawned on me that they were all highly trained bio-scientists with post-graduate degrees and doctorates in 'thermogenics'.

Back to the product. The leaflet added, in small print near the end, that it 'is not intended to diagnose, treat, cure or prevent any disease'. So what exactly does it do? The accompanying photos feature a glamorous woman and a muscle bound man pulling their waistbands out and patting their rears. They are each wearing trousers that are at least six sizes too big for them.

According to the leaflet, this product (I won't embarrass them by naming it) helps breaks down fat in food and turns it into bodily heat and energy. This somehow causes more fat to be burnt off and means less of it is stored in your body. It then uses the super efficient fat disposal caused by the heat to fool your body into thinking it has eaten more often. It makes you feel less hungry, stops you snacking, stops you overfilling your plate at mealtimes, raises your body's metabolic rate, burns off excess calories, increases your energy levels, reduces hunger pangs, drastically suppresses your appetite (only when you want it to), makes you slimmer, restores your waistline, does the same thing for you as going to the gym, stops you buying diet books, provides an emotional experience and best of all, works within the first four hours. All this and it's also a '100% natural' product and not intended to do anything 'medical'.

It has fourteen ingredients in each capsule and I recognised very few of them - a fact that wouldn't instil confidence in users who are advised to consult physicians with their questions. There was 100mg of caffeine in each tablet, the equivalent perhaps of a strong espresso coffee. There was 1mg of powder from damiana leaves. This I found interesting. Herbalists like to tell us that damiana leaves were greatly favoured by Mayan and Aztec civilisations for their orgasmic qualities. In their fervour to praise the horny damiana leaf, they forgot to mention that both of these libidinous communities are long extinct. Other ingredients were common kitchen peppers - black and cayenne, and a handful of chemical compounds that meant nothing to me except that many of them sounded uncompromisingly metallic. It also said it contains an aquatic plant called spirulina. Spirulina, like echinacea, is one of those heal-the-world-and-her-mother potions, beloved of free-range hippies. A quick trawl on the net will persuade you that it cures everything from Chernobyl-related radiation illness to terminal AIDS. I have spent the last few days wondering if there is a particular sort of person who might buy this sort of product in a video shop. Probably the same person who is on first name e mail terms with the wife of the late colonel Udo McGubo (former military leader of a very hot banana republic) who hasn't been heard of since she promised to deposit six billion dollars in their bank account.

EUPHEMISMS
September 2010

Healthcare is a popular resort for confusion as mutual misunderstanding on both sides of the desk is rife. Should the day ever dawn that patients fully understand doctors and doctors completely comprehend patients, the need of one for the other will have passed and the world will be run by quacks. On the patient side of the equation, they provide a never ending source of malapropisms - the humorous misplacement of medical terms. I've always had a hunch that Ireland has a greater concentration of malaprops than any other country in the English speaking world, but perhaps I am unduly influenced by the fact that Mrs Malaprop was the invention of an Irish playwright. Two centuries before Sheridan produced her, William Shakespeare had a lovable character called Dogberry, the incompetent and boastful policeman in *Much Ado About Nothing.* PC Dogberry frequently mangled his words, managing on his night shift to *comprehend two auspicious persons* (apprehend two suspicious persons). It was he who lent the lesser used term dogberryism to our lexicon.

I have devoted previous columns to medical malapropisms and have recently taken possession of some new ones. A lady wrote to me about an event of thirty years ago when her mother's second baby was overdue by a week. A neighbour enquired of a family friend how things were progressing and she was told that if things went on a further week, the lady would be taken in to the maternity hospital to be *seduced* (induced) And a consultant's secretary had two obstetric gems for me, including a more embarrassing variant of the above. A rather loud lady, tired of a long pregnancy, demanded in front of a whole ward round retinue that her consultant *seduce* her straight away.

Proving a genetic propensity for one person to produce many malapropisms, the nurses later overheard the same lady tell another patient that her doctor had to give her a *sexual* for her previous baby. She meant section of course, the caesarean variety.

Misunderstanding is a two way track. Across the pond in the eastern county of Norfolk, nursing staff at the Queen Elizabeth hospital are getting knickers in a twist about patients who use local dialect and medical euphemisms.

The whole thing started off when an elderly lady asked a foreign-trained nurse if she would accompany her to *spend a penny*. The lady was more than a little surprised when the nurse escorted her and her full bladder to the concourse and left her outside the hospital shop. Humorous anecdotes drive state bureaucracies into educational overdrive. Once the story went up a hundred rungs of nursing hierarchy, it was decided the NHS would offer 'euphemism training days' to all staff that weren't from the region. Nurse tutors were assigned clipboards and asked to collect all manner of Great British health expressions that might cause confusion to non-national nurses. Popular in the exhaustive collection were: *feeling a little under the weather, forgotten my jim-jams, back passage is spick and span, tickled pink, a nice cuppa and everything in here is higgledy-piggledy.*

There were murmurings of dissent about the need to treat

the matter so formally. Giving nurses a few hours off their ward duties to attend linguistics has not gone down well with the penny-pinching brigade. A spokeswoman for the UK's taxpayers alliance did little to assist international ecumenism when she said it was akin to 'using a sledgehammer to crack a nut'. But the health authorities in Norfolk do have a point. I have been taking a closer look at their peculiar dialect and there is certainly plenty of room for confusion. Take this example:

Nurse, me lug ache's givin' me serious jip. That fumble-fisted slusspot doctor said one tablet with my cuckoo afore bed would have me la-di-da but he's talkin' a load of squit. I'm covered in muckwash, screws all over, slarvin' at the kisser and more dwainy since he jammed in. Any sour gogs, Mawther?

which roughly translates as:

Nurse, my ear is still very painful. That clumsy drunkard doctor said one tablet with my cocoa at night would cure me but he is talking nonsense. I'm covered with sweat, aches and pains all over, dribbling from the mouth and sicker than I ever was before he marched in. Nurse, have you any better medicine?

Doubtless the many foreign doctors and nurses who have come to Ireland in recent years have had to cope with our own euphemisms, dialects and plain funny expressions.

Lobbin' and Lyin' was one we were all taught at Temple Street Children's Hospital - an expression of serious concern used by inner-city Dublin mothers to indicate the moribund state of a sick child. Doctors who enquire about the possibility of pregnancy could encounter a different feminine description for menstruation, depending on what part of the country they are in. *Munster are playing at home* is a well used euphemism in Cork, whilst in Dublin they might be told exactly what day their *best friend arrived*.

The *trots*, and their close neighbours the *scutters* are well-used Dublin expressions for diarrhoea. More recent variations include *fizzy gravy, rusty water* and *crappucino*. Did you know that the capital's favourite expression for an indoor urination is a *slash* whilst an outdoor one is a *pooley*?

The colloquial term *kaks* is ripe for confusion - some Dublin gents use the expression for their underpants, for others it is their testicles. Ample room for perplexity when one needs to be removed but not necessarily the other. Similarly ladies who use the words *dollies* and *diddies* to describe various parts of their pectoral (chest) anatomy could be sowing some seeds of bewilderment. And I wasn't aware until recently that there is a Dublinese medical term for the gooey trail of green that emanates from the nostrils of schoolchildren in winter time. I am told, on good authority, that it is a *snailer*.

LINCOLN UNIVERSITY
January 2010

Recent lifting of church skirts to expose double standards high up the ecclesiastical chain has been welcomed by many. But stepping quickly into the pulpit are dogmatic do-gooders of a different persuasion. The thin bishops, athletic priests and patronising sororities of the Healthy Lifestyle Church have replaced Sunday's gospels with lengthy sermons that seem to go on all week. Lose one inch from your waistline, and they'll insist you go the full mile.

The carry on at Lincoln University takes the biscuit. Lincoln is the most famous African American University in the whole of the United States. Founded after the civil war, it was given the name of the oft-beatified President, who contrary to official history actually wanted to repatriate or settle slaves abroad rather than allow them remain in his country. Lincoln University was the first American College to award degrees to black people. It's now famous for being the first third level institution in the free world to institute coercive medicine against its own students. You see Lincoln has decided not to allow fat students to graduate. Four years ago, one hundred odd faculty members of the university decided that all future students should have their body mass index measured on arrival. They decreed that those found to be contravening the arbitrary BMI obesity figure of 30, could not graduate unless they took mandatory measures to slim down. They also began measuring student waists and pronounced that they would not allow women with waists over 35 inches (or wide girthed men over 40 inches) to don caps and gowns.

Any student who contravened the college's fat tests, had to

participate in a gym and healthy lifestyle class to receive their parchment. Here, academic fatties would be instructed in walking, cycling and aerobic exercise. They would be given 'healthy lifestyle tips' and taught how to cook properly and manage their own diets. The plan was instigated and devised by the chairman of the college's physical education department who said it was 'all about student wellbeing'. He wept that it would be a 'tragedy' if any student suffered 'a catastrophic health issue associated with obesity' within six or seven years of graduating. God bless America. A once proud semi-tolerant nation, which fought the tyranny of colonial oppressors and guaranteed in its declaration of independence the personal right to 'pursue happiness', has now decided to pursue it on behalf of its own citizens. Whether they like it or not.

Many students who are due to graduate next Spring are less than happy. One sophomore said she signed up to get a degree and not for the college 'to tell me what my BMI should be'. Having forked out annual fees of $20,000 for four years (no mean task for the average African American family), there are now two dozen students who to date have refused to participate. A show-down between these obese students and a tyrannical university administration is in the offing. It has been pointed out to the university that its cafeteria sells very little except pizza, fried chicken, chips and cheeseburgers. Kentucky fried chicken and an assortment of other fast food and barbecue establishments have outlets right inside in the campus. They pay substantial rents to the very same faculty that weighs students.

It's no coincidence that Lincoln's student population is predominantly African American. Long pilloried as the fattest sector of the population, and 'responsible' for much of the current obesity 'crisis' or 'epidemic', it's not easy being a black American. As vaudevillian entertainer Bert Williams once said, 'It's no disgrace to be coloured, but it sure is awfully inconvenient.' It doesn't take long to find a survey telling you that four out of five African American women are overweight or obese and that their men-folk aren't much thinner. It might take a bit longer to find learned criticism of these surveys, where one relatively impoverished population is being unfairly compared with other ethnic groups that have far more advantages - in their weight control genes, in their wallets and in what their nation can generally do for them.

Schools and colleges are best reserved for educations that are free of cant and compulsion. The motto of Lincoln University stands in bright contrast with the ethos of its modern day totalitarians - If the Son shall make you free, you shall be free indeed. To this we now have a small addendum. Provided your weight in kilograms divided by the square of your height in metres is less than thirty.

Postscript: *Two days after this column was filed, Lincoln University rescinded the compulsory fitness requirement for students to graduate.*

HOME ALONE
April 2010

Americans are great folk for finding solutions. Pesky Indians - book them a reservation. Cotton labour shortages - galley ships and shackles. Pearl Harbour - bombs, go extra large. Tricky dictators on oil routes - invade with your friends' soldiers.

Yes, our favourite Uncle Sam, with two hundred years of unworldly experience, has always been first to put his hand up when hard questions are asked.

Just recently, avuncular Sam claimed to have the solution for homelessness. According to a recent *New York Times* report, there is just one homeless man left living on Times Square. Five years ago, he had more than 50 neighbours. Now his cardboard bed rattles alone in the wind under a builder's scaffold. Times Square's last resident is called Heavy - nobody knows his real name and he sees no good reason to give it out when box tickers come calling. The only possession he retains is his personal privacy. Heavy is an African American of more advanced years than his President. He smokes, drinks lots of coffee and has to date declined all offers to move on. Even when the city's sanitation department disposed of his few belongings, he remained in situ.

Social workers say they have no intention of moving him on, like they did to all of his buddies. But their bosses chant from a slightly different hymn book. The executive director of the local 'outreach organisation' says that the general public may not be helping Heavy in the long term by giving him food and clothing. He is now considering posting an outreach worker to stay with Heavy all day, study his movements and talk to neighbours about what is best for him. The trouble with Heavy is that he does not want to be housed like everyone else. He is asked on a daily basis if he would like the key to an apartment and politely declines. He playfully suggests to those who nag him that he is a protector of his community and that they need him. And maybe they do. An old lady who lives nearby and has known Heavy for decades says he is a 'sweetheart' who says 'Hi Mommy' to her whenever they meet. She calls him Honey and greatly values their encounters. An office worker lends him bread at lunchtime. He is renowned for his charm and gentleness of character. He occasionally begs quietly and spends his meager gains on Starbucks and fags. Now that his friends are gone, we are told by the city authorities that Times Square is more commercial, more safe, more tourist-friendly and tellingly, less comfortable for the street homeless.

To find out more about how our American cousins claim to have solved homelessness, you could do worse than peruse the columns of Malcolm Gladwell, described by glossy men's magazines as 'the world's most influential thinker'. Four years ago he wrote a piece called 'Million Dollar Murray' which concerns a homeless man who by the time of his death, was estimated by Gladwell to have cost the American taxpayer more than a million dollars. The expense was calculated principally on health bills and the labour costs of urban officialdom. The message seeping through the pores of Gladwell's polemic, is that 'bums', 'hard-core homeless' and 'chronic inebriates' need to be 'managed' and 'monitored' to become 'successful members of society' and 'good Americans'. Not only that, the actuaries of homelessness estimate that each city can save a pretty fortune by simply offering free apartments and allotting one 'case-worker' to every ten 'down and outs'. Every morning there are mandatory case-meetings where the intimate details of another person's court dates, medical appointments and tablet schedules are crayoned up on a communal white board and dissected and mulled over by all assembled.

Buried within Gladwell's tract on homelessness, and its

pecuniary cost to American society, are many of the prejudicial claims that 'successful' human beings make about those whose street lives are not so fortunate. We hear from downtown merchants who worry that the presence of homeless people is scaring away customers. We hear from an emergency medicine consultant who says that drunks 'run up huge lab fees' and make nurses want to quit their jobs because 'they see the same guys come in over and over'. Gladwell even likens chronically homeless men to the 'bad cops' of Los Angeles. They are a small number of 'hard cases' whom he describes as 'falling down drunks with liver disease, complex infections and mental illness.' In 2002, President Bush appointed Philip Mangano, a homelessness 'abolitionist' to be executive director of the US interagency council on homelessness. Mangano, a one-time advocate for homeless people, set about convincing Americans that providing soup and shelter for their homeless brethren was a waste of money. Under his plan, the homeless would disappear. And they are disappearing. They have been given the keys to their own apartments as the all-American hobo is swept from view beneath a convenient state carpet. Accountants, trained more in financial cost than human value, are in monetary dreamland. We are told that the cost of services comes to $10,000 per homeless client per year and the cost of an apartment is less than $5,000 on top. A far cry from million dollar Murray. According to Mangano the messiah, you should not manage 'social wrongs', you should end them.

Well the end may be nigh here too. Because the London School of Economics negated to teach Bertie Ahern the benefits of planning ahead, we seem to have amassed a peculiar surplus of housing units. With our new state landlord keen for tenants at any price, it looks certain that like their American counterparts, homeless services will be encouraged to trade personal care for bunches of keys. Out of sight, out of mind, and cheap at the price - the all American way.

AGEING
October 2010

The line that once existed between science and science-fiction is becoming lost in a fog of ludicrous health claims and predictions designed for headline-making. What's most depressing is that those in a position to rebuff nonsense masquerading as science, are joining this free-for-all and fuelling it with follies all their own.

Forty years ago, buoyed by modest success against smallpox and measles, the US surgeon general Dr William H. Stewart announced to congress that the book on infectious diseases should be closed as the war against pestilence had been won. Stewart wanted his country to concentrate resources on chronic diseases. The resurgence of TB and the emergence of AIDS a decade later proved his call very wrong. Yet at the time, nobody challenged either his hype or his optimism.

In the mid 1980s Stewart was joined in the eternal optimism stakes by an eminent Irish cardiologist and health promotion expert who proclaimed in the *Irish Times* that 'by the year 2000 the commonest killers such as coronary heart disease, stroke, respiratory disease and many cancers will be wiped out'. Not surprisingly, the newspaper of record, has yet to follow up on this story.

Now I don't want to rain on the recent parade that was Positive Ageing Week. There is much to admire about our elders and they deserve a platform other than that afforded by a free bus pass. But they also deserve to be told the truth, the whole truth and not the varnished and speculative truth that's trotted out on many programmes devoted to positive ageing.

The guff we heard about promises of immortality and the 'end of ageing' is more suited to spiritualists and séance-holders than medicine. I want to rebuff the preposterous notion put forward in Positive Ageing Week that half of all girls born today will live to the age of one hundred. At the risk of suffering a painful torticollis I will stick my neck out and say that the prediction of hundreds of thousands of Irish lady centurions is complete balderdash and should not have been allowed go unchallenged either on the *Late Late Show* or any other forum in which it was reeled off as fact.

It's exactly a year to the month since this 'half of all girls will reach a hundred' fairytale was released to the press by *The Lancet*. It was a Danish prediction, with fairy tale echoes of Hans Christian Andersen. They used very solid statistics showing that we are all living longer, but spoiled them with a ludicrous punt on the future. They assumed that human longevity would keep increasing at the same rate it has been rising for the last century. Just because a football team scores two goals in the first ten minutes of a match, does not mean the final score will be eighteen nil.

Strangely, or perhaps not, their prediction does not tally with the recent shrieks of obesity-mongers. Our public health alarmists and enemies of modest fat reserves have declared war on turkey twizzlers, crisps and chocolate. They suggest that our current wave of parents will be the first generation to outlive their children. Now I'm no Einstein, but these experts can't all be right. In the words of Monty Python's *Life of Brian*, somebody is making it up as they go along. When in doubt, you could do worse than defer to Jonathan Miller - doctor, comedian, historian, philosopher, theatre director and son of a Jewish mammy from Cork city. Writing some decades ago in *The Body in Question*, Miller discussed the limits of human mortality. He suggested that death was and always will be an intrinsic feature of life, not merely an unavoidable interruption. Rather than considering new birth as nature's way of overcoming death, Miller suggested that death is nature's way of giving free rein to the creative opportunities offered by birth. And, as he puts it so well 'in the absence of senescence and death, young hopefuls would enter a very crowded stage. By modest withdrawal from the scene, one generation acknowledges and gives way to the unforeseeable talents of the rest.' Nobody has a monopoly of wisdom on positive ageing. But Jonathan Miller comes very close.

SWEDES
April 2006

I'm old enough to remember a time when babycham socialists would lecture us about the wonderful caring nation Swedes have, and how well we little fir bolg might do if we started to emulate viking society. All social ills could be eradicated if decent citizens gave up the bulk of their taxable earnings and allowed government decide how best to spend it. The idea once seemed as attractive as a night on the town with Agnetha and Freda. But with the passage of time these noble aspirations bore more resemblance to a quiet night in with Benny and Björn. Sweden is not really at the left wing races anymore. Cuba tends to run quite alone there. Everyone's favourite eurovision winners and Nobel prize hosts are struggling to keep pace with the massive volume of illness and disability claims that their once generous society attracted. It was reported recently in the medical press that the Stockholm chapter of Hell's Angel motorcyclists had one of the highest rates of depression in the whole world. But the mood changed when the fraud squad were alerted by social services to the fact that just one doctor was doing all the diagnosing. He had a waiting room full of hairy mollies looking for more bike time.

Sweden is also one of very few countries in the world to recognise a phenomenon called *Electromagnetic Sensitivity*. Now this is a newly constructed disease in which patients describe vague symptoms that are attributed to everything from electrical gadgets to magnetic power lines. EMS is categorised almost everywhere as 'medically unexplained' - code for the fact that most doctors simply don't believe it exists as a distinct condition. Not so in Sweden where all reports of tingling, numb body parts or warm sensations are blamed on the toaster, the kettle or whatever other household appliance is close to hand. The authorities even have a national support scheme to assist sufferers in their homes, their workplaces and who knows, perhaps on their motorbikes too.

Belief in the existence of a medical condition called electromagnetic sensitivity is not exclusively Swedish - in fact support groups and internet forums exist across the world. A team from the Institute of Psychiatry at King's College London had no difficulty recently when recruiting 'sensitive' people to discern whether pulsing signals from GSM mobile phones might be the root cause of their medical problems. One hundred and twenty souls were rounded up. Sixty of them were self-confessed mobile phone hypersensitives who got headache-like symptoms within twenty minutes of taking a call and the other sixty were the control group who had no such problems. The study, reported in a recent

289

British Medical Journal, failed to show that any symptoms were associated with mobile phone radiation. The sensitive group had more severe symptoms than the control group, but the symptoms occurred with precisely the same frequency during sham exposure. This was when all participants were tricked into believing they were being exposed to a continuous wave signal when they weren't. This research is the latest in a steady stream of studies which found no differences between active exposure or sham exposure to electromagnetic fields. The authors believe psychological factors may be at work and suggest a possibility for behavioural therapy, rather than avoidance of modern life, which to date has been pretty much the mainstay of treatment.

CHIROPRACTOR
August 2005

I was greatly cheered by the news last month that the World Series of Poker was won by a chiropractor. Joseph Hachem, a 39 year old Australian bone-cracker who traded his patients for a pack of cards, was crowned king of texas hold'em in Las Vegas and made off with a neat little jackpot of seven and a half million dollars. Whilst genuinely pleased that Mr Hachem had secured lifelong financial security his young family, what particularly contented me was the thought that the world now has one less chiropractor out hunting for patients.

Five and a half thousand members of the poker world, sharks and minnows, entered the tournament, each handing in a $10,000 entry fee. After ninety hours dealing and reeling, Mr Hachem was the last man sitting, scooping the jackpot with a final seven high straight. A fitting hand for a man devoted to the unswerving human spine. The newspapermen swooped in search of a printable quote and Hachem didn't disappoint: "I can tell you I've made more money this week than in many years of fixing people's backs."

There is something rather telling about a member of the chiropractic profession triumphing at the World Series of Poker. Whilst the card game demands equal measures of bluff, bluster, stamina and bravado, Hachen's chosen field of alternative healthcare is little different. Founded by Daniel David Palmer (1845-1913), a one-time schoolmaster, grocery store owner and promoter of medical magnet therapies, chiropractic survived its strange beginnings to become a major player in the health industry of the western world. Whether it contributes in any way to the wellbeing of patients is another matter. Mr Palmer was undoubtedly a quack of the highest order. He was a Canadian immigrant to the USA, who settled on the banks of the Mississippi in Iowa. He first experimented with magnets in his spare time, claiming they could heal all sorts of every day ails. He became interested in the 'manipulation of human vertebrae', a fad he perhaps picked up from a local doctor.

In 1895 he claimed to have cured a janitor of deafness by adjusting his backbone. Soon afterwards he claimed to have relieved another patient's heart trouble by 'racking' displaced vertebrae' into place. The use of x-rays in medical imaging had not come about at this time, so he was free to pontificate at will about the state of his patients' vertebrae - knowing that his medical (or grocer's) opinions were safe from contradiction. Then by oily reasoning beloved of so many branches of alternative health, Palmer declared that all diseases result from pressure of spinal nerves. In his own words he 'created the art of adjusting vertebrae'. With logic derived straight from the Charlatan's Handbook, he hypothesized that energy flow from the brain was the essential force of life and that all diseases were caused by obstruction to this imaginary flow.

A local cleric, the Reverend Weed, had some classical knowledge and helped Palmer adopt the name chiropractic for his new-fangled hobby. *Cheir* is Greek for hand, *praxis* denotes activity. Palmer set up a school in Davenport which pumps out bone-poppers to this day. He also had the wisdom to train his son BJ in the new dogma, which helped to keep his own peculiar brand of nonsense going. His writings on the nature of disease were full of pious and self-promotional waffle, probably not that different from physicians of his day. He wrote about the 'excitability of the various organs' and claimed he 'created the art of adjusting vertebrae'. Though he might have had much to be modest about, Palmer was hardly the self-effacing sort. His 1910 textbook for students contained the following gem.

'I am the Fountain Head of Chiropractic; it originated with me; it was my ingenious brain which discovered its first principles; I was its source; I gave it birth; to me all chiropractors trace their chiropractic lineage.'

Palmer is long gone. His chiropractic legacy over the last hundred years is littered with revolts, schisms, political chicanery and legal wrangles - and that's just amongst its devotees. Relations between bonecrackers and the medical profession have been at best, mistrustful. Medical doctors are quick to point out horrific cases of injury that can result from chiropractic treatment. Chiropractics retort that if they are so dangerous, then why are their malpractice insurance premiums so much lower than doctors of mainstream medicine.

Dr Stephen Barrett is the founder of Quackwatch, and a noteworthy critic of false claims in medicine. He has written that very few health problems can be influenced by spinal manipulation and that there is no logical reason why regular spinal check-ups or adjustments provide any general health benefit or prevent health problems from recurring. The fact that virtually no hospitals employ chiropractors suggests that many agree with him. In support of his views Dr Barrett quotes from an experiment he conducted for the US committee on health fraud some years ago. A young mother took her perfectly healthy four year old girl to see five different chiropractors. The first said the child's shoulder blades were "out of place" and found "pinched nerves to her stomach and gallbladder." The second chiropractor showed a movie which stated that "chiropractic can also be effective in combating most childhood diseases." He said that the child's pelvis was "twisted" and advised that she have "adjustments, vitamins, and a check every four months." The third said one hip was "elevated" and that spinal misalignments could cause "headaches, nervousness, equilibrium or digestive problems" in the future. The fourth predicted "bad periods and rough childbirth" if her "shorter left leg" was not treated. This chiropractor told her that he 'adjusted' his own family once a week and recommended weekly checkups and adjustments for all. The fifth not only found hip and neck problems, but also "adjusted" them without bothering to ask permission. The adjustments were so painful that Dr Barrett abandoned the experiment. It is often claimed, with a modicum of truth, that healthcare can be a bit of a lottery. If you are the sort that would happily gamble your health on a game of poker, chiropractic may well be up your street.

PHONEY WAR
ON FAMILY CARS
March 2005

Doctors shouldn't practice what they preach. I'd prefer if they just practiced, and gave up preaching altogether. Some weeks ago we had a sock-free sandal-wearing medic from the United States staying as a house-guest. We enjoyed his liberal bonhomie and overlooked the fragrance of eau de toot that wafted through the house during the visitation. But our impeccable manners didn't stop our friend passing comments each morning about our family car - a Honda CRV which in his country would be called an SUV (sports utility vehicle). Each day he would utter some remark or other about it being a first world malevolence, responsible for mowing down pedestrians in their prime, the oil crisis in America, warming of the poles, an ozone hole, the war in Iraq and the election of George W. Bush, twice. I had never thought of my beloved car in such a political light. The reason I drive it is because it comfortably accommodates two dogs, a baby seat, a baby, a wife, a driver, a picnic, a hundred books and a ranting American doctor - all on the same journey. What I like most about my Honda CRV is the high visibility it offers from the front and side windows. It makes me feel like a pilot with a great view of traffic ahead, pedestrian lights and those all important speed signs. Rear visibility is not so good, but that's not a major issue since Irish folk all gave up reversing over pedestrians in the Good Friday Agreement.

When our American friend departed for home, he left a gift to thank us for our hospitality. It was a book called *Power Down - Options and Actions for a Post-Carbon World a.k.a. What will you do when the Oil runs out?* It sits happily in an unread state, perched precariously over a deep lavatory cistern.

Anti-SUV activists should take a long wet hike, preferably one way. In the United States they have taken to damaging these cars just as loomadawns in this country take baseball bats to American aircraft. The paramilitaries of the anti-SUV movement also distract drivers at traffic lights, abusing them for their choice of vehicle. They spend weekends at shopping malls, tagging offending vehicles with stickers that cannot be removed. They make up ridiculous statistics. They say that switching from an average car to an SUV for one year wastes more energy than leaving a refrigerator door open for six years.

Next month, at the annual general meeting of the Irish Medical Organisation (IMO), clinical mullahs will decide, like some sort of fashion house, what's in and what's out for good health next season. They too have declared war on my car and have two motions for debate. Patients queue on trolleys for days, operations are cancelled for want of beds, suicides are up and publication of hospital waiting lists has been abolished. But the great IMO nanny doctors of this state have decided that the pressing issue of the day is SUV safety. One motion calls for all such cars to carry a 'very visible sticker' outlining road safety risks to buyers. And another motion calls on the national roads authority to set up a division to monitor SUV cars, their accident rates and deaths associated with their use.

I am not a member of the IMO. Their leaders are too fond of stickers for my liking and their 'group insurance' rates are higher than an individual could get for himself. In a dispute over money some years ago, they decided to issue thousands of "I love my GP" car stickers to patients. The only cars I ever saw them on were those of GPs themselves. The IMO wants more stickers on fags, more stickers on burgers, labels on chips and health warnings on alcohol bottles. Last night I had a terrible dream. I ran over a senior member of the IMO in my SUV. It wasn't my fault. There was a blind spot on the window. It was caused by one of their stickers.

DEFENSIVE MEDICINE
July 2007

If you were to ask patients queuing for scans, blood tests and other investigations why they are there, most would answer that their doctors sent them in good faith, to see if there was anything wrong. Few, if any, would suggest that they were there to cover the doctor's backside or to prevent him being sued. But what we term 'defensive medicine' is rife in modern healthcare and the boom in private testing facilities we are seeing in Ireland is testament to its onward march.

Back in the 1980s when I stalked Dublin's hospital wards as a grim reaper intern in a white coat, testing was just taking off. Men who arrived in coronary care with chest pains were sent for scans of their prostates and livers. I remember one particular inner-city lady arriving for varicose vein day-care being asked if she would object to examination of her rectum. She certainly did object, in the rarest of Dublinese. As interns we were often asked to take blood tests we had never heard of, and have never heard of since now that I think of it. Some of our most senior housemen knew the value of every test in the book, but knew the cost of none. I suspect little has changed. I was reading an article by a young Irish doctor in Boston the other day and he stated quite matter of factly that the United States now spends as much on defensive medicine as it does on protecting its borders. The annual 'premiums and claims' bill there for doctors protecting themselves is $30 billion a year. And if the cost of unnecessary tests was added, the figure would soar even higher into the stratosphere. What this suggests to an old cynic like me is that the 'greatest nation on earth' now fears its own lawyers as much as it fears foreigners.

Our medical predecessors, those wiser doctors of yesteryear, relied on simple observation, astute listening and careful examination of the body before making pronouncements. Don't get me wrong, new diagnostic technology has brought huge medical advances. To paraphrase Star Trek's Captain Kirk, we can certainly now go where no doctors had gone before. But there is a downside that few foresaw. Clinical examination and adequate interrogation have faded into the background as 'tests' assumed an importance above all else. Patients of today are more likely than ever to complain that the doctor 'never even examined them' as they are shunted off into a maze of hospital departments with unpronounceable names.

Nobody knows the precise monetary cost of defensive medicine in Ireland. Based on US figures it probably dwarves the amount wasted on electronic voting and may be in the region of €1 billion a year. It's fuelled by every court case that finds a doctor negligent in their duty. That's not to say that there are not negligent doctors. But our courts system doesn't discriminate between the doctor who is down on skill and the doctor who is down on luck. Patients with simple tension headaches are sent to emergency rooms to await MRI scans of their brains. Youngsters with indigestion are admitted to coronary care for cardiac investigations. Injuries that doctors are quite certain are sprains are subjected to unnecessary x-rays - to be sure, to be sure.

Two years ago, Dr John Murphy, editor of the *Irish Medical Journal*, called for a study of how the practices of Irish doctors have changed in the current climate of high litigation. He opined that if medics turn up to work each day with a sense of apprehension, the drift to defensive medicine will continue. Dr Murphy made a considered distinction between the careful doctor which everyone wants and the defensive doctor who is good to nobody but himself. Sadly we have an Irish legal system that is both adversarial and cost-driven and it does not appear to want to recognise this distinction.

There is little political will to examine the phenomenon of defensive medicine. The status quo suits too many people. Many doctors and clinical entrepreneurs make a good living on the back of tests. And lawyers can make a fee killing from the misery of their clients. Until patients become interested in the adverse consequences, the cost of defensive practice, and the fact that defensive medicine can harm your health, the problem will not be tackled.

In America, there are signs of a stir. A new report has found that the average annual dose of ionizing radiation each American receives has increased by 600% in the last 25 years. The main reason is the proliferation of CT scanning. In 2006, 62 million

Americans had CT scans as opposed to just 3 million in 1980. At current levels, every single American (assuming they can pay for it) can expect to be sent for the test every five years. The principal investigator, a professor of radiology at the University of New Mexico, said that a single CT scan of the chest can give the same radiation dose to breast tissue as 10 or 20 mammograms. 'Most people would get up and leave if they knew that' he said. Food for thought.

LIBEL LAWS
July 2009

An Italian wit once said that newspaper columns are a bit like sausages. You can stuff whatever you like into them. Alas no longer true for those of us who write about medicine and science. The laws of libel are increasingly being used to stifle debate about the veracity of health claims. Freedom of critical speech could be the real loser. Simon Singh is a well-respected UK scientist who has taken the claims of alternative medicine to task. In his book *Trick or Treatment?*, and in subsequent opinion columns, Singh has dished out much criticism of chiropractic, the spine-tingling massage therapy that has operated for a century in an odd quasi-parallel world to mainstream medicine. For perceived sins against their therapy, the British Chiropractic Association is now suing Singh for libel. Rather than debate matters, as people of science usually do, the chiropractors have engaged wigs for hire. The case is proceeding through London's courts and may finish in the European Court of Human Rights. At issue are claims made by chiropractors that they can treat a variety of childrens' illnesses. Singh dismissed these boasts as bogus.

The case will be watched closely by those who value freedom of expression. Already a plethora of figures in science and public life have rowed in behind Dr Singh. Bone-crackers across the water have raised the stakes rather higher than they perhaps imagined. Just two months ago the UK's Advertising Standards

Authority upheld a complaint about a chiropractic clinic that made claims about their ability to treat irritable bowel syndrome, colic and learning difficulties. The ASA also found that references to 'doctors' at the clinic could mislead patients into believing that chiropractors were medically qualified. Many more complaints could follow.

I have written in a previous chapter about Mr Palmer the grocer, the inventor and fountainhead of chiropractic. It's interesting to note that just a hundred miles upriver from Palmer was a disenchanted medic called Andrew Still who became a bone-setter and founded a school of osteopathy in 1892. Dr Still had come to the mistaken conclusion that all diseases are caused by the same misalignment of spinal vertebrae talked about by Palmer, although in Still's case he said that diseases resulted from pressure on the arteries, not nerves. The disciplines of osteopathy and chiropractic are both delusional, they just differ on the precise anatomy of the delusion.

Mistaken theories are six a penny in medicine - they have always been there and will continue for longer than you or I. The ability to discard, learn and move on is what distinguishes the trunk of mainstream medicine from some of the more slippery branches that have angled from it over the years. The textbooks we studied at Trinity College 20 years ago would not be accepted now if I tried to flog them at a student's union sale. Though much remains the same, some of what was taught to us back then is now regarded as pure heresy. One hundred years of scientific progress has clearly shown that the scientific basis claimed by Palmer and Still for their twin therapies of chiropractic and osteopathy are absurd in the extreme. Amply demonstrated perhaps by this popular doctor joke below:

Chiropractor: "Doctors tell me I'm a quack and that my chiropractic techniques are a sham. When are they going to learn that chiropractors are just another scientific profession, providing real help to injured people?" Patient: "I agree. When I was in to see my doctor about my lung cancer, he went off on this long tirade about how the chiropractic profession still relies on pseudoscience." Chiropractor: "Lung cancer, eh? Here, lie down there so I can adjust vertebra number three, it should go away completely."

There is no doubt that some of the masseurs and masseuses who train in chiropractic and osteopathy are skilled with their hands. As with chartered physiotherapists, you will always see patients who find relief from back discomfort on the couches of chiropractors and osteopaths. Most scientists support the benefits of physical massage for a bad back. They will not however support disciplines that overstretch their expertise and move their creed into areas where it clearly has no relevance. Now that chiropractors have moved their benches to the courts of law, they may find the shaky spine upon which Daniel Palmer hinged their discipline, subjected to extreme scrutiny and some very serious racking indeed.

Postscript: *In April 2010, The British Chiropractic Association withdrew their lawsuit against Simon Singh.*

PISSING IN ENNIS
November 2009

Fired up by the global attention it received when Muhammad Ali came to town, Ennis Town Council is now wetting itself about a custom even older than the boxer's ancestors - pissing on the streets. Last month a shopkeeper installed an electric fence so that 'revellers' who lowered their masts anywhere near his premises were in for a nasty shock.

The trader garnered international headlines for his fence and now previously dormant town councillors are falling over each other searching for solutions, each politician trying to pee higher than the next.

At November's meeting of the town council, the chairman set the early mood by saying that 'Ennis needs to be at the forefront of tackling this serious problem'. While the world panicked about swine flu and a posse of bearded hillbillies hiding in an Afghan cave, Ennis led the world in the war on illicit wee-weeing.

First up was the Green Party councillor. He proposed solving the problem by designing a website. Concerned burghers would sneak out at night with heat sensitive cameras, snap images of the offending citizens in full flow, and upload them to the internet.

Naming and shaming appeals to modern Greens who value conformity above all else. The fruit'n'veg party have assumed the position of the fallen church in Ireland - preaching end of the world stuff, only to be avoided through hefty doses of dogma. Their policies seem to be made up as they self-flagellate into work on their bikes each morning. They are living proof of Flann O'Brien's thesis that men who park big arses on saddles for too long, eventually turn into bicycles themselves. At least these modern day Mahatmas haven't ask us yet to drink our own pee. Yet.

Next up was the Labour Party councillor. Ever-conscious of the need to protect the public sector, especially if it involves creating even more superfluous state jobs, he proposed that two 'urine wardens' be employed to patrol the mean streets of Ennis 'on the lookout for revellers' who might stain the fabric of his beloved town. An Independent councillor said he would support the initiative, but only on a trial basis, for he feared for the safety of urine wardens carrying out their duties at three o'clock in the morning when traffic wardens already get spat on at three o'clock in the afternoon.

The Fine Gael councillor, admirably up to date with excretory practices in New South Wales (perhaps it is twinned with Ennis), outlined a more measured plan, proposing that the council hire public urinals at weekends. This radical road-map for the future fired up a hot debate about the current price of day-time peeing in Ennis (25 pence) and the already exorbitant cost of hiring car park superloos, almost €75,000 for a pair. In newspaper reports of the council debate, Fianna Fáil voices were noteworthy for their absence. We must resist cheap shots about what they showered us with in the last twelve years of government.

Ennis is by no means the only town in Ireland worried about the olfactory effects of stale pee in the mornings. Down in Carlow, the judiciary have taken to wearing black hats when sentencing 'revellers' with full bladders and nowhere to go. When a Graiguecullen man recently sprung a leak outside the bus premises on Tullow Street, the learned judge ordered him to pay €1,000 to the Irish Kidney Association.

It's not only nocturnal zombies who have difficulties with

waste management in this country. On a recent trip to Newry, now treasonable as well as seasonal, I couldn't help noticing the number of cars on the verges of the M1, partially hiding mothers as their children voided on the grass. Bertie built us some very fine motorways, but he never cut a single ribbon at a service station or public convenience. Every developer was cosy inside his tent at the Galway Races, there were none outside pissing in.

Some years ago, on a break to the wilds of west Cork, I picked up a copy of the *Southern Star* newspaper. On the letters page was a plea from a retired American kidney specialist who had just returned home from a trip to the land his ancestors had urinated in. He loved Ireland and praised us handsomely for our craic and welcome. But his letter, like a urinary tract infection, had a sting at the end. He was appalled at the lack of public conveniences for natives and tourists alike. He drove for miles on motorways and by-roads looking for places to pee. He mentioned many disorders of the kidney and bladder that necessitate frequent urination - prostatism, stress incontinence, urge incontinence, kidney stones and so on. He described the damage that can result to delicate structures from holding out for too long. And he was flabbergasted that Irish patients, their doctors and their support organisations did not demand better services.

And of course he was dead right. Why do we license 'public houses' which are nothing of the sort. What's public about 'toilets are strictly for customer use only'? Why is it a condition of emptying your bladder that you must fill it up again before you leave? Is it healthy for people to avoid hydrating themselves before a long journey because they know there is nowhere to stop for relief? Why do we tolerate road safety zealots talking down to us about the need to pull over for cappucino, when they know quite well you can't get a beverage, lavatory or even a safe place to pull over on hundreds of miles of Irish motorways. When it comes to pee, this country is always caught short.

Postscript: *Almost one year later, in September 2010, Ireland's first motorway service area opened in Lusk, Co Dublin,*

GEORGE VANDELEUR LEE
February 2010

'*Over the years, we Irish have tried every medicine for our ails, including Catholicism, drink, nationalism, assassination, apathy and Mr Haughey.*'

I miss that razor-sharp nib of Hugh Leonard. It dried up a year ago this month. Had the bard of Dalkey survived longer, he might have appended George Lee to his finely crafted list. It's just a fortnight since the aforementioned Mr George Lee TD detonated his political suicide bomb at the gates of Leinster House. The 'great party' he had joined revealed itself to be little more than a classroom of jibbering squeals, who ran to teacher, stroked his knee and told ill-proportioned tales of runaway George, the gunpowder plotter. What set the country's sympathies firmly on the Lee side, were the hoity-toity tones of his Fine Gael canvas team who flooded the airwaves with a very singular intention, to damage the George Lee brand. They ended up, as they always do, sounding every inch the uptown snobs that have dominated the party since it was founded. Lee's 'how dare you talk down to me like that' riposte certainly hit home. He had been treated by the Fine Gael jesuits as the kid from the poor side of town, the scholarship boy to be patted on the back, wished well and left out of decision-making at all costs. There was a real meanness of spirit about the party that carried Lee high on their shoulders just months before. Many ordinary folk felt a great pride in George Lee. He quit the turf, explained himself as well as I have ever heard a politician explain anything, and retained a dignity of the sort that has long been in short supply on Kildare Street.

Interestingly, he is not the only George Lee to have found himself feted by polite society in south Dublin before being cast out to foreign climes. In the latter half of the nineteenth century, an 'original Svengali' of the same name cast a spell on the ladies of the capital. George Lee was an inner city boy from Caroline Row, son of a coalman and educated by the Christian Brothers at O'Connell Schools. He re-launched himself as George Vandeleur Lee, conductor and teacher of singing, and became quite the wheeze in Dublin musical society. Those of us with a conspiracy bent, like to believe he was the real father of George Bernard

Shaw. Close comparison of early photographs of the young Shaw with those of Lee, and of his official father certainly tell a tale. Michael Holroyd, Shaw's celebrated biographer gives the story of the original George Lee some welly in his five volume series on Ireland's most celebrated polemicist. George Vandeleur Lee told the ladies to whom he taught 'the Method' that he was the son of Colonel Crofton Moore Vandeleur, a member of parliament. Lee is described as mesmeric and gypsy-like, sharply-dressed with such confidence and zest that women 'came alive under his spell'. For many years, Shaw, his mother Bessie and George Lee shared accommodation near Dublin's Portobello quarter, then Dalkey and later in London where the family migrated.

It's reckoned that Shaw developed many of his idiosyncrasies about health and his particular disdain for doctors directly from this man who so influenced his mother and early life. Lee always slept with the windows open and ate brown bread rather than the more usual white. He walked with a pronounced limp, on a badly deformed foot that had been poorly treated when he fell down a stairs in childhood. Distrust of doctors and other 'professionals' ran deep. George Lee put on operatic productions in Dublin's Theatre Royal and ran fundraisers for various hospitals and deserving charities. He did have some medical friends, and together they dissected human corpses, with particular reference to the larynx, in search of the secret of bel canto.

What happened to make George Lee quit his successful and self-made career in Dublin is not clear. He may have had ambitions for his 'Method' in London, but it is known that that there was an amount of professional jealousy from 'more qualified' musical academics who noticed his rise from nowhere. Lee was making serious amounts of money on his ventures, enough to purchase outright Torca Cottage in Dalkey, a residence he had previously leased. Often anonymous and dismissive reviews of his work appeared in the national press. Academic detractors sent word around that he was an impostor. Lee gave his last concert in Dublin in May 1873 and he died fairly anonymously in London at the end of 1886. A sudden cardiac arrest as he was putting on a nightshirt. He was only in his mid 50s. These promising George Lee fellows just don't seem to last.

DEATH OF A SALESMAN
August 2005

Two deaths to report in the last month, both of which cast interesting clouds on the doctrine of health promotion. For the past twenty years, Deborah Hutton was the doyenne of health journalism. She pored out umpteen remedies for longevity, eternal happiness and wellbeing in the pages of *Vogue* magazine. Known to friends and work colleagues as 'Miss Fit Pants', Ms Hutton died at the age of 49, succumbing to a particularly virulent form of lung cancer. She had smoked cigarettes for a period of just seven years in her youth and had spent the majority of her adult life preaching healthy lifestyles, detox diets, colonic irrigation and whatever other fads took her fancy. A self-described anti-smoking fanatic since quitting at 24, it may be seen by many as a cruel blow of fate that she lost her life to a 'cigarette disease' before reaching her 50th birthday. Deborah Hutton was also a firm believer in regular health screening and therein lies another story. When she took ill suddenly last year, Ms Hutton had a very advanced aggressive Stage 4 adenocarcinoma of the lungs. All that remained for her doctors to do was to manage the symptoms of her last months rather than treat her condition. Breast screening, cervical screening, bowel cancer screening and all the other screening proved of no benefit, to a woman simply died of something else. Ms Hutton will be missed by the many thousands who followed her career in health journalism, but the knowledge that her sermons on life extension didn't do her much good herself, should ring bells amongst even the most ardent health propagandists. It's interesting that in the many fulsome tributes to Ms Hutton, some mentioned that recently she was coming around to the idea that life, death and the diseases we meet in between, are more heavily encoded in DNA than health preachers acknowledge.

Last year a senior figure in the pharmaceutical industry admitted a truth that we doctors have been slow to acknowledge. Namely that Medicine is a much more complicated business than we let on. We are light years away from offering guarantees with our work. Dr Allen Roses admitted that many modern drugs simply don't work for particular individuals, on account of our limited knowledge of genetics. Newspapers around the world proclaimed 'The Drugs Don't Work' but the truth was a tad more complicated than the headlines. Many drugs do work, it's just that we often don't know why they work for some people and not for others. The science of genetics, half a century old since Watson and Crick unravelled the first strands of DNA, is still very much in nappies. What Dr Roses was signalling was the start of a new medical frontier, where patients may be tested for their response to particular medicines, before they are prescribed in the first place.

And the other death that took place last month. That was of Gerry Thomas, a once obscure American salesman who had the bright idea of packaging frozen meals in disposable foil trays, divided into compartments to keep the foods from mixing. His brainwave came upon him in 1954 whilst working as a representative for a small Nebraska food company. Thomas christened it the TV Dinner and the first product rolled out was a turkey breast smothered with dressing and gravy, sweet potatoes and well buttered peas. It cooked up in less than half an hour, sold for a dollar and ensured dinner time never interfered with family television viewing. Compulsive television watching was taking off, grabbing a nation of couch potatoes by the waistline. His company shifted more than 10 million products in its first year. This change to American eating habits was described once as the biggest shift since the discovery that raw food cooks nicely on a fire. Mr Thomas's small operation was soon acquired by catering giant, the Campbell Soup Company. Thomas left the business in 1970 when he had a heart attack.

Never having never eaten a TV dinner in my life, I cannot comment on the culinary experience, but I do know that it has been long vilified by fervent devotees of health promotion and life elongation. Mr Thomas was no shrinking violet and defended his invention to the end. Well used to a bad press, he liked to tell stories about the hate mail he regularly received from men who wanted their wives to cook from scratch like their mothers did ! Perhaps he had the last laugh. He died a very wealthy and fulfilled man last month at the respectable old age of 83. His final resting place, the well named Paradise Valley.

COMIC RELIEF
February 2006

News coverage of recent natural disasters has been wall to wall. First we had the carnage and misery caused by the devastating Asian tsunami. This was followed by twenty four hour reportage of the New Orleans flooding which initially greatly exaggerated the loss of life and then changed tack to heap blame on the President for spending too much time with his Scotch Terriers Barney and Miss Beazley, and Tony his Downing Street poodle. Less visible, less accessible and less media-friendly was the devastating earthquake last October high in the Kashmir mountains above Northern Pakistan. If one was to pick and choose a statistic to convey the sheer scale of this disaster, the fact that the quake caused ten thousand schools to collapse gives you the picture. Millions of surviving children are homeless, in one of the most inhospitable winterlands on earth.

The current issue of the *British Medical Journal* carries a report from two doctors, a hospital consultant and a GP, who have just returned home from helping Pakistani disaster patients. What they had to say about the relief effort does not make for pleasant reading. Dr Hasan Tahir and Dr Zafar Iqbal spoke of the massive outpouring of charity and the chaotic rush to the scene by emergency relief organisations, individual doctors and health workers. So far so good, but sadly that's where the pleasant news ended. They wrote about the chaotic nature of the disaster relief provided to survivors. Limbs that were not broken being immobilised in plaster for weeks on end leading to muscle wasting and stiff joints for life. Doctors, who meant well, were working away with no understanding of the language, no understanding of the symptoms and without the benefit of translators. Some local people said they felt like they were being used as guinea pigs. The two doctors found many patients suffering from perfectly avoidable complications. There was a child with stomach pain who was prescribed aspirin, a no-no class of drug for all children, and certainly not for those with tummy discomfort. Inexperienced surgeons were performing operations that left many patients with further complications. Cocktails of painkillers and antibiotics were being prescribed with abandon for indeterminate periods. Doctors would treat one lot of patients and then move on. A second group of doctors would come in and do the exact opposite. Daily medical care of whole camps was left to medical students who were growing frustrated by the continual influx of volunteer doctors who invariably changed treatment plans. In summary, the two doctors were led to question whether volunteer medics do more harm than good in relief situations. Even their own team of 'senior doctors' turned out to be nothing of the sort. Junior doctors were passing themselves off as senior consultants, nurses and physiotherapists were passing themselves off as doctors.

The Pakistani relief effort is not alone in this regard. Another doctor who worked on tsunami relief in India related his own experiences in a follow up letter. He spoke highly of Medicins sans Frontières, UNICEF and the Red Cross who he said are well organised, adequately staffed by professionals who are well trained and experienced, and work with clear goals and plans. On the other hand he wrote about unnamed organisations who quickly assemble teams of final year medical students, junior house officers or doctors who want to improve their surgical skills. Controversially he claimed that some are primarily motivated by media exposure. He described how one organisation brought a team of novices to the coastline of south India and then bragged to a leading television channel about they saved hundreds of children and women and rehabilitated them to a nearby camp. The damage he saw ranged from inappropriate medications, incorrect fluid management, blatantly wrong surgical procedures being conducted and inadequate anaesthetics.

In my own medical school days in the 1980s, I cannot recall a single lecture or any tuition on the field of disaster medicine, or even military medicine. Yet we had hundreds of lectures on subjects that were of absolutely no consequence to a qualified doctor. I believe this still to be the case today. Some would say that with the state of public health services here, the absence of disaster relief from the curriculum is a surprising omission. But really, it's no laughing matter. In a country the tiny size of ours, there is absolutely no call for our proliferation of relief organisations. The crying need is surely for them to come together as one. Where they could play a real role in the education of future doctors, nurses and others, as to how they can respond best to real suffering.

REFLEXOLOGY
July 2009

You don't need to have a disease to claim on your health insurance these days. You can have your baby's head massaged, your teeth whitened, your toe-nails clipped and even claim discount at the gym.

Even reflexology, most nonsensical of non-sciences, is now being paid for by some health insurers. Its practitioners must be tickled all the way to the bank. Reflexology and acupuncture have something important in common. They are both based on a primary psychiatric delusion, namely that all of your body's organs and most of its functions are projected on far-flung parts of your body. What's worse, is that only those who have paid exorbitant fees to train in these branches of imaginary medicine know where to find them. The footie fetishists of reflexology are bred to believe that by twiddling their fingers and thumbs on the soles of your feet they can correct unspecified hormonal imbalances, cure infertility and even affect the course of arthritis.

Reflexology's claims of antiquity date back to the pyramids of Egypt and the caves of dynastic China (depending on whom you consult). But it was actually a middle-aged American lady, Eunice Ingham, who propagated the idea that your whole being is conveniently mapped out on the soles of your feet. Seventy years ago, Nurse Eunice, a physical therapist too, published a very strange book entitled *Stories the Feet Can Tell*. In true quackery style, it mapped out imaginary 'reflex points' on the feet and arbitrarily twinned them with anatomical parts of the body. Her book was every bit as deserving of a fiction award as *The Hobbit* by JRR Tolkien, which was published just a year before. For the last four decades of her life nurse Eunice became a kind of Gandalf in the twilight moon world of reflexology. She toured the United States peddling bizarre theories, particularly amongst fellow nurses. Few doctors have entertained either the practice or theory, but the annals of reflexology do mention a certain Dr William H. Fitzgerald who in the early 20th century tried to quench pain by prodding his patients' feet. He was actually an ear, nose and throat specialist. Any lasting contribution he made to medical science is not recorded.

Reflexology was first introduced here by the well-known Doctor Gay Byrne back in 1985. On Ireland's most important clinical forum, the *Late Late Show*, the eminent broadcaster had his feet massaged in front of the nation by Sister Rosario - her of the Medical Missionaries of Mary in Drogheda don't you know. History does not record what exactly greeted her seven senses as she knelt before those sensitive hairy toes but there may well have been a large piece of fluff for every member of the audience. Certainly the whiff of reflexology lived on rather longer than many might have wished.

In Ireland you can 'train' to be a reflexologist in less than a year, in fact just one hundred hours will do the trick. The onerous module usually takes two hours once a week or a full day every month. But it will cost you a tidy four figure sum, excluding course books, T-shirt and materials. In fact it may well debit your account more to become a new-age reflexologist than it would to pay your family's health insurance premium for a whole year.

In preparation for this piece I've been roving a sceptical eye through some websites in Ireland dealing with reflexology. One member of the guild specialises in 'depression, bereavement, giving cancer advice and panic attacks'. In what particular order, is not made clear. The same member does not list any medical or even nursing qualifications that I can decipher but rather reassuringly, has appeared on television and radio, exhibits at the RDS, hosts workshops on flower remedies and has written a book about feet. So that's alright then. One wonders just what sort of regulatory system we have in this country when 'specialists in cancer advice' can be found so easily.

We are told by the powers that be in Irish reflexology that research is ongoing and that they are 'continually kept informed of research projects in many parts of the world'. They are also greatly heartened by the fact that the Green party are 'active supporters of complementary medicine research'. Not mentioned however is actual research showing that reflexology after gynaecological surgery is not only completely ineffective but can actually increase pain. Nor could I find any confirmation of the research showing that reflexology has zero effect on asthma. Nor is there any mention of the fact that it has no diagnostic value whatsoever. The bald truth is that reflexology is a plain foot massage masquerading as a clinical therapy. Patients are charged for participating in a work of fiction. Pass it by. Stopping for a rub just encourages them.

CAFFEINE
September 2010

For me, the life of professional rugby players has just got a whole lot duller. I was fascinated by a recent column I read on rising Irish rugby player Jonathan Sexton, which detailed both the medicalised monotony and daily routines he has to follow for the privilege of playing out-half for province and country. There ain't much fun left in sport these days.

His day begins with breakfast, usually a porridge sprinkled with protein supplement. This is followed by a bewildering array of supplements - fish oils, vitamins, minerals and caffeine to 'kick start the day'. Sexton explains that Leinster have a new nutritionist and that 'she's quite into supplements'. Evidently. She also bans fried breakfasts.

Players must weigh themselves every morning and record results precisely. They collect their own urine each day, not for drug testing, but for 'hydration tests' which they are trained to conduct on themselves. If their wee is too yellow, or heaven forbid, too brown - they are prescribed more supplementation in the form of Dioralyte - a soluble powder containing sugar and salts more commonly used to correct fluid losses in protracted diarrhoea.

Then it's off to the gym. Serious reprimand awaits if you are late. Even if caught by traffic, you may be degraded to 'towel boy' duties. Make it a habit and you are issued with serial monetary fines. The first workstation is a computer where you have to answer a series of questions from fitness coaches. You detail how well you have slept, your feelings, your worries, your level of tiredness, your mood - everything is relayed back to the same people who assign you to collect dirty towels if you are late.

The application that is now demanded of professional sportsmen is quite extraordinary, especially in the case of Sexton who is studying for degree finals in UCD. Pre-season training majors on running, weight-lifting sessions and yoga. All weight sessions are followed by more protein supplements and all foodstuffs consumed are tightly controlled. Running sessions are micro-managed to the extent that vests contain heart-rate monitors and satellite positioning software to alert coaches to how hard you are working, running and tackling. As Leinster and Irish goal-kicker, Sexton also has sponsored sessions with a specialist kicking coach and engages sports psychologists to assist him with mental preparation for matches. Training is often followed by medical massage where the emphasis is more on the painful pummelling of injuries than essential oils and candles.

Irish rugby has changed. It's a long way from half-time trays of cut oranges, Ciaran 'where's your effing pride' Fitzgerald and Ginger McLaughlin's rusty old head rampaging to the try line like a gored bull from Pamplona. But when you consider the dire and soul-free performances of our naturally talented team at the last rugby world cup, you might query the benefits of these overarching military regimes. Those in charge will doubtless argue that they are simply following new norms and adopt that perennial excuse for everything new and untested - best international practice.

But Sexton's description of a big game aftermath is enlightening.

'After the game you're exhausted, but it's hard to sleep because you have got so much caffeine in you. And then there is the adrenaline rush. You could be playing things over in your mind and then you don't sleep.' The column finished with his daily 'bed by eleven' routine, because 'they insist that we get at least eight hours sleep'.

The use of caffeine to temporarily improve physical prowess and mental agility is as old as mankind. It's a drug, it's a stimulant and these days it's everywhere. It was first identified two centuries ago in Germany by analytical chemist Friedlieb Runge, following a tip-off from a writer friend called Goethe. Coffee and tea have long been the traditional vectors of small doses, but now a whole sports 'energy' drinks market is founded on the premise that adding titrated doses of sugar and caffeine to cold water will 'boost' whatever you're having yourself.

If some of the endurance and performance claims being made for caffeine supplements and caffeine-laced drinks are true, there is a valid argument to be made for banning them as performance enhancing. But sports federations express little interest in travelling down that particular road. With growing pressure on field sports to abandon long-held sponsorship deals with alcohol makers, manufacturers of caffeinated sugar drinks might be expected to take up much of the slack. It's widely accepted that the banning of cigarette advertising in magazines simply led to it being displaced by a glut of alcohol advertising. The same will happen here. If alcohol advertising is banned, caffeine and other stimulants will fill the berth. The world anti-doping agency (WADA) has caffeine on a list of products that are not prohibited but are 'monitored in competition' to detect 'patterns of misuse'. Fudge is the word that comes to my mind on reading that.

There have long been naysayers, medical and religious, who have warned of the dangers of caffeine. But our long and relatively safe experience of small doses in hot mugs has tempered and moderated the more extreme views. Consumption of moderate amounts can be deleterious, resulting in headache, heart palpitations and difficulty reaching sleep. Psychiatrists have also taken an increasing interest in caffeine. Aside from its well recognised (but rarely discussed) effect of loosening the grip of the anal sphincter, they have identified mania, depression, delusions, loss of inhibitions, hallucinations and psychosis as potential consequences of caffeine overdose. The lethal dose in humans depends on both your size and your sensitivity to the drug but is relatively large and such overdoses are rare.

I don't think we have heard the last about the encroachment of caffeine and other psychoactive supplements in sport. More pace and more alertness on the pitch may be exactly what coaches and nutritionists desire. But caffeine is and always has been a drug, and drugs, especially psychoactive ones, do affect different players in different ways. What causes one player to become more focused on his duties, might well induce another to start fisticuffs in the changing room. And we wouldn't want that now.

A CHILDREN'S HOSPITAL
October 2009

A strong sense of déjà vu has overtaken me on hearing Madame Harney the health minister announcing a brand new children's hospital on the cramped and land-locked Mater campus at Eccles Street. The first little mites will be admitted 'by the end of 2014'. Four years ago, the exact same press release was issued - Crumlin, Temple Street and Tallaght were to merge. A few years before that we heard that international management consultants were looking at our organisation of paediatric care. In 1999 we had the council for children's hospital care which was going to promote collaboration between all the various interests. In 1969 a study group was formed to advise on paediatric services. At the time there were nearly 600 children's beds on the southside of Dublin alone. It was proposed to merge all of them into one unit. It never happened - irreconcilable differences about who would get on the board. In the 1940s it was proposed that all existing children's hospitals on the southside of Dublin would merge . The plan was opposed by Archbishop Byrne on religious grounds, and his successor, Charles McQuaid subsequently purchased 16 acres at Crumlin, got the state to build him a Catholic theme hospital and appointed himself chairman of the board.

There is little comfort for the distraught parents who braved the cameras on Pat Kenny's *Frontline* programme last month, to complain about the dire state of affairs their acutely ill offspring find themselves in. For decades, sick children have been the innocent victims of medical turf wars, religious battles, political gombeenism and sheer managerial uselessness. The Children's Hospital at Temple Street and Our Lady's Hospital in Crumlin have grabbed most of the headlines. But history may perhaps be kinder to the oldest sibling in the family, the National Children's Hospital at Tallaght, formerly of Harcourt Street.

This old hospital traces roots much longer than all the others and the other day I tried to trace its origins on a personal walking tour of Dublin. It began in 1821 as the Institute for Sick Children at Numbers 8 and 9 Pitt Street, beside a farmyard that is now Dublin's Westbury Hotel. The operatic composer Michael Balfe, he of *The Bohemian Girl*, was born at number 10 and it is his surname that now adorns the street. The Pitt Street Hospital, the first dedicated children's teaching establishment in the whole of the British Isles, was not founded by politicians, HSE ancestors, foreign management consultants or property speculators. The instigators were three medics, Henry Marsh of Galway, Charles Johnson of Wexford and Philip Crampton of Dublin. Marsh and Johnson were wannabe surgeons, but the former lost an index finger to infection through a clumsy corpse dissection and the latter had to retire his scalpel because of failing eyesight. They diverted their attention to the care of newborn infants and children, who in truth were not doing too well at the time. Back in the 18th century, the workhouse at St James's opened a foundling wing to care for abandoned babies. The boat to Britain was not the semi-accessible option it is now, and admissions averaged 200 infants a month. The Irish parliament became concerned in 1797 when it was discovered that of 10,000 infants admitted in a 20 year period, only 45 survived. A tribunal started up which resulted in the sacking of two senior doctors, the pharmacist and the voluntary board. As in the blood contamination scandal two centuries later, political hands were washed rigorously. Admission of inadequate resources and ultimate responsibility was a foreign concept back then too.

The other founder of Pitt Street, Sir Philip Crampton, was a well known surgeon and a colourful one at that. Nicknamed 'Flourishing Phil' by his colleagues, Crampton was tall, thin, and a natty dresser who wore white pants and a blue-tailed coat adorned with gilt buttons. He had his own personal pack of hounds and three times a week he would hunt with them at home in Wicklow. Like today's medical alicadoos who pace sidelines at rugby or soccer matches, Phil's weekend nixer required that a spare shirt be kept in the wagon as he was surgeon-in-attendance at duels. He was a founder of Dublin zoo and even had the eye muscle of a bird named after him - musculus cramptonius. He became quite expert at paediatric surgery, especially in the repairing of cleft lips. Crampton's eldest son went on to marry the soprano daughter of the aforementioned Michael Balfe.

The Pitt Street Institute treated children of all creeds and means. There was no McQuaidian figure running dark fingers and beady eyes over hospital staff lists to ascertain their particular brand of Christianity. It developed an international reputation for training and for the quality of medical papers and books written by its specialists. Dr Charles West, founder of Great Ormond Street in London, learned his paediatrics here in Dublin. In 1884, without any managerial assistance whatsoever, the doctors at Pitt Street and colleagues at a Children's Orthopaedic Hospital on Kevin Street decided to merge. Three years later (note that timeline), in 1887, the National Children's Hospital opened on Harcourt Street. It led the world in the training of paediatric nurses and developed expertise and an international reputation in the treatment of blood disorders, childhood epilepsy, kidney disease and growth problems. The first bone marrow transplant in Ireland took place there in 1976 under the direction of Professor Ian Temperley and the hospital received worldwide acclaim and visits when Professor Prem Puri developed his teflon injection to cure reflux kidney disease, sparing thousands of children the distress of open surgery. In 1998 it moved to Tallaght where half the population were young enough to avail of its proximity.

Its reward for almost 200 years of excellence, and for being the only applicant to tick all the boxes demanded by the management consultants, is banishment to a high tower on Eccles Street with inadequate beds, premium parking rates and zero expansion room. And doubtless our new mirage hospital will retain that peculiar Irish apartheid, the 'mix' of public and private that has allowed the Department of Health under-fund paediatric care for decades. Suffer little children? I'm afraid they will, for some time yet.

Postscript: *The Mater was abandoned as the site for the new Children's Hospital in 2012 following an adverse planning ruling. It is now proposed to build a new unit in a tight space at another hospital. The new opening date is 2018. Children born in 1969 when plans began, will be getting ready to celebrate their fiftieth birthdays.*